The Notebooks for Crime and Punishment

The Notebooks for

Crime and Punishment

Fyodor Dostoevsky

Edited and Translated by Edward Wasiolek

The University of Chicago Press
CHICAGO & LONDON

The translation is based upon the Russian edition of Dostoevsky's notebooks: *Iz arkhiva F. M. Dostoevskogo: "Prestuplenie i nakazanie," Neizdannye materialy,* edited by I. I. Glivenko (Moscow & Leningrad, 1931)

The University of Chicago Press, Chicago 60637
The University of Chicago Press, Ltd., London

Published 1967. Third impression 1974
Printed in the United States of America

ISBN: 0-226-15959-0 (clothbound); 0-226-15960-4 (paperbound)
Library of Congress Catalog Card Number: 66-23702

Contents

Illustrations

The illustrations included in this edition of Dostoevsky's *Notebooks for "Crime and Punishment"* are facsimiles of original pages of the notebooks.

Introduction

I

The notebooks for *Crime and Punishment* first came to the attention of the general public in 1921, when a representative of the Soviet government in the presence of A. V. Lunacharsky, Assistant Commissar of Education, opened a white tin case left to the State Archives by Dostoevsky's widow. Among articles, letters, and various documents was a listing by Anna Grigorievna of fifteen notebooks kept by Dostoevsky. She had numbered each of the notebooks and briefly described its contents. The notes for *Crime and Punishment* were contained in the first three notebooks. They were subsequently published in full by I. I. Glivenko in 1931, and the present volume is a translation of Glivenko's edition.

The notebooks today are housed in a special archive of the Central Government Archives in Moscow. In 1963 I obtained permission to examine a number of them. They are hard-covered copybooks, about nine by ten inches in size, bound in faded darkish maroon cloth. Dostoevsky's handwriting is remarkably clear, uniform, and regular; he evidently took pride in it. On a number of pages he practiced calligraphy and has left us specimens of his skill. He also left examples of his skill at drawing, for the notebooks have many sketches, most frequently of male figures and medieval churches. Some of these pages are reproduced as illustrations in the body of the text.

The Soviet edition is a good and faithful edition. The task of editing was not easy, despite the clarity of Dostoevsky's handwriting. His notebooks are in every respect working notebooks. They contain drawings, jottings about practical matters, doodlings of various sorts, calculations about pressing expenses, sketches, and random remarks. The text itself is often scattered about the pages: there are crossings-out, insertions, marginal matter in great abundance, and writing slanted in various directions across the pages. Sometimes Dostoevsky begins in the middle of the page and fills in the right-hand side before turning to the left. Sometimes he crosses out and puts the variant above or below the crossed-out material or in the margin. In addition, he apparently used the notebooks in a random and unsystematic manner, skipping pages and then returning to the empty pages with different matter and even with comments on a different work. At times too he turned the notebook upside down and proceeded from back to front.

Dostoevsky's capriciousness makes the dating of the notebooks difficult; but it seems fairly clear that his wife Anna Grigorievna misnumbered them and that Notebook Two was used before Notebook One. We have a few indications in the notebooks themselves that permit us to date them approximately: the dated rough drafts of two letters to Katkov, the editor of *The Russian Messenger,* and a few dates scattered here and there. On the basis of these hints, we can assume that the material for the second notebook covers approximately September to October of 1865, the first notebook November to December, and the third notebook from January to February of 1866, or in sum the notebooks date from September of 1865 to February of 1866. In the absence of incontestable evidence, however, I have not changed the numbering of the notebooks. In September of 1865 Dostoevsky had written Katkov that he had been working on *Crime and Punishment* for about two months, and the serialized publication of *Crime and Punishment* began the following January. The three notebooks, therefore, start about two months after Dostoevsky began writing *Crime and Punishment* and continue for a few months after the first instalment appeared in *The Russian Messenger.*

We have no idea, of course, whether this material represents the bulk of his working notes for the novel. They have a fragmental and partial character, and it seems reasonable to assume that they are only a part of what Dostoevsky actually wrote, the rest being in all probability lost irrevocably. We have in these notebooks two extended passages. One in the first notebook corresponds to the last pages of the first chapter and the second chapter of the first part of the novel, or essentially to Raskolnikov's meeting with Marmeladov in the tavern. In the second notebook we have a variant corresponding to the first four chapters and part of the sixth chapter of the second part of the finished version. This corresponds to Raskolnikov's immediate actions after the murder: his attempts at hiding the stolen articles in his room, the visit to the police station, his sickness, his conversations with Razumikhin and Zosimov in his room, and his attempts to flee from his room and his friends. The rest of the notes contained in the third notebook are varied and cover in fragmental form almost every character and situation in the novel. There is, of course, every reason to believe that Dostoevsky left notes of corresponding fulness for all parts of the novel. One would wish for them all, but what he has left is of great significance to those who have interested themselves in the creative imagination of this great Russian writer.

II

The notebooks of a great author are a peculiar kind of biographical fact. A painful experience in childhood, a disappointing love, a cruel father, and numberless facts of personal biography may be windows on the work of the author, but notebooks such as these stand closer to the work than does any event. Dostoevsky's notebooks for *Crime and Punishment* are the embryo of the novel: his intentions, trials, mistakes, uncertainties. In the final version we have one book; in the notebooks we have the shadows of other books. The novel offers us what Dostoevsky finally chose to say, but the notebooks offer us what he considered, and what he discarded. The notebooks are a dialogue between Dostoevsky and his novel; and only here do we have the author interrogating himself.

But is not the work enough? Will we be committing the "intentional fallacy," "the genetic fallacy," "the psychological fallacy"—some kind of fallacy—if we go outside the work to the notebooks? Many have told us, again and again, that to go outside the work, whether to life or time or rough draft, is fruitless, unilluminating, perhaps even dishonest. The novel is before us, and it alone contains what Dostoevsky wanted to say. What we want, to use Ivanov Razumnik's words, is "what was said" not "what was talked about."* The confusions of this view are legion. Everyone is interested in the work itself, but the work itself cut off from the mind that made it and the age that nurtured it may be, as Tynianov has reminded us, an abstraction.** The vocabulary of *Crime and Punishment* is more than its lexicon, and unless we accept Kenneth Burke's ideal of criticism as using "all that there is to use" we risk substituting our age and its eccentricities for Dostoevsky's. When it is so hard to see clearly a work as complicated as *Crime and Punishment,* it would seem less than wise to shut our eyes to anything that might help us to see even a little. And the notebooks for *Crime and Punishment* help us to see more than a little.

---

* Russian historian, social philosopher, and literary critic. Quotations are from his untranslated "Creative Work and Criticism" (*Tvorchestvo i kritika;* 1906), to be found in *Works,* II (St. Petersburg, 1911), 1–6.

** Yurii Tynianov, a brilliant Formalist critic whose best work was written in the twenties. Reference is to his untranslated essay, "On Literary Evolution," to be found in *Traditionalists and Innovators* (*Arkhaisty i novatory;* Leningrad, 1929).

What do the wrong turns, mistakes, blind alleys, and unmined possibilities tell us? How do we go from possibilities to the fact itself? They remind us, first of all, that the marvelous coherence of *Crime and Punishment,* the creative logic that takes us with what seems to be inevitable movement from beginning to end, was once uncertain, halting, and far from clear. They tell us something about the way Dostoevsky's creative imagination works: its habits, mannerisms, logic; something about his concern for technique; and something about what was recurrent in his thinking about the novel. The notebooks tell us much about the content of the novel itself: what was left out, what was different, what was undeveloped, and what was at some point more fully developed. At times they may help us clear up what is obscured in the novel, and resolve what has been critically disputable.

One of the first impressions we get of the notebooks is the different *Crime and Punishment* we find there. The similarities are, of course, much greater, but it is the deviations that stand out. Some of the characters and some of the relations between characters are different; some actions that Dostoevsky returned to over and over again never appear in the novel; and there is a whole array of little facts that die abortively in the notebooks. Lizaveta has a daughter; Raskolnikov has had his shirts mended by Lizaveta and still owes her ten kopecks; Porfiry and Zosimov are running after the same woman. More significant differences and omissions are: a fire at which Raskolnikov is a hero and presumably begins his redemptive process is spoken of at least half a dozen times; a vision of Christ for Raskolnikov is briefly considered, as are new crimes that Raskolnikov thinks about committing; and more than once Dostoevsky has Raskolnikov go off to put a bullet in his head. Some narrative lines considered in the notebooks are never followed up: Raskolnikov, for example, is repeatedly tempted to take money—and on occasion does help himself to the stolen hoard under the stone—in order to aid his family after they split with Luzhin. One is tempted to believe that Dostoevsky gave up this narrative line as he realized with increasing clarity that the real motive for the crime was not economic.

Relations between some of the characters are at times significantly different: Dunia, who has very little to do with Sonia in the novel, has a complex emotional relationship with her in the notebooks: "The sister becomes Sonia's worst enemy; she sets Razumikhin against her; gets him to insult her; and afterward when Razumikhin goes over to Sonia's side, she quarrels with him. And then she herself goes to have things out with Sonia; at first she insults her, and then she falls at her feet." Raskolnikov denounces Sonia at one point, and on more than one occasion treats her to some coarse words. Sonia, on the other hand, recoils from Raskolnikov when he confesses the murder. Perhaps the most significant omission in the final version is a love affair between Raskolnikov and Sonia that Dostoevsky toyed with repeatedly. In the novel itself Raskolnikov is, of course, fatally drawn to Sonia. Both have been swept out of the company of humankind, and they share the spiritual bond of those who have crossed the line of the accepted and the permitted. Spiritual love, yes, but of physical love there is not a word, although she is a prostitute. But love in the ordinary sense is something that Dostoevsky returns to again and again in the notebooks: "Suddenly he falls in love with her [Sonia] and becomes hopelessly attached to her." Or, "Sonia fell in love with him on the evening her father died." And, apparently on the same evening, "Sonia and Raskolnikov cry silently while embracing." They act like lovers: they write letters, embrace, argue. Dostoevsky decided apparently that love in this sense was not compatible with the sacrificial and purifying humility that Sonia was to represent. Yet one cannot help wondering whether Dostoevsky lost one dimension of realism in purging their relationship of at least the temptations of romantic love.

This is not the only respect in which Sonia is different in the notebooks. In general she is a more complicated personality: she argues with Raskolnikov, rejects him, feels insult, and becomes hysterical. Here are a few examples: "N.B. *She* thinks of herself continually as a deep sinner, a fallen profligate beyond salvation; she is terribly modest, but once insulted she is beside herself." Also, "*Sonia,* always meek, always without humor, always serious and quiet; then suddenly, she would burst out laughing terribly at trifles, and this affected the young man as gracious." Sonia in the novel itself is an uncomplicated expression of humility and self-sacrificing love. Some have found her unreal in her unvarying perfection. And yet this is the way Dostoevsky wanted her. The notebooks make abundantly clear that he successively purged her of contradictory and complicating traits. In the novel, he wanted her to represent that unconditional love to which Raskolnikov was drawn and which he did not find in his family.

Luzhin, too, is different in the notes, and it seems that Dostoevsky originally destined him for a larger role in the novel. At one point he puts forth a theory justifying murder; he, like Svidrigaylov, overhears Raskolnikov's confession; and he is not only the persecutor of Sonia but also Raskolnikov's rival, since Dostoevsky has him fall in love with Sonia: "Despite himself he is forced all the same to notice the fine qualities of Sonia; and suddenly he falls in love with her and becomes hopelessly attached to her." In the novel he hurts Sonia only to hurt Raskolnikov, but in the notes his ill-will is personal. We are told that he "conceived a hatred for Sonia, a bitter personal hatred and even entered into a pact with Lebeziatnikov to humble Sonia." In general, Luzhin's role in the novel strikes us as unessential, as a mere accessory in the plotting of the intrigue. The larger significance that Dostoevsky seemed at first to reserve for him disappeared as the narrative lines in which he is important faded away in the process of writing.

Svidrigaylov, on the other hand, is for the most part as he appears in the novel: an embodiment of one side of Raskolnikov, an ironic expression of that bronze man that Raskolnikov admired. We never feel—as we will later in the portraiture of Stavrogin—the terror that Dostoevsky wanted us to feel in the presence of someone beyond good and evil. Yet, there is no doubt that this was his intention, and those who have attempted to see some redemptive traits in Svidrigaylov because he takes care of the Marmeladov children and the five-year-old girl in his dream, simply have not understood the logic of Dostoevsky's morality. The character who does only "evil" must sense the distinction between evil and good, but Svidrigaylov is meant to express indifference to any moral distinction, and one way of showing this indifference is to have him do what we conventionally call "good" acts as well as evil acts. These are just a few examples of the many omissions and changes that occur in the passage from notes to novel, and the exploitation of their full significance will undoubtedly provoke discussion and dispute. In many respects, however, insights into Dostoevsky's concern with the craft of *Crime and Punishment* and his general concern with technique may be the most significant information we gain from the notebooks.

The notebooks make abundantly clear that Dostoevsky thought and worried about technical matters: about factual accuracy, style, probabilities, tone, point of view. The smallest details are fussed over: "Don't forget that he is 23 years old" he reminds himself. "Do it more skilfully" is an injunction that he is at pains to underline more than once. He concerns himself with pace and tone: "Have it all pass more quickly," and "very serious, but with subtle humor"; with the relations of inner and outer: "The event first and the distortion of his own psychology begins." Long before Henry James, he knew the value of dramatic implication: "About his love for Sonia—say little; only give the facts"; and more than once he reminds himself: "All the facts without reflection." Motivation and probabilities occupy him repeatedly. He wants, for example, Porfiry's visit to Raskolnikov to be probable, and he tells himself "There has to be an incident, a pretext, so that Porfiry would take hold of the pretext readily to visit Raskolnikov."

The right point of view evidently gave him a great deal of trouble, for he returns to reflection on it again and again, and he considers a variety of modes of narration. He experiments with three forms: the first-person as diary and as memory, and the third-person, which in a kind of limited omniscience constitutes the narrative manner of the finished version. He also briefly considers two other forms: the first-person as "confession" and a mixed form of drama and diary. He left the "I-form" with reluctance, taking it through several variations and leaving us with two large fragments in the notebooks. These fragments invite analysis since the content of both is essentially what we are given in the final version. The point of view is the variable, and even a quick reading impresses us: how radically a change of mode of narration affects the content of the experience! Dostoevsky, I hazard, thought of the "I-form" as a way of gaining immediacy, of dramatizing the self in touch with its own crisis, but the long extended passage in the second notebook shows us that the "I-form" took him away from the immediacy he sought, turning what was meant to be immediate into something analyzed, self-conscious, and schematic. There were even practical difficulties in giving the narration to the hero, who at significant moments is in a half-delirious state. Dostoevsky attempted to solve this by putting the experience at a remove, in memory and diary, but a hero who cannot remember significant moments of experience is not a great improvement. Dostoevsky learned, to judge by the finished *Crime and Punishment*, that he wanted to dramatize more than the self could be consciously aware of. He solved this, with considerable success, by centering, but not limiting, the point of view on the hero, permitting Raskolnikov to become absorbed in his experiences (whether of action or reflection) in a way that was impossible with a first-person narrative. In this way the action is given to the hero, and the consciousness and significance of the experience are given to the author. Some of his exasperation with this problem of craft and his determination to find what was right is caught in this quotation: "Rummage through all the questions of this novel. But the plot's structure is such *that the story must be narrated by the author and not by the hero.* If it is to be a confession, then everything must be made clear *to the utter extreme.* Every instant of the story must be entirely clear. [Complete frankness, completely serious even to the point of naïveté, and narrate only what is necessary]." And he was close to his final solution when he wrote: "Narration from the point of view of the author, sort of invisible but omniscient being, who doesn't leave his hero for a moment, even with the words: 'all that was done completely by chance.' "

Point of view, tone, probabilities are specific matters of technique, and the notebooks also tell us something about the larger matters of Dostoevsky's creative process. We learn that his creative imagination moves usually from conceptual framework to circumstantial elaboration, from general to particular, from schema to narrative fact. Henry James had a way of elevating the accidentalities of his own genius into universal laws, so that today, because of his influence, we are apt to see the artistic process as a natural or inevitable movement from chance impressions to the delicate elaboration of the "implication of things." Dostoevsky's notebooks—these and others—confirm what he said again and again in his letters: the birth of a novel is the birth of a "living idea" in his soul.

What we get of this process in the notebooks takes the following form: he gives us a rapid schematization of some large block of action, a kind of précis of the events he plans to fill out. The following is characteristic:

1) He went to pawn his watch and *to look things over.* Reflections. N.B. (so that the reader be given to understand that he did not go there to pawn his watch but for another purpose).

2) Meeting with Marmeladov in the tavern.

3) Home. Relations with the landlady. Letter from his mother about the fiancé. No, they must not suffer. Skeptical arguments. Lizaveta at Hay Market Square.

4) Before the preparations [memories] reasonings. Murder.

5) To the police. Under the stone. On the boulevard. 20 K He returned the translations.

6) Illness. His mother's letter. Money.

7) He runs. Tavern. Terrible arrogance. Quarrel with the workmen. Marmeladov's death.

The usual movement of Dostoevsky's imagination from schematic generalization to specific elaboration permits us to see his creative intention more clearly in the notebooks than in the final version. Not infrequently he is definite and explicit on points in the first sketches in the notebooks that are obscured in the finished version by the shadows of descriptive and reflective detail. In the novel itself we can discern, for example, that Sonia is a counterpoise to Svidrigaylov, but the notebooks tell us explicitly that this was Dostoevsky's intention; we can discern that she is meant to be a Christlike creature, but in the notebooks she is explicitly tied to the image of Christ. Raskolnikov is a rebel, but it takes some refined analysis to see that he craves what he is aggressively against; in the notebooks his self-punishing traits stand out sharply: "Oh, I'm a scoundrel; I'm a scoundrel! I call them base and disgusting, but I crave their good opinion. I'm not good for anything, for anything. Life has [still] not given me anything." Indeed, the notebooks as scheme make much stand out sharply that otherwise might be subject to debate. To be sure, we are not obligated to accept what the notes tell us, but this is hardly the problem at those junctures where notes and finished version coincide. Some of the facts left deliberately vague in the novel, for example, are given explicitly in the notebooks. Svidrigaylov's crimes are hinted at darkly in the novel; we are told exactly what they are in the notebooks. We guess from his dream the night before he kills himself that he had violated a young girl who then drowned herself. In the notebooks Dostoevsky writes: "He says about the landlady that the daughter was raped and drowned, but he doesn't say who did it.: Later, it becomes clear that it was he." It is also rumored in the novel that he had been responsible for the death of a servant; in the notes, Luzhin's gossip is fact: "Relates without any twinge of conscience that at the time of serfdom he had whipped two men to death . . ."

One is tempted to use the notebooks as evidence for points that have been critically disputed and for parts of the novel that have been insufficiently explained. Raskolnikov's relations with his mother have never, to my knowledge, been examined adequately. W. D. Snodgrass has given us the best discussion of their relationship and has suggested that Raskolnikov sees the moneylender as a mother surrogate, presumably because the mother, in a subtle and perhaps unconscious way, has manipulated and oppressed her son. The notebooks seem to bear this out. On several occasions Dostoevsky writes, "His mother's caresses are a burden," and once he writes, "Even thoughts of his mother are painful." The mother is not very admirable in the notebooks, nor for that matter in the novel, although there her negative traits are veiled and obscured. In the notebooks she is conscious of how Raskolnikov has hurt her; she loses her temper with him, reminds him of his duty toward her, and in general fills him with feelings of guilt and shame. His feelings toward her, as a consequence, are contradictory and unclear, a compound of love, duty, anguish, fear, and aggression: "And my mother? God, what will happen to her? Won't she have to curse me? Me, her womb and her love? Can it be that she will? Can she really? No, it is impossible, impossible." Sometimes the aggression becomes bald and open, as in the following quotations, where his violence is directed at sister and mother: "He sells his sister to a dandy from K boulevard. He beats his sister and takes everything from her." And, "He beats his mother." The mother is frank about what she expects from Raskolnikov: "He is my son; he must obey me." Raskolnikov is apparently confused between the feelings he actually has and those he is expected to have: "Went to see his mother, wanted to be good and was very bad." One wonders why Dostoevsky felt it necessary to veil the love-hate relationship that comes out clearly in the notebooks and only dimly in the novel. There may be something to those who have suggested Freudian explanations here, and indeed it does not seem outlandish—in the light of the notebooks—to suggest at least incipient incestuous feelings between sister and brother. Raskolnikov's anger against Luzhin the suitor seems a bit excessive for the reasons given, and Dunia in the notebooks becomes Sonia's worst enemy. That apart, Dostoevsky would have helped the reader a little if he had made clearer the negative feelings, especially for his mother, Raskolnikov felt for his family. Structurally, the negative feelings help explain, I think, why he is so strongly attracted to Sonia, who asks nothing of him, and so repelled at moments by his family, who ask everything of him, and perhaps the most intolerable burden of all: that he be good, honest, and the strong, virtuous support of a virtuous mother and sister. In Dostoevsky's moral logic, there is little that is more burdensome than a conditional love, and it is not inconceivable that Raskolnikov's murder of the old woman is in part a revolt against an image of himself, unfree and determined by the expectations of those who love him. We get something of Raskolnikov's anguish in the following reflection: "N.B. *About the Mother.* She loves me because she sees in me everything beautiful, an unattainable ideal, but if she were to find out, then she would come perhaps to hate me very much. (Lack of faith, doubt, estrangement from his Mother. From his sister, all the more.)" And he tells us exactly why he has been attracted to Sonia: "Why have I attached myself to you?

because you alone are mine; you are the only person who is left for me. The others, mother, sister, they are all strangers. We will never again be at one. If I don't tell them, then I will not go to them; and if I reveal everything to them, then they will not come to me. But you and I are damned; therefore our road is the same, even though we look in different directions. [You are my sovereign], my fate, my life—everything. We are both *damned,* society's pariahs."

Whether the notebooks shed light on the nettlesome problem of Raskolnikov's motives for killing the moneylender is not immediately apparent. They do show rather clearly, however, that Raskolnikov vacillates sharply between sympathy and contempt for the people for whom he is, according to one set of motives, presumably sacrificing the moneylender and himself. The love and sympathy, whether for family or for the flower of St. Petersburg youth, correspond to the humanitarian motives, and the contempt and hate correspond to the superman and self-willed motives. This is a familiar division, but it is interesting to see how Dostoevsky himself seemed unable to decide which was the true set of motives. The following suggests the mixture of determination and frustration with which Raskolnikov struggles: "After the illness, etc., it is absolutely necessary to establish the course of things firmly and clearly and to eliminate what is vague, that is, explain the whole murder one way or another, and make its character and relations clear. Only then start the second part of the novel: Clash with reality and the logical outcome in the law of nature and duty." The Soviet critic I. I. Glivenko* saw these two motives—as have Mochulsky** and many others—as contradictory. And it would seem that the motive of sacrificing one's self for humanity or sacrificing humanity for one's self are contradictory. But the real relationship between them, I am convinced, is one of appearance and reality, of evasion and truth. The "pretty" humanitarian motive is flattering to Raskolnikov's ego, evasively presented to the conscious mind as a rationalization of an ugly truth. I don't think the notebooks help us to establish what the "real" motive is—for the evasions are so complex that they may obscure impenetrably, as in *Hamlet,* the real motive—but they do help establish the evasive and unreal-

---

* I. I. Glivenko is the Russian editor of the notebooks for *Crime and Punishment.* He expresses these views in the Preface to his 1931 edition of the notebooks.

** Konstantin V. Mochulsky, *Dostoevsky: Life and Works* (Paris, 1947), as yet untranslated into English, but available in French: *Dostoievsky, l'homme et l'œuvre* (Paris, 1962).

nature of the "humanitarian" motive. These two motives are not contradictory because they are not equally real. One is believed in, even though we may know only its manifestations in the superman theory and the self-willed rejections of the family; the other is not believed in. The relationship is dramatic and psychological, not logical.

These problems as well as many others await the work of those who may find these notebooks useful in confronting or reconfronting Dostoevsky's creative process. It is hoped that these notebooks will put to rest, as did their publication in Russia, careless references to Dostoevsky's ineptness in matters of technique and craft. In the West —Symons and Murry* are good examples—and in Russia—Solovyov and Rozanov** are examples—Dostoevsky was looked upon as visionary, thinker, seer, but seldom craftsman. This view may have been influenced by Dostoevsky himself in his repeated plaints that the conditions for good work had never been granted to him. Indeed, the letter to M. Katkov, a rough draft of which is to be found on pages 171–73, makes pointed reference to such conditions. If these plaints have had some influence in keeping alive the idea of Dostoevsky's careless workmanship, then the conclusions were non sequiturs and based on a naïve view of Dostoevsky's character. Non sequitur because less than ideal conditions for writing in no way implied that Dostoevsky did not work hard at his craft—they probably made him work harder—and naïve because we know enough about Dostoevsky to know that he could not work effectively unless he was complaining: about money, creditors, living conditions, lack of time. No one can read much about his life without realizing that, like one of his characters, he looked for untoward conditions in order to complain about them.

Those like Murry who were ecstatic over Dostoevsky's works but still apologized for his lack of technique were themselves contradictory, for no writer could move his admirers as Dostoevsky did the English in the early years of this century without possessing the technique, in the broad and perhaps most meaningful sense, to do so. The notebooks for *Crime and Punishment* are convincing proof that Dostoevsky had technique in the conventional sense. Although these

---

* See John Middleton Murry, *Dostoevsky* (London, 1916), and Arthur Symons, *Studies in Prose and Verse* (New York, 1922).

** See Vladimir Solovyov's untranslated "Three Speeches in Memory of Dostoevsky, 1881–1883," in his *Collected Works,* III (St. Petersburg, 1912). Also, V. Rozanov's untranslated *The Legend of the Grand Inquisitor* (St. Petersburg, 1894), originally published in 1890.

notes are doubtless but a small fragment of all the jottings Dostoevsky made for *Crime and Punishment,* they are priceless testimony of how Dostoevsky worked, what he worried about, and what kinds of things attracted his attention. They are sure evidence that Dostoevsky did not dash off his works unthinkingly to satisfy some journalistic deadline. True, he worked on his novels while parts of them were being printed, but he worked on them painstakingly, lovingly, intensely, and with all the care, attention, and suffering that a great writer gives to his craft.

The translation of the notebooks that follows is offered for the consideration of all those who admire *Crime and Punishment,* and who would like to explore further the fascinating intricacies of Dostoevsky's imagination and creative processes. The specialist will find his way, and should find his way, to the originals; although there is no substitute for Dostoevsky's own words, whether in novel or notebook, I do not share the professional's passion for exclusion. Some of our finest work on Dostoevsky has come from brilliant non-specialists —Snodgrass and Howe are examples; and though it would be hazardous and foolish to attempt certain kinds of criticism without knowing Russian and consulting the original texts, it would be both selfish and foolish to make of Dostoevsky a private domain. Dostoevsky belongs to the world, to professional and amateur alike.

III

Notes on the Translation

I have tried to make this a readable translation, unencumbered by apparatus except where the apparatus serves some conceivable critical purpose. I have not followed Glivenko, for example, in reproducing the original pagination of Dostoevsky's notebooks. This seemed to me to be interruptive, pedantic, and to no special purpose. On the other hand, I have included material that Dostoevsky crossed out and have preserved by appropriate devices two kinds of variants. The bracketed material in the text is in almost all cases additions by Dostoevsky and material that fits easily into the text. The material in the numbered notes consists of variations, either in fact or wording, of material that already appears in the text, elaboration of points made in the text, or remarks suggested by something in the text. Crossed-out material has been made part of the text itself, appearing just before the wording that was substituted for it.

I was strongly tempted to eliminate the brackets in order to have a smooth, unencumbered text. Since the bracketed material represents, for the most part, additions to the text, and thus points to the processes of accretion, qualification, and elaboration, it may be at times critically significant. To give a few examples: a phrase like "dirty satin vest" becomes "dirty [black] satin vest," or "She married an officer out of love" becomes "She married [her first husband] an [infantry] officer out of love." Undoubtedly, the preserved distinction at times may seem trivial, but it seemed advisable to preserve a distinction that might tell us something of Dostoevsky's creative process. Parentheses are Dostoevsky's; ellipses are Dostoevsky's, but where the ellipses appear in parentheses (. . .) they indicate words that were undecipherable in the notebooks themselves. Punctuation has been anglicized, and variant spellings of names have been preserved. Finally, Dostoevsky's three notebooks have been divided into ten sections for the convenience of the reader.

Except for two long narrative fragments, found in Sections I and IV, the material of these notes are jottings of great diversity set down in a random manner: queries, snatches of dialogue, embryonic characterizations, philosophical generalizations, brief drafts of scenes. The subject matter may change from sentence to sentence, sentences may be left unfinished, and often there is no context to provide us with a definite frame for the meaning. Dostoevsky did not set down these notes, as Henry James or André Gide set down theirs, with one eye on posterity. These are notes written in the lonely and exultant moments of the creative process. They were never intended for publication; they were in a sense the transcription of the nerve ends of Dostoevsky's creative process.

I have no theory of translation, unless the following remarks constitute a theory: there is no such thing as a "literal" translation, but only a translation from idiom to idiom. To translate Russian syntax "literally" would be nonsense, and to pause at half-idiomatic English in deference to some concept of literalism is also nonsense. It is my conviction that the idiom of a great writer exists in a specific, not a public, environment, in this case the dramatic and ideological purpose embodied in the novel itself. It would seem to follow then that the more we know of the specific dramatic environment—in this case the more we know of *Crime and Punishment*—the better the translation will be.

Notebook One

I

Raskolnikov's meeting with Marmeladov in the tavern—Marmeladov's confession

The following section corresponds very closely to Part I, Chapter 2, of the final version of *Crime and Punishment:* Raskolnikov's meeting with Marmeladov in the tavern; Marmeladov's long speech—to the chorus of jeers from inmates of the tavern—about his character, his perfidy, the character of Katerina, and the destruction he has wrought on his wife and daughter; the return of Marmeladov and Raskolnikov to the Marmeladov apartment, the description of Mrs. Marmeladov, her hysterical reception of Marmeladov, and Raskolnikov's departure.

Despite the fact that the two versions correspond very closely, there are a number of differences. Dostoevsky did not include details and incidents like these in the final version: In the notes, Katerina's first husband in addition to being a gambler and a squanderer of public funds is a drunkard; the 30 rubles that Sonia brings home to Katerina as wages for her first night of prostitution are "thirty rubles in silver"; the scene in which Marmeladov tries futilely to borrow money from a distinguished gentleman develops at great length the humiliation Marmeladov has to suffer. The significance of such omissions—and there are more—may be variously interpreted, but one might argue that Dostoevsky does not want to identify too explicitly the first husband and Marmeladov; Katerina, like her husband, has a way of choosing what will hurt her. The "silver" that Dostoevsky omits from the final version obviously links Sonia's fate—perhaps too explicitly—with the betrayal of Christ. The scene in which Marmeladov goes to great lengths to forestall the need of Sonia's prostitution by trying to borrow money conflicts with Dostoevsky's intention to show that Marmeladov is the cause of the family's misery. There are, too, significant additions to the notes which Dostoevsky made later and which are included in the final version. I will give only one example: just before Raskolnikov leaves the Marmeladov apartment, he reaches into his pocket and leaves 30 kopecks on the window sill. He then consciously upbraids himself for this involuntary act and calls it a stupid deed. Unable to retrieve the kopecks, he sarcastically dismisses them as necessary for Sonia's "cleanliness." None of this is to be found in the notes, pointing perhaps to Dostoevsky's late need to pattern more explicitly the alternation of Raskolnikov's unconscious sympathy and conscious indifference to the fate of others, a pattern that is worked out in other parts of Part I.

The two texts differ very little. The similarity of content throws into relief the changed point of view of the two versions: the notes are in an "I-confessional" mode of narration, the final version in a limited third-person omniscience centered on Raskolnikov. The difference in effect is considerable. The "I" point of view leads to analysis and statement rather than to the portrayal of action. We are told about madness rather than shown it, as for example: "Five days ago, I was walking around like a madman." Or, in the notes: "Was I hungry or not? I didn't even feel the hunger. Everything, everything was devoured by my project, by the need to put it into effect." In the final version, Dostoevsky merely notes that Raskolnikov had not eaten for two days. Quite appropriately he does not give us Raskolnikov reflecting on his hunger; a Raskolnikov devoured by his project will not be reflecting on whether he is hungry or not. Rather, by third-person narration Dostoevsky expresses how Raskolnikov is devoured by his project, leaving him in a stupor of self-absorption and contrasting it with the world to which he is insensitive. In the final version only what touches his project touches his consciousness.

The effect of an "I" point of view on similar subject matter is various and important. Section IV of these notes contains an even longer passage, corresponding to Chapters 1, 2, and 3 of Part II of the novel, and is narrated in the first-person. The effects of this mode of narration on similar subject matter are perhaps better gauged there, since much of this first section is taken up with Marmeladov's long speech in which in the novel necessarily he talks in the first-person.

The wife of the collegiate assessor, Julia Prokhorovna Zarnitsyna
Aleksandr Grigorovich Zametov
Afanasii Ivanych Vakhrushin
Italia
Petr Petrovich Luzhin
Civil Counselor Chebarov
Il'ia Petrovich Poruchik—gunpowder
The merchant Shelopaev sent the money
Shil's house. Raskolnikov
Bakalieeva, manor, ladies, fiancée
Andrei Semenych. Lebeziatnikov
Pochinkov's house. No. 47. The civil servant Babushk
Razumikhin
Nikolai Dmitriev, worker
Mitrei*
Semen Semenych, Merchant in (Afan. zag)
Aleksei Semenych, worker for Vakhrushin
Babushkin's house

His Excellency is as good as an angel of the Lord . . . I will take you back, but be careful, be careful. And he gave him money for a uniform. A well-groomed lady. She was completely transformed, yet still in the same dress. They know somehow how to do things: dainty collars, new armlets, clean children—just as if she were getting ready to visit someone or was expecting guests. Important. Ivan Makarych, *she says,* was tired after coming home from the office. I lay down on the couch—I almost killed the children, they were so noisy—silence! And, she couldn't stand it;—she invited her enemy, the landlady, whom she herself had upbraided, for coffee. They sat in a corner, drank coffee, and talked in whispers in order not to awaken me, but

---

* Popular diminutive for Mikhail (Michael).

79.

[illegible]

Под судом.

[illegible] Я все записку. Я [illegible] себе [illegible]

[illegible] и другие и все [illegible] мои. [illegible]

[illegible] исповедь. [illegible]

[illegible] не [illegible].

Как это начал — [illegible] говорить. [illegible]

[illegible] это все [illegible]. [illegible] до этого дня [illegible]

[illegible] сумасшедший. [illegible]

[illegible] сумасшедший и не хочу себя оправдывать [illegible]

[illegible] не хочу. [illegible]

[illegible] сумасшедший. Я все по городу [illegible]

и до того [illegible] что [illegible]

Это впрочем [illegible]

что, [illegible] право [illegible] что [illegible]

[illegible] обладал [illegible]

себе принесть. Впрочем [illegible]

[illegible] что я [illegible]

[illegible] хочу — [illegible]

[illegible]

[illegible] совершенно. [illegible]

This manuscript page corresponds to pp. 23–24, beginning with the phrase "On Trial" and ending with the words "I was no longer thinking it over . . ." Despite the crossings-out and marginal material, Dostoevsky's handwriting is clear and readable.

I heard everything. Now, she said, Ivan Makarych has a position; he is going to receive a salary; and he has been in to see his Excellency. His Excellency himself came out to greet him, received him very politely, had him sit down, and after listening to him, said: I remember well, Ivan Makarych, your services; and I know that you were formerly *addicted* ~~sometimes~~ to that weakness; but since you give me your word, since I appreciate your talents, and since things have been going badly here without you (take note, take note!) I'm going to take you back, putting my trust in your honest and honorable word. That is, she thought up all this, not in order to brag, but to comfort herself, but perhaps also to look good before Savishna, an ambitious woman. We're going to rent an apartment, she went on, and only the question of housekeeping details remains. Then they talked about how to set up housekeeping, and they couldn't get their fill of talking. They talked to each other like old friends for two hours [and I lay there and could hardly keep the tears back]. When I brought home my first wages a week ago, she called me darling; you darling, she said.

And I lay there and thought about how I would arrange things for them, how I would bring back my daughter, how everything would be fine, and how I would dress the children and give her some peace. But then the next day I stole her keys to the trunk where the money was hidden and left home. Since then I haven't gone back, and he poked his finger at a bottle of liquor.[1, 2]

On Trial.

[I am on trial and] I will tell everything. I will write everything down. I am writing this for myself, but let others and all my judges read it, [if they want to]. This is a confession [a full confession]. ~~I am writing for myself, for my own needs and therefore~~ I will not keep anything a secret.

How did [all] this begin—it's useless to talk about it. ~~It will be self-evident [clear].~~ I will begin straight off with how it all came about.

---

[1] Young Man take me home because I am afraid. Suffering on your face. It forced me to be frank . . . Because I am afraid; because Katerina Ivanovna is going to beat me and scream and torture herself. I'm afraid of that, but I'm not afraid that she is going to beat me, because I find pleasure in that. She can (. . .) Katerina Ivanovna, if she didn't beat me, I would suffer. If she were as gentle as my daughter, my heart would bleed from suffering . . . Do you understand that, dear sir? Do you understand?

[2] Don't worry, dear sir, don't worry. Everyone knows everything about me here. Here everyone knows everything about me.

Five days ago, I was walking around like a madman. I won't say that I was [really] mad then and I don't want to justify myself by [lying]. ~~I will not say [a single false word] even though my [salvation] depends on it. No~~ I don't want, I don't want! I was completely sane ~~I want to say only that I walked about then, only to say~~; [I've been telling myself this all month]. [I say only that I walked around like] a madman [and that was the truth]. I walked all around the city like that, loitered about, and it got to the point that I even began to fall into a kind of unconsciousness. But that could have been in part from hunger, because I really don't know what I ate for a whole month. The landlady ~~seeing that I was no longer giving any lessons~~ had stopped sending me dinner. Only Nastasya would bring me something of her own. But [what's the matter with me! The most important reason was certainly not that]; hunger [here] was a thing of tertiary importance, and I remember very well that I did not even pay any attention to all that during these last days: was I hungry or not? I didn't even feel the hunger.[3] Everything, everything was devoured by my project, by the need to put it into effect. I was no longer thinking it over then, recently, when I strolled about, because everything [had been] thought through before and everything had been decided. I was drawn [even], somehow drawn mechanically [to do it as quickly as possible and to have it over with] [so as to have it off my hands one way or another. But I couldn't give it up . . . I couldn't . . .] I was getting ill; and if it had continued any longer, I would have gone crazy and would have given myself up, or . . . I really don't know what would have happened.

To tell the truth, I've remembered [well and clearly] from the whole past week only how I met Marmeladov. [However, that may be because I had not met anyone for a long time, and had kept to myself, so that a meeting with anyone, as if (. . .) in me. I will write about Marmeladov especially, because this meeting plays an important role later in my own plan.] That was [exactly] ~~three~~ four days before the ninth. I see the rest of the week as if through a fog. I remember some things with unusual clarity, and other things as if I had seen them in a dream ~~I have to tell about Marmeladov; I met Marmeladov in the evening~~,. I remember absolutely nothing about that whole day [when I met Marmeladov]. [Absolutely.] At nine o'clock in the evening—I think it was so—I found myself on S——m

---

[3] And expelled from the university; and I left the university.

Street near a tavern. [Up to that time] I had never gone [into] taverns, and now I went in not [only] because I was [really] tortured by a [terrible] thirst and wanted to drink beer, but because suddenly—and I don't know why—I wanted to be with people ~~on the street~~ of any kind. Otherwise, I would have collapsed on the street and my head would have burst. Even though it was dangerous then for me [to enter], I was no longer reasoning and I entered.

~~As if in a haze, I remember that~~ I don't even remember very clearly how I went up to the counter and took off my [small] silver ring,[4] and somehow or other made a bargain to get a bottle of beer for it. Then I sat down and after I drank my first glass, my thoughts suddenly [in a single minute] cleared up for the rest of the evening from that first glass. I remember the evening as if it were imprinted [on my memory].

There were not many people ~~One, very drunk, lay~~ in the tavern. When I entered, a whole crowd, five [with a girl and an accordion] had just left. After they left, there remained a drunkard who was sleeping [or drowsing] on a bench, his companion [fat in a short overcoat] who was sitting ~~and drank nothing~~, a little drunk and drinking a beer, and Marmeladov [whom I had never met up to then]. He sat drinking a half bottle. ~~I had never seen Marmeladov before.~~ [From time to time he drank a little from it, pouring some into a small glass and looking around in a kind of agitation, or so it seemed to me.] [Then during all that time two, three men entered; I don't remember exactly what kind. In rags. I [myself] was completely in rags.]*

The proprietor (of the tavern) was in another room, but he would come into ours often [coming down some steps to us]. He wore high boots with red top flaps, a short coat, and a frightfully dirty [black] satin vest. Behind the counter there were two boys, one of whom served what was asked for. [There were also on the counter some sliced cucumbers [rye crusts] and some kind of big fish.] The atmosphere was stuffy, and the weather then ~~It was agonizing~~ was burning hot—[it was that kind of July]—in the tavern. It was [even] unbearable to sit there. Everything was so impregnated with the odor of wine that it seemed to me that one could get drunk [in ten minutes] from the air itself.

---

* Material within brackets was first crossed out and then reinstated.

4 I got it from my mother, from some kind of convent.

Without meaning to I turned my attention toward Marmeladov, perhaps just because he himself was turning his attention to me. [From the very beginning] he seemed to want terribly to start talking to me [and precisely with me]. [He looked at the others who were in the tavern beside us with apparent disdain, even a little down his nose, as if he considered himself as belonging to a higher social group.] He was a man of forty-five, of medium height [with greying hair and a large bald spot] with a swollen, yellow and even greenish face from [continual] drunkenness and with swollen eyelids behind which his vivid small slit-like eyes sparkled. His look attracted attention [even mine]; but I at that time was interested only [especially] in one thing. His face shone with exultation and with [perhaps a special significance and] meaning and, [at the same time] immediately after, with a sort of a madness—I don't know how else to express it. He was dressed in some kind of ragged coat with all its buttons gone, a nankeen vest. From beneath the vest you could make out a dickey, which was all crumpled, spotted ~~with something or other,~~ and dirty. He was shaved in the manner of civil servants, but it had been some time ago so that a [thick] grey-bluish bristle had begun to grow ~~Hands frightfully soiled with black.~~. In his bearing and manners there was something really of the settled civil servant. He was restless; he would ruffle his hair. With his elbows on the table he would prop up his head with his arms. Finally he looked right at me and broke into conversation loudly and firmly.

"May I, dear sir, ~~despite my appearance"—he pointed to his clothes—~~"turn to you with polite conversation? For although you don't look important, I can tell from experience that you are an educated young man and someone who is not accustomed to drinking. I myself have always respected education when joined to sincere feelings; and besides I am a titular counselor.* [Marmeladov is my surname.] May I ask—have you served?"

"No . . . I am a student," I answered, surprised by the particularly courteous tone with which he spoke.[5]

"A student [perhaps, or a former student]. That's what I thought. That you were a student or were engaged in educational work.

---

* The ninth grade, of fourteen, in the civil service.

[5] I turned my attention. He was apparently unwashed and had black hair. Did you ever spend the night on the hay barges of the Neva? Well, I have spent nights on them.

Please." He got up, swayed a bit, took his half bottle and small glass, and then quickly sat down at my table, a little to one side of me.

"Dear sir," he continued, "Poverty is not a vice, that is true. I know that drunkenness is no virtue, and that's even truer. But destitution,* dear sir, destitution is a vice. They jail you for being destitute. They don't chase you out of the company of human kind with a stick; they sweep you out ~~like garbage from the kitchen~~. Because of destitution the worst rascal can hold [you] in contempt and he has a right, for when destitute, I will be the first to feel contempt for myself [and more so than the rest]. Poverty is permitted, but destitution is ~~severely~~ not permitted. In poverty you can [still] hold on to the ~~dignity~~ gentility of [natural] feelings, but no one can ever do so in destitution. Dear sir, Mr. Lebeziatnikov beat up my wife two weeks ago, but my wife is not me. Yes, not me! ~~Look, I'm drinking~~ . . . Do you understand? Hmm . . . Let me ask you [yet] have you, dear sir, ever passed the night on the Neva on a hay barge?"

"No-o," I answered ~~in part, a little~~, surprised by the question.

"Well, I've come from five nights on such a barge, and look at me!" He poked at the half bottle with his finger, poured himself some, and drank it.

To be sure, wisps of hay were to be seen sticking to his clothes. I looked him over, and it was quite probable that he had not undressed or washed himself for five days. His hands in particular were frightfully soiled, and his fingernails were very dirty.

His conversation seemed to awaken the attention of the others in the room. Even the boys behind the counter came to life and began to snicker. The proprietor[6] [yawning] came down from his room and sat down some distance away, listening with curiosity to Marmeladov. ~~He also was, it seemed, a bit drunk.~~ Marmeladov was apparently known here. [In all likelihood his speech had taken on a certain ornateness from the frequent habit of holding forth with these extraordinary monologues.] Although he was drunk, he spoke volubly and smoothly, but ~~dragged out his speech~~ lost the point only a little. He took a long time finishing what he had to say. [But that was near the end of his speech.] He was one of those drunkards who

---

* The Russian word here is *nishcheta,* a state of poverty in which man's self-respect has been affected. The French word *misère* is a better translation than "poverty."

[6] also, it seems, a bit drunk.

drinks by fits and who needs a glass or two ~~each day~~ in order to shake everything loose in him again.

"Permit me, dear sir, permit me," [he continued heatedly; "I foresee your objections": as if I had already objected to something]. "You will say [perhaps] that I am responsible [more than anyone] for my destitution. I agree and I agree completely. But permit me [to ask you], young man: Have you ever had to beg for money when you knew you had no chance of getting it?"

"I don't know . . . perhaps. What do you mean by no chance of getting it?"

"That is, no chance, sir, no chance whatsoever. Look you [know], for example, [know fully beforehand] that this man, this beautifully decorated and benevolent old man will not give you any money under any circumstances. Why, I ask, should he give me any? He knows that I will not pay it back. From compassion? Well [Mr. Lebeziatnikov, who keeps in touch with the currents of thought, explained the other day] that [compassion] in our time is forbidden even by science. Well, why then [after that] should he give you anything? And yet knowing full well that ~~you would drown before he~~ he will not give you anything, you go just the same begging to borrow some sum from him."

"Why go?"

"But suppose there is no one else to turn to? [And suppose there is nowhere else to go? You've got to go somewhere.][7] Suppose besides him there is no longer anyone, anyone to turn to? So you go ~~to this decorated and perfumed~~. And so I went before my only daughter went out for the first time with a yellow ticket.* Because my [older] daughter makes her living by walking the streets with a yellow ticket. [My good sir]," he added with a certain anxiety as he looked at me. "But don't worry, my dear sir," he said when both the little ruffians behind the counter let out a chuckle and even the proprietor smiled. "Don't worry, everyone here knows everything about me, and I look at all this not with disdain but with humility. [The hell with it.][8] Some man! ~~In your face [young man] I noticed something akin to suffering, and that's why I have turned to you at this time. And so I turn only to you at this moment, and I speak only with you~~. Dear sir, [do you know] I kissed the cleaned and lacquered

---

* Official identification card carried by prostitutes.

[7] Every man must have somewhere to go.

[8] What a man! He is a vital man.

boots of the old man, kissed the dust under his feet, and then I returned home drunk ~~after kissing his boots~~. Because, dear sir, when you have to kiss the boots of another for the first time, a ~~man~~ being just like you [even a very decorated old man], then you will most certainly return home drunk. If you are sensitive by nature, you will return home even the third and the fifth times drunk."

He grunted and took a drink.

"Idler!" muttered the proprietor. "Why don't you go to work? Why don't you serve, if you are a civil functionary?"

"Why don't I serve, dear sir," Marmeladov went on, turning only to me, as if I have asked him [this] the question. "Why don't I serve? Don't you think my heart pains? Don't you think it pains? Don't you think I feel the same things? When Mr. Lebeziatnikov beat up my wife with his own hands ~~three weeks~~ a month and a half ago, and I lay there drunk, don't you think I suffered? Permit me, permit me, dear sir. Can you [I'll even say] will you dare state definitely, looking at me at this time, that I am not a pig?"

"Well, dear sir," he continued after[9] the ~~the owner smiled again~~ little ruffians sniggered again, "I am a ~~wild~~ pig, but she is a lady! I am a monster, but my wife is ~~a lady~~ an educated woman, has a lofty heart, and carries a noble name. Dear sir, if I look like a pig, then know that I am a scoundrel, and she was a ~~noble person and~~ educated as an officer's daughter ~~brought up in a wealthy house~~, [endowed with wealth and nobility]. And yet, if only she would take pity on me; for it is necessary to take pity on (every man).[10] Whoever he may be (whoever the man, you have to, have to), (it is necessary) that someone take pity [on him also]. [Because] my wife is a generous lady but is also unjust. ~~Didn't I suffer?~~ And even though I ~~and I know~~ [feel at the bottom of my heart] that when she pulls me by the hair (every time I come home), dear sir, she does so only from pity. (For she does pull me by the hair), but, dear God, if only she could pity me without pulling my hair? My dear sir, dear sir, I might be myself again. Yes! No, I would not regain my senses! . . ."

And now ~~having come to, he added~~ [awakening] the owner [yawned]. Marmeladov banged resolutely on the table with his fist.

—No! I would not regain my senses, dear sir. ~~Because there had been experiences before. And on top of that I have lied to all of you,~~

---

9 There followed a general burst of laughter.

10 Otherwise a man will perish; he will not be able to lift himself up. Ask him to—and—and he will lift himself up.

~~because it is useless to pity him who does not pity others. But don't you think I feel, don't I feel?~~ Do you know, do you know, dear sir, that I once sold her stockings in order to get money for liquor? Not her boots, for that would still be rather in the order of things, but I sold her stockings, her stockings for drink. I had drunk up her mohair scarf just for a small glass. We live in a corner, in a cold corner; the children [three small ones] and Katerina Ivanovna, who works from morning to night, scraping and cleaning, washing the children, because she has become accustomed [from childhood] to cleanliness. Yet she has a bad chest and is prone to consumption. And when I drank up her scarf, she caught cold [that winter], and began to cough, and now she spits blood. And I feel that. Don't you think I feel [that]? ~~Don't you think I suffer?~~ [Just because I'm drunk, don't you think I feel it? No sir, I] may lie drunk, but I suffer.[11] Because the drunker I am, the more I understand. ~~I am a pig and a scoundrel . . . but I suffer.~~ Without this suffering I would not want to live . . . And I do not look for pleasure but for suffering in drink." ~~for that reason I drink~~

"Dear sir, I perceived a certain suffering in your face. And therefore I have not made an exhibition of my shame, but have talked to you alone. ~~You will understand about my wife, and therefore I will tell you about my wife from the beginning.~~ She was brought up in comfort. [Dear sir, my wife, Katerina Ivanovna was brought up in comfort.] She was educated in an honorable provincial institute, and when she graduated she danced with her scarf [before the governor and other personages]. And for that she received a [gold] medal and a letter of praise. The medal was sold, a long time ago [previously] sold, [yes], but she still has the letter of praise printed on parchment, lying in a chest of drawers. Indeed, not long ago we showed it to the landlady, for even though we live shabbily, and have endless arguments with our landlady, still she has to take pride in her letter of praise before someone. I don't condemn her! I don't condemn her! This is all she has left [of her memories]. [The rest has all gone up in smoke.] She is a fiery, proud, and unbending woman; she washes her own floor, and eats only bread, but she will not permit disrespect to be shown her.[12] When Mr. Lebeziatnikov beat her up in our corner, she went to bed not so much from the

[11] I suffer precisely from the fact that I feel all that, and from the rest.

[12] Because of that she wouldn't overlook Mr. Lebeziatnikov's vulgarity.

beating as from what she felt. She was a widow with three small children when I married her. She married [her first husband] an [infantry] officer out of love; she eloped [with him], fleeing from ~~from relatives~~ the home of her parents. She was mad about her husband, but ~~he retired~~ [he] didn't want to serve, and he began to play cards, became a drunkard. [He ended up in court because of that], and he died. He used to beat her near the end, although she [herself][13] would fight with him. I know this to be a fact [from documents].[14] But up to now she remembers him [with tears] and she [keeps] reproaching me with his example.[15] She was left [with two] small children in a remote province, where I happened to be [then]; and she was left in such hopeless destitution that although I had seen much, I couldn't even describe it to you. ~~I can. Meanwhile, the relatives died, and~~ All her relatives had deserted her. And she was proud [proud]. And then, dear sir, then I, also a widower with a twelve-year-old daughter from my first marriage, offered her my hand, because I couldn't look on such ~~poverty~~ suffering. You can judge for yourself, my dear sir, how poor she must have been, when she, who was educated and of good family, consented to marry me. I was already addicted to drink. But she married me; crying and sobbing [and twisting her arms], ~~she married in tears~~ she married me [because there was nowhere else] to go.[16] And then I, dear sir, feeling [all this], didn't touch a drop for a whole year. And for a whole year ~~I stood it~~ [I] fulfilled all my duties, but calumny suddenly, and not because of my fault [but because of changes in the office]. And then I began to touch again . . ."

He touched the bottle with his finger [so as to show what he had touched].

"A year and a half ago we found ourselves [here] in this capital [which is decorated with countless monuments]. [And] Here I got a position. Got it and . . . lost ~~my position and salary~~ it again. Do

---

[13] did not permit him.

[14] I know it to be really a fact from documents.

[15] If he were alive, perhaps she ~~would have stopped loving him long ago . . .~~ but dead [she would have poisoned his existence]. But dead he remained a comfort to her. [And I was happy about it, I was happy, I was happy that ~~at least~~ she had something to remember.] Yes, I am not angry.

[16] Do you understand, dear sir, what it means to have nowhere to go? [And I would go to my well-decorated old man and kiss his boots.] Oh, dear sir.

you understand, sir? We live [now] in a corner, at Amalia Fyodorovna Lippevekhzel's, but I don't know how we live and how we pay. There is always a crowd in our rooms, a veritable Sodom." ~~And the whole day Katerina Ivanovna washes and cleans and irons and washes the young children without stopping. But what can a woman make [and blames and criticizes me every minute] and furthermore in gold~~.

"Well [during this time], [my] dear sir, during this time, my daughter, [from the former marriage], grew up, and what didn't she suffer, my daughter, Sonia, at the hands of her stepmother [in growing up]—I can't even tell about it. For although Katerina Ivanovna, my wife, is a generous woman, she is also impetuous, unjust and cutting. Sonia didn't receive any education; ~~She was gentle in soul and heart like an angel of the Lord;~~ she received only her gentleness from God. I tried to teach her some geography five years ago and also world history, but I myself knew little about these subjects, and what is more we didn't have the right handbooks[17] [because we have nothing worth while in books]. Hardly necessary to talk about it [they went the way of everything else and with them the whole education][18] and with that her education ended: ~~we got up to Cyrus, King of the Persians, [more or less].~~ Later, when she had matured, she read several books, [the contents of which for the most part] were romantic. Then not long ago, ~~six months ago~~ about half a year ago, she read some book about the earth and what there is inside of it [Do you know it, sir?], and she was very taken by this book. [She even read portions of it aloud to the children and we all listened to her reading.] And that is the long and short of her education. [Mr. Lebeziatnikov recommended it to her, for he had some designs on her.]"

"Now I will ask you, dear sir, can a woman earn [more in a day] than 15 kopecks (silver) on the average, and then only by working without stopping?[19] [Perhaps even 12.] And then the state counsellor, Klopshtok, Ivan Ivanovich—Do you know him? He not only did not pay her for [sewing] a half-dozen shirts [of fine linen] [to this day], but he even insulted her and chased her away. He stamped his foot and called her things no woman should hear just because

---

[17] Because I had sold them for drink.

[18] And there were books, but soon, yes, they disappeared.

[19] And now a question: how much do you think a woman can make a day?

she had sewn a collar wrong [crooked]. On top of that the children were hungry still! Katerina Ivanovna wrings her hands and red spots appear on her cheeks, as they always do in that illness when you get excited. ~~Katerina Ivanovna is a generous but unjust and cutting woman.~~

" 'You live,' she says to Sonia, 'with us, you free-loader, eat and drink and soak in our warmth.' But how can you speak of eating and drinking[20] when for three days not only we but the little ones have not seen as much as a crust of bread. I, dear sir, was lying there drunk and (heard) my dear little Sonia answer—she is ~~an angel of the Lord; she is gentle and mild~~ so gentle with a voice so tender, 'You don't really, Katerina Ivanovna, want me to go out to do that.' Daria Feklistovna, an ill-intentioned woman, well-known to the police, had already stopped by three times for that purpose. 'Well, what do you think,' says Katerina Ivanovna, 'what are you saving it for! You think it's a treasure!' But do not blame her, do not blame her, dear sir, do not blame her! She no longer was in the possession of her senses when she said it; she said it when the children had gone ~~hungry~~ two days without eating and were crying, when red spots had appeared on her emaciated cheeks [when her mind had got unhinged, and she said it more to hurt [to insult] than in earnest]. ~~Well, continuing, things went along that way for two or three days.~~ And then [precisely on that day, in the morning] the civil counsellor Klopshtok insulted ~~my daughter~~ her because of the shirts; he spit in her face and pushed her with his own hands, and dressed her down with coarse words. She returned insulted and without the money. Katerina Ivanovna was waiting impatiently for her return with the money ~~because the children could no longer wait~~.[21] It's useless to go over what happened, because once the children begin to cry, whether from sickness or hunger, Katerina Ivanovna begins immediately to beat them. Sonia suddenly got up, put on her kerchief, her coat, and left the apartment (about 6 o'clock). When she returned ~~completely pale and shaken~~ at nine she went straight up to Katerina Ivanovna and put thirty rubles [in silver]

---

[20] and what warmth

[21] I lay there then and heard everything, heard all their confused mumblings, because I was lying there. But what was said, I cannot, that is, Katerina Ivanovna seemed more to be reproaching, tormenting herself, and crying; finally she became quiet.

on a small table in front of her; she did not say a single word [when she did that], but took her [green, large winter] shawl, covered her head and face with it and lay down on the bed with her face turned toward the wall. She lay there without looking at anyone, but with [her shoulders and] body trembling all over ~~from sobbing. And I~~ I lay there drunk ~~but I heard and saw all~~. And I saw, my dear sir, how my wife, my Katerina Ivanovna ~~also without saying a word~~, went up to my little Sonia's bed, knelt down, and for two[22] hours [without the slightest sign of wanting to get up] kissed her legs. Later they both fell asleep in each other's arms ~~crying~~, both . . . martyrs. [God! . . .]"

He took a drink . . . and then knocked the glass against the table.[23]

"What are the reasons, dear sir?" he said and his chin trembled. "Ugh," said the owner [yawning] and left the room. "From that time on, dear sir," [he continued after having been silent from that

time], "because of an unpleasant incident and because some spiteful people had reported her [Daria Feklistovna had a hand in that because the appropriate respect had not been shown her], my daughter, Sonia was [forced] to get a yellow ticket and therefore could no longer live with us. [For even Katerina Ivanovna could not permit that, let alone Lebeziatnikov.] Since that time [Sonia] supports our whole family and lightens Katerina Ivanovna's lot. She stops by to see us, but[24] lives herself at the tailor's, Ukhvatov [where she rents an apartment], who is tongue-tied with a wife who is also tongue-tied and all the children are also tongue-tied. They are the poorest of people and ~~very good~~ they let her have a room . . . [and tongue-tied, humm . . .]. A folding screen has been set up, and behind the folding screen . . . Well, yes. What am I saying! But yes! Behind the screen . . . [what are you saying!] Well, as soon as I got up in the morning, I ~~got dressed~~ put on my rags, stretched out my hands to heaven, and went off to his Excellency, Ivan Afanasevich [and dropped down before him at his feet]. ~~This is the way things are, I said. Take me back, defend me, [have mercy on me].~~ Do you know his Excellency, Ivan Afanasevich? You don't know him? Well then you have missed knowing a man of God. He is a candle

---

22 three

23 Because I don't look for pleasure, but for suffering in drink.

24 Now she lives at the tailor's

held up to the face of the Lord. He had the patience to listen to [all] and his eyes were filled with tears: 'Well,' he says, 'Marmeladov, you have already deceived my expectations once; you gave me your word and then went back on it. ~~You yourself forced me to fire you.~~ Watch out! I'm giving you another chance, but watch out. Remember that I am taking you back on my own responsibility . . . [and after this don't hope for any mercy]. Go.' I kissed the dust of his feet, in thought that is, because he would not have permitted me to do it physically, since he is a high dignitary, a man with advanced administrative and educated thoughts. When I returned home and announced that I had got my job back and that I was getting paid again—God! You can't imagine what happened then!"

Marmeladov stopped, evidently ~~strongly~~ excited. At that moment a whole gang of drunkards entered, already drunk, and the sounds of a hired barrel organ resounded [and a child's voice singing] "The Little Farm"* at the entrance. It became noisy. The owner and the help busied themselves with the newcomers. Marmeladov, paying no attention to them, continued his tale. He was ~~apparently~~ [already very] drunk; he repeated [at times] the same words [two or three times], would get off the point, but nevertheless he continued fluently and volubly. The memories of his recent success [concerning his job] glowed in his face.

"Only a month and a half ago, my good man, this happened. As soon as [both] Katerina Ivanovna and Sonia learned about it, God! It was as if I had moved to paradise itself. Before I was treated like a brute, and heard only abuse. And then they walked on their tiptoes; they kept the children quiet. 'Zakharii Semenovich has been tired out by his work; he needs his rest.' They served me coffee before I went to work. [They boiled the cream. They began to serve me actual cream with my coffee.] And how they were able to scrape together ~~70 k.~~ 11 rubles [and a half] for a decent uniform for me. [Sonechka. Yes, it was Sonechka's work . . .] Boots, calico shirt fronts of the best sort, a uniform, everything of the best sort was somehow found for 11½. I returned from the office the first day in the morning. I looked: Katerina Ivanovna had prepared two dishes. Soup and corned beef with horse-radish sauce. And what was even more remarkable: she didn't have any dresses [everything . . . well in one word, everything had gone down the same drain, even the last rags]

---

* A popular song.

and yet I looked and she had dressed up as if she were getting ready to go visiting, as if it were a holiday of some kind in our home. And how they know to get such things done [do it somehow]: they do up their hair, put on a small collar [of some kind], clean armlets, and (a completely) different person stands before you; she had grown young, got prettier, and begun to live again. My Sonia, my angel, helped only with money, and added that it was not seemly that she visit us frequently [any longer]; perhaps at dusk so that no one would see her. (Note that, that!) I lay down after dinner, and tried to fall asleep ~~on the couch~~, but can you imagine Katerina Ivanovna couldn't stand it. Only a week ago she had almost come to blows with our landlady [with Amaliia Karlovna]; they had called each other the basest names, and now she ~~couldn't stand it~~ invited her for coffee [so as to tell someone about all this once again][25] ~~while I was sleeping, and only,~~ solely to brag before her. ~~She spoke in a whisper, so as not to awaken me.~~[26] She said, 'Well now Zakhar Semenych is back at the office; he is receiving his salary and has been in to see his Excellency himself. His Excellency himself came out, left everyone else, gave word to have everyone else wait, and took Zakhar Ivanovich to his office [and seated him].' (Note that, note that!) 'I remember, of course,' he says, 'Zakhar Semenych, your services, and I know that formerly you suffered from this (thoughtless) weakness. But now seeing that you have given your word, and valuing your abilities, and seeing that things went badly without you . . . (Do you hear that, that!), I put my trust,' he said, 'in your honest and honorable word.' That is, she thought up everything, not only to brag[27] but to find comfort for herself, my God! [And I do not condemn it, do not condemn it] dear sir, don't you understand? It may be funny to you, but I understand, I understand . . . I feel it. It's not funny to me.[28] ~~To be sure, she also wanted to brag a little before Lippevekhzel. She is an ambitious woman: We, she says, now will rent a decent apartment, and we will have only to set up housekeeping; there followed discussions and calculations as to how to set up housekeeping [for two hours they exchanged ideas];~~

---

[25] to have someone before her

[26] And I do not condemn, do not condemn, he says; that's how they chatter.

[27] I'm not much to look at, and not much of a husband. Yet she pinched my cheek when we were alone and she said: you dear little thing.

[28] (They raised me to the rank of general)

~~they were getting up to thousands [got up to 6]; they even got [finally] to making me a general! Note that! Note that! Oh, dear sir!~~ [And] when I brought her my first wages in full a week ago, 23 rubles, 40 kopecks [Can you understand it?], she called me her little darling. 'What a precious thing you are!' And alone! Do you understand? [The important thing is that she did it when we were alone, with no children about.] What is there in me that is attractive? What am I good for ~~in understanding a woman~~ as a husband? No—She pinched my cheek: 'Oh, what a pretty little dove you are,' she said."

Marmeladov stopped[29] again and his chin trembled. [But] he managed to restrain himself. That bottle and that [boundless] love for his wife and his family bewildered me . . .

"And I spent that whole day and that whole evening, dear sir," added Marmeladov, "in winged dreams: how I would arrange [everything] and dress the children and give her peace and save my only daughter from ruin and bring her back into the bosom of the family. Well, the next day, that is [exactly] five days ago, about evening, like a thief in the night I stole the keys to the trunk from Katerina Ivanovna, took out all ~~that was left~~ of yesterday's wages, and that's it. Five days away from home; they're waiting for me there; my job is over and my uniform is lying in a Stremyanny Street tavern in exchange for the clothes that I'm wearing . . . That's it.[30] Now, dear sir, may I ask what I may expect from Katerina Ivanovna when I return home?"

"Well . . . Nothing good, that's for sure."

"Hmm. Yes, [to be sure? O. K. But I have just come from Sonia's]; I stopped by this morning ~~at her place~~. This very half-bottle was bought with her money. [She brought me thirty kopecks with her own hand.] I went there for that purpose, to beg (her) for money for drink."

"And ~~Did she give it?~~ did you beg her? ~~at her place~~ And she gave you the money?"[31]

"She didn't [even] say a word, [and she gave it]. ~~She took her last money, brought it out, and gave it.~~ [I know that afterward] only she looked at me this way silently. You know how angels suffer

---

[29] wanted to laugh but suddenly

[30] I drank not for pleasure but for suffering . . . I redeemed my guilt by suffering.

[31] And you took it? I took it.

for people, cry, but never reproach them, dear sir. ~~That is more difficult. That is more difficult than meeting Katerina Ivanovna now.~~ Since morning, ~~her face is before me, her~~ Sonia's face haunts me. The thirty kopecks were her last, that is, her very last,[32] do you understand. ~~Do you understand, young man? And what's more,~~ Do you understand that she has to take care to be clean? Do you know what it means to be clean? [A clean skirt] a small jar of pommade, clean stockings, a clean little boot so as to show off on the street when she has to cross over a puddle, do you understand? Understand? And yet I took her last 30 kopecks.[33, 34] I came to beg for drink. Do you understand [everything now]? Have you heard everything now, everything? Well, tell me then. Who [then] will take pity on someone like me?"

"Yeh, why pity you!" the proprietor cried out; he was again at our side. The others, both those who had been listening and those who had not been listening, began to laugh, looking only at Marmeladov.

"Take pity, why take pity [on me]!" yelled Marmeladov, [getting up in veritable inspiration]. "[Why take pity, you say. Yes!] True there is no reason to take pity on me! I ought to be crucified [and not pitied] crucified! But crucify [judge, crucify] but take pity on him! Who, who will take pity on us, if there is no one to take pity? Don't we have feelings, don't we suffer? Do you think, merchant, that I enjoyed this half bottle? No, I was looking for suffering, suffering at the bottom of it, suffering and tears, because I know whose money I put on your counter! [And I found them, and that is why I drink and that is why I went to beg money for drink.] One will take pity. One. [In order to take pity, you have to understand. Who will understand? One will!] For he took pity on all, the good and the evil, the very wise, and the fallen! For this they laughed at him, ~~and laugh at him to this day~~ they insulted him. He will come at the appointed hour and he will ask: 'And where is my daughter, who sold herself for an evil and consumptive stepmother and for someone else's young children? Where is my daughter who took pity on her flesh and blood, on her revolting drunk of a father, and who was not repulsed by his bestiality?' And he will say: 'come to me! I have already for-

---

[32] Sir, and now how can I go to Katerina Ivanovna; Sonia to me.

[33] Sir, what can I hope for myself? It's impossible to return to Katerina Ivanovna's. I went to Sonia's.

[34] What was most of all, most of all difficult for me was going today to Sonia's.

given you once, I have already forgiven you once. Your many sins are forgiven now because you loved much![35] Come!' And he will judge all [then], the good and the evil [the just and the unjust, the meek and the cynical] and the very wise and the reasonable. And when he has judged all, ~~the very wise and the reasonable~~ then he will call us: 'Appear' [he will say, 'You! Come out] drunkards, come out you who were weak and shameless.' And we will appear, all of us, without shame and [we will all stand up and] we will say: 'You come also.' ~~He will say: you are pigs.~~ And, and the very wise will cry out, and the reasonable will cry out: 'Lord, why do you take such as these to yourself; because they bear the image of the beasts and they alone have made themselves such?' And he will say 'I know all that, you who are very wise, and I know all that, you who are reasonable, but I am receiving [them], because not one of them considered [and does not consider] himself worthy of this.' [And he will forgive all because of their suffering.] And he will stretch out his very pure and crucified hands and he will say, 'Come': And we will fall at his feet and . . . we will cry. And he will understand everything . . . Then, Katerina Ivanovna and ~~I will become reconciled.~~ I will embrace and we will burst into tears. And he will understand . . . everything . . ."

"Lord, thy kingdom come!"

And he sat down, as if he were exhausted and sunk in thought.

"Do you think by any stretch of the imagination that you're going to heaven?" cried out one of the customers.

"Well, not to paradise!" grumbled Marmeladov without lifting his head, "but, they'll find somehow a little corner ~~where we will all find peace, so~~ for us somewhere. [Yes, a little corner, a very small corner.] By rank—by rank—by rank—by rank . . ."

"He's lost his marbles."

"Let's go . . . dear sir," [he said, lifting his head] . . . "take me home, I live . . . in the Kozel building, in the courtyard. It's time to go to Katerina Ivanovna."

I myself wanted to get away from him as quickly as possible, and therefore I agreed to take him home. It turned out that his legs were weaker than his speech, and he leaned heavily on me. We had about two or three hundred steps to go.

"Don't think that I am afraid of Katerina Ivanovna, young man,"

---

[35] For the same thing as before. For the same thing. For the past! Marmeladov began to sob.

he muttered on the way [very excited]. "But it's true. I am afraid of Katerina Ivanovna, but not because she will begin to pull my hair, and beat me. No [not because of that]: I am afraid of her eyes; [yes, her eyes], I am afraid of the red spots on her cheeks and [also, and also . . .] [I am afraid] of [her] halting breath. Have you seen how hard it is for consumptives to breathe when they get excited . . . I am afraid of children's crying also . . . [because if Sonia doesn't feed, then . . .] And the fact that I will have my hair pulled and my face beaten; well you know [young man] that this is ~~not only not pain~~ a pleasure for me [without which I couldn't live and couldn't return home]." ~~For if they do not say anything to me [now], that will mean more suffering; if they do not say anything [absolutely nothing] as Sonia had not, then that [still] will mean more suffering.~~

"Well, here's the building, Kozel's building . . . the locksmith's. Kozel's . . . [the rich German's] . . . Lead the way."

I took him almost to the fifth floor. The farther we went the dirtier and darker the stairway became. Besides, it was already 10 o'clock outside; and although it was not yet night at that hour, it was [very] dark on the top of the stairs. A small dark door at the very end of the stairway on the very top, right under the roof, was open.[36] A candle stub illuminated a very small [very poor] room. Everything was ~~dirty~~ scattered about in disorder, and especially children's rags. You could see the whole room from the entry. There was a folding screen in one corner, and very probably a bed behind the screen. There were ~~three~~ two chairs in the room and a terribly torn couch covered with oilcloth; a [plain pine bare] table stood in front of the couch. A nearly burnt-down candle in an iron candleholder was on the table. It turned out that Marmeladov lived in an actual room and not in a corner, but the room itself was a passageway. The door which led to further rooms or cages, which made up the apartment of Amaliia Lippevekhzel, was open. Noise and shouts came from the other rooms. People were laughing. People seemed to be playing cards, and someone was drinking tea. From behind the door, the most unceremonious words would come flying.

I recognized Katerina Ivanovna immediately. She was a [terribly] thin and pale woman [but tall, and well-shaped with beautiful dark hair] truly with cheeks spotted with red. She was walking back and

---

[36] The door was open; before the door the sound of crying. Do you hear? Go in because I can't.

forth in the room; ~~wringing her hands~~ her lips were feverish [and she was breathing unevenly. Her eyes were glittering feverishly]. She was a woman about thirty, ~~still not old~~ still attractive with a sharp ~~at the very least with an intelligent~~ [and sort of fixed] look. You could make out everything in the dark by the bright but dying light [of the candle end] flickering on her face, but she did not notice us. It was stuffy in the room, but she kept the windows closed. An insufferable smell came in from the stairs, but the door to the stairs was ~~also~~ kept open. Waves of [foul] tobacco smoke came from the half-opened door. She was coughing, but she did not close the door. The smallest girl, about five, slept on the floor, sort of sitting and burying her head in the couch. A boy [probably only a year] older than she [very thin and weak] stood in a corner trembling all over [and he was crying]. Apparently he had been beaten. The oldest girl, about ~~eight~~ seven, [tall and thin like a matchstick] took him by the arm, whispered to him, pleaded with him, pressed him against her, restrained him so that somehow he would not begin crying again; while she was doing this, she followed her mother's actions fearfully. All the children were in ~~frightful~~ rags. Marmeladov did not want to go in. He went down on his knees at the doorway, but he pushed me ahead. The woman, seeing me, stopped in front of me ~~not knowing~~ [as if considering and trying to figure out] why I had entered. But then she seemed to decide suddenly that I was going into the other rooms, since their room [was] a passageway. [Not paying any attention to me] she walked [past me] to close the entry door and suddenly[37] she saw her husband on his knees.

"Ah!" she yelled [in a frenzy]. "It's you! [Wretch!] The money? Where's the money? The money?" And she threw herself into searching him. Marmeladov opened wide his arms to help with the search of his pockets. There was no money of any kind.

"The money!" she kept yelling, and then suddenly grabbing him by the hair dragged him into the room.

"And this is a pleasure for me! This is not painful, but pleasurable, yyyyoung man," Marmeladov ~~was repeating~~ kept crying out, [shaken by the hair] and his forehead hitting against the floor. The baby awoke and began to cry. The young boy began to cry also . . .

"He spent it all on drink, everything, everything, everything on drink!" She screamed in despair ~~wringing her hands~~. And he doesn't

---

[37] she shouted

have his clothes.[38] Hungry! Hungry!" she continued wringing her hands. "Aren't you, aren't you ashamed?" Suddenly throwing herself on me, "You've come from a tavern! You drank with him. You helped him drink ~~his money~~ it up. Get out!"

And I myself was glad to go. The inner door was opening and a great number of people were pouring out. People with cigarettes, pipes, cards, and in skullcaps stretched their hands out; they were grinning and laughing [especially] [when Marmeladov was being dragged by his hair and yelling that he liked it]. An ominous screech was then heard: that was Amaliia Lippevekhzel cutting her way through to restore order and terrify for the hundredth time the poor woman [with the abusive] demand that she get out of the apartment the next morning. I went away as quickly as possible. I thought only of how careless I had been in entering [the tavern and now here], showing myself to so many people. But what was done was done. I cursed Marmeladov and all the others. I felt no pity. I wasn't concerned with that. That wasn't in my thoughts.

---

[38] and he drank up his clothes

II

Raskolnikov and his mother—Raskolnikov's love for Sonia—Confession or suicide—Sonia's character—Technical notations

These pages contain very diverse material, but Dostoevsky seems to call special attention to these points: the relations of Raskolnikov and his mother and the contradictory feelings he has for her; Dunia's love-hate relationship with Sonia; the characterization of Luzhin and an exposition of his theory of permissible killing; Raskolnikov's love for Sonia; his confession to Sonia and her contradictory reactions of sympathy and recoil; various reflections on point of view and the development of the story; several references to a heroic deed Raskolnikov accomplishes at a fire, the beginning, apparently, of his redemption; repeated references to Raskolnikov going off to shoot himself; the alternation of Raskolnikov between loving and hating the oppressed multitudes.

Dostoevsky seems unable to make up his mind as to how the novel should end, and what Raskolnikov's feelings should be toward his act, his confession, and Sonia. Whether Raskolnikov should confess or kill himself is a dilemma that expresses itself in snatches of confessional scenes and repeated references to Raskolnikov going off to put a bullet in his head. The confessional scenes throw into relief the complex and unresolved relations between Raskolnikov and Sonia. References to a love affair, which appear here and at other parts in the notebooks—but not in the final version—complicate the relationship between the two. Raskolnikov insults Sonia at one point, and charges her with not loving him when she advises him to repent. Sonia's reaction to Raskolnikov, expressed with such eloquence and beauty in the final version in her unhesitating and unconditional sympathy for the harm he has done to himself, is ambiguously expressed here in admonitions to repent, the tone of which is a bit too peremptory. Curiously, on more than one occasion she expresses horror rather than sympathy.

Indeed, the Sonia of this section is in many respects different from the Sonia of the novel. As in the novel she is humble, thinks of herself as a sinner, and embodies love and humility. But she also feels insult, has definite views, and even attempts actively to impose her views on Raskolnikov. For example: "She says to him *afterward:* 'we could not say we loved each other until you had given yourself up.' " We hardly recognize Sonia in the following note: "Finally, she wrote him a letter. I love you. I will be your slave. She was attracted by his pride, independence, and by his preaching that she was not humbled." A Sonia united with Raskolnikov in revolt against society is, of course, what Raskolnikov invites her to be in the novel, but which she is most definitely not. In the notes Dostoevsky seems to have first conceived of her as something of a "double" character: "*Sonia,* always meek, always without humor, always serious and quiet; then suddenly, she would burst out laughing terribly at trifles, and this affected the young man as gracious." Some of her conflicting traits are caught in the following: "N.B. *She* thinks of herself as a deep sinner, a fallen profligate, beyond salvation; she is terribly modest, but once insulted she is beside herself."

Dostoevsky was, of course, right in purging her of these conflicting traits. In the novel itself she is unrelievedly self-sacrificing and humble. She moves Raskolnikov powerfully by dissipating the hostility he tries to provoke in her. He confesses to her because she does not want anything from him, because she alone is ready to accept all of him, even the murderer in him. For everyone else—friend, society, mother, sister—he is an abstraction, a partial Raskolnikov. And Raskolnikov wants, of course, to be accepted; one is even tempted to say that one of the reasons he commits the murder is to provoke the rejection which he suspects in others. If Sonia is to accept Raskolnikov unconditionally, then she must be purged of many of the qualities she has in these notes.

References to Raskolnikov's relations with his mother are sprinkled throughout the section, and some of them throw light on these complex relations. Much that is veiled in the final version is explicit in these notes. It seems clear in the novel itself that Raskolnikov feels the burden of his mother's love and expectations, and resents the guilt she makes him bear for failing that love and those expectations. She makes him feel that he is hurting her and his sister, but the hurt she feels in the final version is veiled by a repeated love and concern that she expresses for his welfare. But in this section of the notes, we find the mother saying: "He hurt me very much before (by his love for the landlady's daughter)." And on more than one occasion Dostoevsky tells us explicitly that Raskolnikov feels his mother's caresses as a burden.

Raskolnikov's attitudes toward the people for whom—according to one set of motives—he has committed the murder are ambiguous: Raskolnikov alternates—as he does in the final version—between sympathy for the oppressed multitudes and arrogant indifference to them. This is not significantly different from the final version, but Dostoevsky's irritation at his inability to fix the course of things is different: "After the illness, etc. It is absolutely necessary to establish the course of things firmly and clearly and to eliminate what is vague, that is, explain the whole murder one way or another, and make its character and relations clear." I think it is clear, finally, that Raskolnikov loves the people abstractly, but feels contempt for them in reality. The theme of loving humanity "from afar" is found throughout Dostoevsky's work; one might even say that the Grand Inquisitor resolves the conflicting Raskolnikov's attitudes by loving the people contemptuously.

Throughout this section Dostoevsky is concerned with technical matters: point of view, tone, development. He is particularly concerned with "tone": "Very serious, but with subtle humor," he says of one scene. When he sketches out in brief the scene of Raskolnikov's first visit to the pawnbroker's apartment, he realizes that background information will have to be given; but dramatic in instinct, he is reluctant to give such background information by exposition: " 'I began by going to her to pawn my watch. I had heard about her a long time ago (student).' N.B. Who this old woman was, the visit, the apartment, etc. How he looked it over (N.B. *Not Clear,* but for the reader, *something of this kind* must be given.)"

Finally, readers may find two other scenes interesting for comparison with the final version, and a commentary on Raskolnikov's moral development anticipatory of one of Dostoevsky's provocative paradoxes. In this section we find Dunia hating Sonia, plotting against her, and then inexplicably falling at her feet. In the novel itself the relations between the two are superficial. Curiously, too, Dostoevsky has Luzhin put forth a theory that justifies murder. In the final version (see Part II, Chapter 5, of the novel) it is Raskolnikov himself who points out that Luzhin's rapacious individualism leads logically to murder. Finally, Dostoevsky says of Raskolnikov: "N.B. His moral development begins from the crime itself, the possibility of such questions arises which would not have existed previously. In the last chapter, in prison, he says that without the crime he would not have reached the point of asking himself *such* questions and experiencing such desires, feelings, needs, strivings, and development." Dostoevsky is referring here surely to the good that comes from Raskolnikov's suffering, but he may also have in mind that ambiguous good that comes from the criminal act because it is a free act. Freud has reminded us of the unbounded compassion Dostoevsky felt for the criminal and explained it by similar criminal tendencies in Dostoevsky. But there was more than neuroticism in this view: Dostoevsky saw the criminal as one who had justifiably defied the judgment of other men and placed himself into contest with the true judge, God.

The mother lost her temper and parted with him forever (?); the next day she came to fawn on him, to smooth over the matter. But not his sister; his sister loves him more, and because of that is more angry; so much pride and indignation.

The sister becomes Sonia's worst enemy; she sets Razumikhin against her; gets him to insult her; and afterward when Razumikhin goes over to Sonia's side, she quarrels with him.[1]

[1] N.B. The sister says: "I want to live more originally, after my own fashion; everyone is afraid to do so, but I want to live as I want."

And then she herself goes to have things out with Sonia; at first she insults her, and then she falls at her feet.

N.B. N.B. N.B. The sister comes to know all.

Then he admits: up to the time I received the letter from my mother, I was still only dreaming. The letter was like a bolt from the blue. Everything turned upside down in me. I had either to give it up or go ahead. At the most decisive moment, Lizaveta.

Razumikhin says: "I have already been to her (to Sonia's) to ask for forgiveness; how happy she was that I had come.

At Razumikhin's party—the student who had knocked at the door with Kokh. "Ah! It was you then."

About Kokh: he still cringes about, and then suddenly! . . . "How base he is . . ."

N.B. Toward the end of the novel some begin to think that he had imagined that he had killed the old woman. Razumikhin believes this and he convinces Sonia of it. Zametov communicates this thought to him.

Beginning with Dec. 7

"That's not the truth," says Sonia.

"You might not have seen anything of the poverty of people if you had lived in comfort and wealth. God sends much unhappiness to him whom he loves and from whom he expects much so that he might learn and see more for himself; because one discerns the suffering of people more easily when one is unhappy than when one is happy."

"But perhaps there is no God," he says to her.

She seemed to want to object, but suddenly she burst into tears.

"But what would I be without God?"

"There is (sometimes) more happiness in suffering."

Razumikhin, defending his paradoxes, insists that no one robs a dead person, that no robbery had taken place, and that the old woman had left a will leaving her money to a convent.

He demonstrates at Razumikhin's what he believes is important: that you need *a guarantee* (5,000) at the very beginning in order to get a solid start; otherwise you'll have to be a scoundrel, fawn and give in to everyone.

"Do you consider this guarantee important?" (Zametov, inspector)

"You are curious to know whether 5,000 is sufficient, even three." (a description of what effect a development of one's strength and a defense of one's freedom may have on one) and the contrary, a picture of the baseness one would have to commit before people like Luzhin if one were poor.[2]

N.B. *About the mother.* She loves me because she sees in me everything beautiful, an unattainable ideal, but if she were to find out, then she would come perhaps to hate me very much. (Lack of faith, doubt, estrangement from his Mother. From his sister, all the more.)

Sonia wins him over.

The mother about Rodia. "He hurt me very much before (by his love for the landlady's daughter)."

His mother calculates what she'll have when she arrives. She'll have three rubles left; she always counts rather on the best because of her ardent desire to see him.

"Better for my sister to be a Negro, better for her to be a slave, better to be Sonia than the concubine of a 'Monsieur' holding down two positions."

Chebilov says to Raskolnikov. *Tant que** I've put my affairs in good order, I am useful to others, and therefore the more I am an egoist, the better it is for others. As for the old beliefs: you loved, you thought of others, and you let your own affairs go down the drain, and you ended up being a weight around the neck of your neighbor. It's simply a matter of arithmetic.[3] No, you know, I like the realists of the new generation, and not those romanticizings, the shoemaker and Pushkin; and although I do not agree with them in parts, still the general tendency.[4]**

Individualists. It is given to me for one instant and that instant.

---

* French: "as long as."

** Chebilov's speech is to be compared to one made by Luzhin in Part II, Chapter 5, of the final version of the novel.

[2] N.B. *At Razumikhin's.* Zametov says: "Perhaps you acted like a scoundrel before Il'ia Petrovich then because you were sick."

"No, I did it simply because I am a scoundrel. But you know you were very good when that thought about illness came to you."

"And you are very proud; you don't even want to justify yourself."

N.B. "Still it's true what he said about my acting basely when I was panic-stricken," Raskolnikov thought to himself when he was home.

[3] After the arithmetic, he went out on the Hay Market: And why have I got the ax ready? Why have I thought it over? Why have I counted the steps?

[4] He reads and thinks: about Neofitov, about Gavrilov (Kokh), etc. About causes and detachments.

That a civil crime—agreed, but well we are such (. . .) will do (. . .) in Siberia.

And (. . .) that the civil witness (. . . . .)

I agree with that, agree.

28 December

N.B. The fiancé (Luzhin) outlines fully a theory to him by which it is permitted to kill. N.B. He even talks about the murder of the old woman; "to be sure you can" (according to the theory of the fiancé).

Do it once, but only once.

N.B. *Important:* when he is walking, a whirlwind. No, that was not stupidity; it was not youth; it was not chance; but it was a conviction, a disrespect for his own self.

After the boulevard. Coming home; why did it seem to him that the ax was better . . . etc. The throbbing in his head was so bad that he went out. And then Lizaveta . . .

N.B. *She* thinks of herself continually as a deep sinner, a fallen profligate, beyond salvation; she is terribly modest, but once insulted she is beside herself.

Trait: At the get-together at Razumikhin's they blame him for almost always staying away from others, despite the fact that his friends appreciate him. Razumikhin also reproaches him for this.

Sonia, always meek, always without humor, always serious and quiet; then suddenly, she would burst out laughing terribly at trifles, and this affected the young man as gracious.

N.B. When he returned from Hay Market Square, after hearing Lizaveta, he fell asleep, and then a few words (a page) about how he thought about the ax and why he went to the old woman's to look things over.

Tone. N.B. N.B. N.B.

Third or fourth chapter. I ought to admit that I thought about the idea more than once. N.B. Therefore, explain the crime more naturally, but so as to keep it serious. How utterly serious he is must be made clear at the evening at Razumikhin's by his satanical pride.

N.B. *When he felt drawn to the murder* [narrated by him]. That happens. The baker of fine rolls. The fiancé about the civil servant: There are such; I knew one like that.

This manuscript page corresponds to pp. 49–51, beginning with the word "Tone" and ending with the words "My God." This is a very clean manuscript page. The lines are straight and evenly spaced, a habitual feature of Dostoevsky's handwriting. The picture of the formally frocked gentleman reminds us that Dostoevsky's drawings are mostly of men (usually depicting heads) and the outlines of churches. The drawing has no apparent relationship to the text.

Panic-stricken fear, also to be narrated from his point of view (tone).

Make it clear.

His skeptical views; more skeptical and ironic when he thinks about the future.

The dream and the requiem.

Love in humiliation between the worst of beings.

The delight in the fire.

Saying goodbye in the presence of Razumikhin, and then the first confession of love.

Then: leave me. Come in two hours, or tomorrow if you can. And you, mother. And now leave me.

And then the last chapter: summer, dust, lime, Lieutenant Gunpowder, etc., as base, foul, and prosaic as possible.

Gunpowder: "Why are you all burned? Ah, yes, ugh my God!"

Nevertheless, action at his mother's: What's the matter with him? Razumikhin. The mother is afraid of being a burden to him? They all go together to him. They find her. She is insulted. He quarrels. Razumikhin quarrels with him. *She,* a letter to him. His mother is glad that she has discovered the real reason for his foul humor, and that it is not from greed, nor bad feeling, nor fear that they had come to be burdens around his neck. He goes to her. She is insulted on the street. He bumps into Razumikhin at her place; a quarrel; [Razumikhin goes away]. He reveals [to her] who he is and that he is worse than her. A scene. She is terrified. He returns home self-assured. Mrs. Marmeladov is on the street with children. He says to Razumikhin [to his mother and his sister] who is there: there you are! A fever and off to the hospital. The children have been taken to a foundling home. His mother asks: Not to her place? At his mother's place: Razumikhin is announced as the fiancé. ~~He is in doubt. A perspective of the future. She looks for him.~~ His doubts. Perspective of the future. He speaks to Razumikhin. The latter busies himself trying to save. *She* looks for him. He is sick at her place. [Razumikhin comes many times.] He runs away from her [and their compassion] and roams about the city. Whirlwind, Christ, *Veuve Capet,** why don't they groan? *Crevez chiens si vous n'êtes pas contents.*** Fire. [Razumikhin is there also.] Everyone is there also. [His mother's

---

* French: "The Widow Capet."

** French: "Croak, you dogs, if you're not satisfied."

triumph.] ~~On Hay Market Square; he bows down.~~ All burned he goes home. [Says two words to Razumikhin.] [He] is at first horrified, then fascinated. He bows down on Hay Market Square; he goes to her to beg for forgiveness.[5] Tell your mother. Lieutenant Gun Powder. Discovery.

Rummage through all the questions in this novel. But the plot's structure* is such, *the story must be narrated by the author and not by the hero*. If it is to be a confession, then everything must be made clear *to the utter extreme*. Every instant of the story must be entirely clear. [Complete frankness; *completely serious even to the point of naïveté,* and narrate only what is *necessary*.]

N.B. *For information.* If a confession, then in parts it will not be chaste and it will be difficult to imagine why it was written.

But from *the author*. Too much naïveté and frankness are needed. An omniscient and infallible author will have to be assumed; he will have to appear as one of the members of the new generation.

After the panic-stricken fear the next morning, he awakens in a strange state of soul, that is: completely calm in regard to *that* matter. He is even surprised himself. The thought comes to him that he compromised himself yesterday in the tavern. That must be made right, he thinks. Then continuing his thinking, he goes through all the circumstances of the matter and sees to what extent everything was done in awfully risky fashion. He is astonished. He admits to himself and realizes that the whole thing was done almost accidentally (attracts relentlessly, *draws*), that perhaps now he would not risk it again, if it were not finished, even with the best of guarantees. Surely, he would not risk it. He realizes, however, that everything had followed from a correct logical idea. There was no madness. Definitely not. He rejects this with indignation. But since it's already done, he'll take advantage of it. He'll make up for it. But, nevertheless, you have stolen! God, the bargains you can make with your conscience!

---

* The Russian word here translated as "plot structure" is *siuzhet,* for which there is no exact English equivalent. For the Formalist critics in the twenties it came to refer to the order of narrative events as distinguished from the temporal-causal order of events. As used by Dostoevsky, it refers to the structural implications of the story.

[5] His mother comes and cries. Silently the tears flow. Then he runs away. His mother kisses his hand in the hall. Take care of him. Take care of his poor head.

Why don't I feel any shame inside of myself?[6] Is it not because there's no sin involved? But it's horrible to kill. Picture of spilled blood, the old woman, poor Lizaveta. Oh, I will make up for it, but how hard it is! . . .

The fiancé enters at that moment. A most unpleasant impression. He says that he is renting an apartment and that he forestalled it by only two days. The other person with him is non-committal. Reserved. He went to Marmeladov's requiem. *She* is (slighting and disdainful); a conversation with her. She is humbled. Shaken, assured, and proud he goes to the evening at Razumikhin's. Satanical pride.

Marmeladov's burial. After the burial. A long conversation with her. She is clearly shaken. Nevertheless, Razumikhin looks for her. They arrive. Everyone is at their place. Razumikhin became acquainted by chance. "An efficient young man." He has a sudden quarrel with the fiancé. The fiancé is insolent.

A scene. He is driven out. They remain alone. His mother says crying that she was getting married for your sake. I don't want it. *We have only you now.* A letter from the fiancé. Razumikhin gets 300 rubles but he is in despair because he can't take his money. He remains alone. He asks himself: Why has he refrained from taking the money for so long? Why in the water? Why didn't he dare offer it now, saying that he got it somewhere? Sonia visits him. He insults her.

Another Plan

Narration from the point of view of the author, sort of invisible but omniscient being, who doesn't leave his hero for a moment, even with the words: "all that was done completely by chance."

After the letter, his fury and answer, he went out on the boulevard, roamed, "No they ought to be happy!" He couldn't go back home; he had to roam. An idea planted itself in his mind.

Chapter N.B. This idea had already been fixed in his mind a long time ago; it is difficult to say how it came to him. Mathematics—what—that (the hardest chapter, point of view of the author. Very serious, but with subtle humor.)

He returned home. To complain. Scene with his landlady. He went out again. Lizaveta.

And it all happened so unexpectedly. [Murder and]—panic—fear—

---

[6] N.B. He didn't look long.

Then: Here are the kinds of thoughts that came to him: And why do I want to be nobler than the rest?

Main Idea of the Novel

And during the whole time while talking *to her* and afterward, he comes to insist that he can redeem things, that he can be good and that it's all mathematics.

He would go to Sonia not out of love, but as if to Providence.

The worker gives testimony against himself [he had become religious] and wanted to suffer, [gets mixed up]. They began to badger very much. And an old man sits there: You have, he says, to suffer.

N.B. Wanderings:

Can one love them? Can one suffer for them? Hate for humanity. N.B. (During his wanderings memories about the horse and about insults).

At first: a visit to the old woman and the pawning of the watch. He *nevertheless* looks the place over.

Then a letter, boulevards, troubles [dislike for humanity] and then suddenly the idea about the old woman, not completely by chance. He had to *admit* that the idea had been there for a long time, but now for the first time it had formed itself wholly and clearly.

Then and completely by chance, Lizaveta. Turmoil and torments follow. And then suddenly it was done and panic fear.

A New Plan

The Story of a Criminal

Eight years before (in order to keep it completely at a distance.)

"That was exactly eight years ago and I want ~~to begin~~ to narrate everything in an orderly fashion."

"I began by going to her to pawn my watch. I had heard about her a long time ago (student)." N.B. Who this old woman was, the visit, the apartment, etc. How he looked it over (N.B. *Not clear* but for the reader, *something of this kind* must be given).

"I left her place; I was even trembling all over. I was walking past a tavern, but since I want to narrate everything in good order, I will tell how I became acquainted with Marmeladov." A detailed account of Marmeladov and a note [at the end] that Marmeladov affected his fate.

I came home; I lived at that time at a landlady's; I was afraid. Letters from home. They made me furious. I will send some money. [I wrote a letter, posted it, and] went to Razumikhin's. On the boulevard. I didn't go, and decided that I'd go next day when the thing had been done. The Neva. I wandered about. Insults. Why does that old woman live. Mathematics. I returned home. Scene with the landlady. They are going to complain (Nastasya said). Went out. Lizaveta.

And it happened so completely by chance that I didn't think really that I myself would have to do the killing. Torments. Oasis water.[7]

The murder.

Panic terror, to Razumikhin's. Then getting well. Death of Marmeladov.

The next morning the fiancé. Rent an apartment. Rage and justification of himself. Conversation with her. In the evening to Razumikhin's. *Peace*. [Inflamed temper.] Marmeladov's funeral. The widow. Serious conversation with her. Sick.

They arrive. They drive away the fiancé. He was expecting something from the arrival of the family. Even thoughts of his mother are painful. Razumikhin: you are hurting your mother. They quarrel. Razumikhin is the fiancé. Walked—roamed. The whole perspective. Sonia insulted by him. He didn't answer the letter. Insulting of her on the street. At her place. Confession. ~~Bullet in the head. Admit it.~~ Insolence.

Sonia. Requiem.

Goes to her.

Scene with the widow Marmeladov.

Quarrels at home.

Fire.

He brings a package to her. Say goodbye.

I can't live home, unclean, disgusting, "If you knew" [My friends]! She says to him *afterward:* "We could not say we loved each other until you had given yourself up."

"Where are you pushing to?"[8]

The young girl is singing "The Little Farm."

Lebeziatnikov beat her up because she took Sonia's part.

---

[7] Then I thought for three days.

"I thought for a week."

"And this is what wouldn't leave my thoughts: the whole process."

I do not remember how I lived then. [His sister gets married.] Scene with the landlady. I went out on the street, Lizaveta.

[8] We get together here every day in a small tavern.

She took the children, sewed them costumes; under the window, to sing and dance.

And perhaps you robbed her of moments of repentance in killing her.

(N.B. Letters to the public)

To make a bit more famous.

There is everything in Piter.* Only no father or mother.

IN THIS CHAPTER. I can't give up life. I understand my calling in life to be life itself. I am not the kind of man who will permit some scoundrel to destroy the defenselessly weak. I want to take their part [And to do that] I need power. To do that I want to become a man. I must start with education, because education is strength and even more all of life . . .[9]

And this is why: the spilled blood shook me and this is why I became weak. And now I want life, [I am thirsty] for life. And I will be the life.[10]

This blood—I will have a Mass sung for her. [He laughs.]

Poor Lizaveta.

I found 10 rubles more, consequently I gave only 40. Take Sassia. Perform, my father, a Requiem Mass.

Finally she wrote him a letter: I love you, I will be your slave. She was attracted by his pride, independence, and by his preaching that she was not humbled.

(Create her letter skilfully)

He goes to her after receiving the letter. Insult on the street.

Confession to her.

She recoils.

He leaves her. The fire. Rescue. Ur! Life exists.

His despair. Walk——He examines every point *Veuve Capet.* How nasty people are.[11] *Dreams of a new crime.* Saves from death. Razumikhin also works. Requiem. Dream. *Inspector.*

---

* A popular diminutive for St. Petersburg.

[9] N.B. THOUGHT. Night wandering. Sun, life, life! And then to Razumikhin, and there all those reflections. [And only then he tells her about his mother and sister.]

[10] And not humbly again: I don't want to. The masters of life did not do things that way. They turned the world upside down. They pushed around hundreds of thousands as if they were pawns on a chessboard! Why didn't they waver? Because they were strong . . .

[11] He bustles about to take care of the three children.

On Krestovsky* for one morning only and drops of rain; after the drops of rain—*the natural* and psychological need of people *of this planet*. Hints at Razumikhin's (get 3,000—do the deed); rut, etc. unoriginality, etc.[12]

Thoughts Hinted At

Then the entire *confession* to her, after she had been insulted and humiliated and she had wanted to justify herself.

And then after she had already rejected him, among questions of *Veuve Capet* and so forth—the question: why haven't you looked into purse so far? and why did you want to throw it into the Neva?

(N.B. She, by the way, asks him during the confession how much money there was? How is it that you yourself don't know? Didn't you look? And she looked at him strangely. So that he then (thinking of *Veuve Capet*) asks himself: yes, by the way, why haven't I yet looked into the purse?

And only before saying goodbye (gives himself up) does he go to the purse and see with a sad smile that there is little money.

It is only afterward, near the very end, that he finds out what is in the purse.

The chief nota bene

When he ran out, he ended up in a tavern, at first with Zametov, and then with Razumikhin and the whole company.[13] And that instead of the evening at Razumikhin's. His defense lay in a quasi-delirium. Why on earth don't you take? Take. He went out. Razumikhin ran out after him. Under the street lamp. Razumikhin forewarns him that they think him mad, and that he should be on his guard. He goes then to the apartment where the murder had taken place; he quarrels with the workmen.[14] Then Marmeladov's death. Home.

"But still, is it a crime?"

"Are you a lawyer?"

"Yes."

"Is it possible that you have never noticed that no one who has

---

* An island at the mouth of the Neva River.

[12] Things ended up so that he quarreled with everyone at Razumikhin's and begged Razumikhin himself to leave him alone.

[13] trait of a twenty-three-year-old.

[14] I would confess, but how nasty they all are.

power ever obeys these laws? Napoleons trampled on them and changed them; those who were weaker used them; those who were weaker still avoided them. The ruler of a nation."[15]

"There is one law—the moral law. Agreed, agreed! Well, and that law?"

"Well, if my conscience doesn't bother me, I take power, I seize strength, whether money or power, but only for a good end. I bring happiness. What, because of a stupid barrier must one stand on the other side looking, envying, hating, but standing without doing anything? That's base!"[16]

"Can it be that you are even denying that there is any question of crime here?"

"No, I am not denying that."

"You are not denying it? Is there a crime?"

"There is. But, after all, it's question of mathematics. (If your heart [torments you], bear it.)"

The Chief Anatomy of the Novel

After the illness, etc. It is absolutely necessary to establish the course of things firmly and clearly and to eliminate what is vague, that is, explain the whole murder[17] one way or another, and make its character and relations clear. Only then start the second part of the novel: Clash with reality and the logical outcome in the law of nature and duty.

He begins with her in this way. He talks to her about her terrible position on the street, about how one need not obey fate, about being in a rut, etc.

He receives a letter from her (he goes to Razumikhin, legal inspector).

He meets her at Mrs. Marmeladov's place, behaves rudely, so as to keep her from falling in love with him.

Another letter the next day. (Not a drop of love, but at the same time timidly.)

---

[15] Why is it that people generally know how to die better than to live? Because you have to live for a *long time,* but you can die *quickly*.

[16] Damn it, that's true in part. Look, I am in part a cherub (. . .) because (. . .) I don't know. I know, after all, that this is not good, but it's not so important, and I permit myself; I don't permit, of course, what is more important.

[17] pride, personality, and insolence.

This manuscript page corresponds to pp. 58–60, beginning with the title "The Chief Anatomy of the Novel" and ending with the phrase "Full explanation." Dostoevsky tends to leave generous space between lines of writing, as here. The prominent dash in the center of the page is frequently used by Dostoevsky. In this edition a space is left to indicate a dash.

He goes to her. Contempt, didn't recognize her. [Because she is gadding about all dressed up.] And suddenly she is insulted on the street. He defends her and takes her home. Full explanation.

Lizaveta

ALTERATION

ALTERATION.

1) Finally his mother and sister arrive. At first the fiancé of his sister. Even before the murder he had sent a letter to her about his sister's fiancé: *not to marry*. Now they themselves arrive. Vrazumikhin falls in love. They throw out the fiancé. The mother says: all our hopes are now placed in you. What must be done?

2) He gets Sonia's advice. Looks for her: she has moved.

3) He behaves strangely at home: I can't study, can't translate. His mother says to Razumikhin: Aren't we a burden to him? Razumikhin proposes. Having learned of this he goes to Razumikhin. He says: Well? Dream. In a dream he goes to his mother.

Having learned about everything from him, Razumikhin *remue ciel et terre** to make right the stupid mistakes he had made: hide! hide! But when he learns near the end what he had done: Vassia!** You have washed everything away, washed everything away.

His mother says to him: "And haven't you suffered?"

The Marmeladov children in an orphanage.

Marmeladov's daughter follows him to Siberia.

The old woman is a consumptive. She has a will: everything is to go to the monastery in Novgor province in memory of her soul. *A Hundred Rubles* for the repose of Lizaveta's soul.

His mother attributes the whole affair at first to Sonia Marmeladova; she interrogates her and then insults her.

If in the form of a diary.

N.B. 1) Hole under the window sill

1) He went to pawn his watch and *to look things over.* Reflections.

N.B. (so that the reader be given to understand that he did not go there to pawn his watch but for another purpose).

2) Meeting with Marmeladov in the tavern.

---

* French: "moves heaven and earth."

** A nickname for Raskolnikov.

This manuscript page corresponds to p. 60, beginning with the staggered titles "Alteration" and "Lizaveta" and ending with the phrase "The Marmeladov children in an orphanage." On this page Dostoevsky practices calligraphy. The name "Lizaveta" appears twice in the margin, and twice he begins to write "Man" or "Mankind." The calligraphy and the drawings have no apparent relationship to the text.

3) Home. Relations with the landlady. Letter from his mother about the fiancé. No, they must not suffer. Skeptical arguments. ~~He went to Razumikhin. Meeting on the boulevard. He returned the translations. 20 K.~~ Lizaveta at Hay Market Square.

4) Before the preparations [memories] reasonings.[18] Murder.

5) To the police. Under the stone. On the boulevard. 20K He returned the translations.

6) Illness. His mother's letter. Money.

7) He runs. Tavern. Terrible arrogance. Quarrel with the workmen. Marmeladov's death.[19]

His sister's fiancé. (various episodes) He arrives to make his acquaintance. He gives money. Rents an apartment for them. He is avaricious and wants to keep their life lean.

Marmeladov's funeral and conversation with her. The judicial inspector.

At Razumikhin's evening (Terrible pride).

He comes home. Arrival of his mother and sister.[20] Explanation. The fiancé is not wanted, because of him.[21]

They get rid of the fiancé.[22] A note from Sonia Marmeladov.[23] She comes to him.[24] His mother and sister (insult her). He tells where he put the money. Razumikhin is there also. *He* makes a scene before *her*. He tells her that he can't love her. ~~They insult her.~~

The scene with Mrs. Marmeladova and the barrel organ.

His mother and everyone takes part.[25] N.B. They insult her. He tells *her* everything. Don't say that I love (but that is clear).

---

[18] (about the ax). Frank discussion with his landlady. The girl on the boulevard—reasonings. Memories of insults; the courier. [suicide].

[19] 1) How base they all are. 2) Youth alone still [gives] inspires pity. 3) What is Marmeladov? 4) I am not thinking [about that thought, but why does it live?] Lizaveta entered.

[20] His mother says: "Your sister is sacrificing herself for you." He: "She mustn't! She mustn't!" He quarrels with the fiancé. Razumikhin is there; the fiancé feels insulted and leaves; then a letter to his fiancée. Her answer. They owe money. *He runs to count the money*. Razumikhin gets 300 rubles.

[21] From that moment he gives himself to a terrible pride.

[22] After the fiancé: God sees that I did it all for them.

[23] You are all we have left.

[24] Arrival of his mother and sister at this point.

[25] His mother suspects her influence: they look into the matter. Quarrel with his mother.

She rejects him and is afraid.

His wanderings. He doesn't want to do anything, neither translate nor work. Razumikhin makes friends with his mother. He proposes. He comes once at night and sees that Razumikhin is the fiancé. He accompanies Razumikhin back. At the street lamp. [Hints but only not about everything.][26]

Dream

Better a bullet in the head. All the wanderings and reasonings. He asks once and for all Razumikhin; he does not refuse.[27] Torment his mother. He goes to her to say goodbye. He puts his mother in Razumikhin's hands. He tries to talk him out of it and then is enthusiastic about it. He sells himself.

Farewell to his mother: Haven't you suffered?

Mother with Miss Marmeladov.

[*I'm in everyone's way.*]

["I was foolish, for example, to tell her. I should have used the love and then thrown her over."]

["But is that honest? Can one carry it off?"]

[I'm in everyone's way: bullet in the head.] [He comes to say goodbye.]

She stops him.

"Free yourself in some other way."

"Repent and start another life." A new perspective from despair. [*Fire*]

"Only by your heroism will you make amends, redeem."

"Re-educate one's self."

The Beginning of the Novel

The tone.

At first:

He would go, for example, to the old woman to look things over, but without giving it much thought and practically without believing himself that he would do it. Just in case.

Then develop it and bring in extraneous matters, even a sort of humor. As if he himself does not expect that this might take place.

Further. The murder takes place almost by chance. [I myself did

---

[26] Examining magistrate.

[27] I myself will be a man.

not expect this.] Account of panic fear and illness. This ends with Marmeladov's death.

Finally. Suddenly: gloomy sadness and infinite pride and a *struggle* to keep[28] life from being completely destroyed, so that life would continue.

N.B. His moral development begins from the crime itself; the possibility of such questions arises which would not have existed previously.

[In] the last chapter, in prison, he says that without the crime he would not have reached the point of asking himself *such* questions and experiencing such desires, feelings, needs, strivings, and development.

N.B. 2d part. The confession. Narration of the murder: I myself did not expect it; during the whole narration there follows a sort of astonishment at himself, a sort of astonishment of seeing himself from the outside. And then he judges himself completely; [in two weeks he is at peace].[29]

3d part. Extreme pride. Arrival of his mother and sister. They drive out the fiancé. Whims. Against Razumikhin. Scene with his sister. Talk under the street lamp. Sonia's suspicion: *I cannot* love you. Finally, sudden terror and despair. Wandering. Meeting with Sonia: he explains everything to her, bullet in the head. She renews him. Runs away from him. She cleans up Sassia. Vision. Christ. Why don't they grumble? He goes to say goodbye—she renews him.

renews

First Part. Beginning.

Boulevard. Young girl.

My first personal insult, the horse, the courier.*

Violation of a child.

---

* As a youth (in 1837) on his way to a military engineering school in St. Petersburg, Dostoevsky witnessed a scene that remained in his memory for the rest of his life: he saw a state courier beat his coachman with his fists, and the coachman beat the horses. The rhythm of hurt passing from one being to another was an early instance of what was to be a premise of his mature psychology. References to the beaten horse are made a number of times in the notes.

[28] ideas

[29] About the fiancé and others slightly.

Why does that old woman, who has outlived life, continue to live? Mathematics.[30]

He came home: letter from his mother. [He loses his temper] with the landlady because of the soup.

In *10 days.*

2d part. Here's how it happened. Overheard Lizaveta talking. Then I asked myself in terror: Can it be that the idea I had in my mind was real and not just an idle idea?

THE MAIN IDEA

His love affair begins with Sonia when he is in the depths of despair and humiliation. When the widow of Marmeladov dies, she goes to bed.

Argument at his place with Sonia. She says repent. Shows him the perspective of a new life and love (not a word about love).

He gives himself up conquered.[31]

N.B.

His mother's caresses are a burden.

I am a fool who made a mistake in his calculations.

He talks about everyone caustically.

Doesn't want to work at anything; is preparing translations.

He argued with everyone on Sonia's account.[32]

A bullet in the head, because suddenly the perspective [confusion] of the future became illuminated and he saw himself as a family man, father, husband, good citizen, etc.[33]

Sonia says: "Repent." Arguments about true pride. Base torments about *what people will think,* etc. Walking, vision, episode with Mrs. Marmeladova, and the barrel organ.

Why don't they moan?

One of the chapters begins: "I don't understand this foolishness that has happened to me."[34]

---

[30] Can it be that my thought is not just? His mother is against Sonia, scenes.

[31] Life ends from one point of view and begins from another.
On the one hand the funeral and damnation, from the other resurrection.
Even his mother's caresses are a burden to him.

[32] And yet he is not in love with Sonia at all.

[33] (Realizes that he does not respect people.)

[34] I am astonished at myself: how I can [yet] feel, think, reason, and even laugh. *Dream* and has a Requiem Mass celebrated and then laughs at himself.

When they have to return the money to the fiancé, he runs off to count his. Razumikhin got it. He could not count his. In the evening Razumikhin makes a plan for work on translations. Everyone is happy; he is not. They joke with him, but his mother is uneasy. Razumikhin says that he has lost his senses.

Even the caresses of his mother are burdensome. He goes out, roams about, and dreams how he will be a good husband, father, etc. I will pray and will earn the right! From despair to hope. A letter from her. She is insulted by him, by his contempt; he has pity; he goes to her. She is insulted by others. At her place he reveals everything to her; her terror; his pride.

At home they suspect a tie with Sonia. Scene at home.

Mrs. Marmeladov's death. Bullet in the head. Razumikhin is the fiancé of his sister. The fire. The last convulsions.[35]

2d page

"Well, is this your son?"

Razumikhin says to him: "You are hurting your mother."

He says to him: "Is it possible you don't understand?"

And he becomes dumb with terror.

"Well, what's the matter with you? What's the matter with you?"

He wrote *everything* and left it for his mother. He went off to say goodbye to Sonia.

His mother says: "I thought at first: Isn't it a burden for him to have us around his neck, and I thought this until Razumikhin's proposal, but after the proposal I began to think of other things."

For the structure of the novel (definitively)

It's necessary that Lyzhin (who is staying at Lebeziatnikov's) be struck with Sonia. He finds a *corrupt* woman at his place. He was at Marmeladov's at the time of Marmeladov's death and he saw Sonia. He informs Pulkheriia that her son is spending money to keep a prostitute. (a slanderer by birth)

He insults Sonia on the street with Lebeziatnikov (his ferocity against Sonia is not even understandable). I will bend you completely to my will. Sonia flees him.

Finally, it is revealed that he is falling terribly in love with Sonia

[35] Is there a law of nature that we don't know and which cries out in us? Dream.

(nature); he makes acquaintances in Petersburg and is himself astonished how he is falling.

Reisler heard (everything about Reisler). He gets friendly with Reisler and guesses at (the whole story), that he committed a murder. He warns Sonia that he will destroy him.

And why did you get 50 r. for him?

He gets acquainted with the inspector and Zametov's.

They interrogate him (at Filipov's) and keep him under surveillance. He destroys all their convictions. At Zametov's, at Bakalin's, and at Razumikhin's they are convinced that he is crazy in believing *that he had committed a murder*.

Aristov (who had been with Zametov at Razumikhin's and in the tavern) comes to him still at the beginning and lets him know all his convictions and hints at there being a sister and that it can be done with counterfeit money. He is Lyzhin's spy. They are tormenting Sonia.

Razumikhin. At times he persecutes Sonia; at times he defends her. The sister visits Sonia. *Aristova* is her friend.

Don't forget 1) When Razumikhin told him that he was interested in his own socks, Razumikhin looked at him strangely. 2) After the evening at his place, Razumikhin mentioned that they had strange thoughts, but that he had dispersed them. 3) Then he says to himself that he talked about arithmetic at Razumikhin's because he knew that *after that* no one would suspect him. (rapturous state)

Important N.B. He says: To rule over them! All the baseness about him fills him only with indignation. Deep contempt for people. Pride. He tells Sonia about his contempt for people. He doesn't want to out of pride. He argues with her. *Oh, I cannot reconcile myself* with them. Finally he reconciles himself with all. Vision of Christ. He begs forgiveness of the people. Pride. He goes. Sonia and love broke him. Can it be that such a one as she was unhappy; is that justice?

He accomplished some *striking* deeds at the time of the fire. Sick after the fire. The fire decided everything. A short period.

N.B. After the scene in the office (the fainting), there would have been a search if suspicion had not fallen on the worker. Nevertheless, they came to the house and asked questions; Razumikhin told him about this later. Razumikhin also helped out a lot, while he was lying sick, to dissipate the suspicions of the police.

Toward a Characterization of Sonia

After the death of Marmeladov, when he calls her a saint, she says with terror: "Oh, what on earth are you saying! I am a great sinner." When he thinks that she is speaking about the prostitution and says so, Sonia (tired of his indecent words on this theme) says to him: *I am not speaking of that,* but I have been ungrateful; I have sinned against love many times (and she narrates here a[36] story—write it well) how once Mrs. Marmeladov, humiliated and downtrodden, had taken a liking to an embroidered collar of hers, and had asked her for it, but Sonia had not given it to her; later the collar disappeared. Now if she only had the collar and if she were to ask for it, she would give it to her; she would give everything to her.

Sonia also narrates many anecdotes about her father; sometimes they were cheerful, but at other times filled with suffering and torment.

N.B. Create all this.

N.B. Very important in the novel.

After Razumikhin has a talk with Bakalin* in the 6th chapter, he has the thought—run; but after Bakalin says that one mustn't stir, he says: nonsense, I am strong; I can walk.

And in reality at night near daybreak, he runs away.

And then a whole day of wandering ([N.B.] Razumikhin looks for him). The day ends with Marmeladov's death.

But because of that day and later, he is suspected.

The Inspector who interrogates him; his answers are proud (new interest in the fact that he is being pursued and that he is wriggling out of it).

He awoke at 10 o'clock in the morning after the illness. Razumikhin has breakfast. ~~After the purchase of clothes leave me.~~ He brought the clothes. ~~Luzhin enters. Conversation and he chases him out [wanted to go out during the conversation]. Razumikhin is a witness.~~

When he went away: Leave me, leave me.

He fell asleep; he awoke in the evening in anger—to rent another apartment. Tavern; Zametov; visit to the apartment of the murdered

---

* Bakalin is called Zosimov in the final version. In these notes he is variously called Bakalin, Bakavin, and Zosimov.

[36] touching.

woman. Marmeladov. (Lord have pity on me;[37] arithmetic.) [He cried out falling.] (Repentant element.) In the morning she, then Razumikhin, then Luzhin. [Sonia comes to tell him that they are burying her father today.] He has her sit down and has her stay. Razumikhin wanted to go but he sits down. He sends Luzhin packing; Luzhin insults her. He stands up for her. After Luzhin leaves [he says] to Razumikhin: "I insulted you yesterday, but leave me."[38] "You're strange," Razumikhin says, "but as you wish; I'll leave you." And he goes away.

He goes to the Marmeladov's requiem. Sonia. He speaks to her. He wants to beg her forgiveness, and she says to him: I am guilty.[39] He takes Sonia home; he speaks obscenities to her; ~~she bursts into tears~~ she answers him modestly ~~and proudly.~~ He goes to Razumikhin. Evening. ~~He returns, Mother~~ He arrives repentant and demonically proud: Complete defense.[40] He arrives home ~~and defends himself~~: Mother N.B.[41] The inspector has suspicions; they call him in; he gives his testimony with a smile. And why were you in the apartment of the old woman? I dreamed of her. I was looking for an apartment.

Razumikhin quarrels with Zametov, the inspector, and others and refuses to give the reason.[42]

(He learns about the visit to the apartment later.)

That evening in a scene with his mother, a quarrel with her and with his sister [despot]. Razumikhin is a conciliatory person; he assures the mother that he is not yet himself after the sickness.

You could have talked to your sister differently! No need of sacrifices. Of course! Pyotr Petrov. finds you with a shady woman. That woman, yes, she is a shady character; she walks the streets but she is not worth a little finger.

After that we [cannot remain], and they leave.

---

37 His prayer after returning from Marmeladov's: [meekly] Lord! If this crime against an old, blind, stupid, and useless old woman is a sin, after I wanted to consecrate myself, then reveal it to me. I have judged myself severely; it was not vanity, and if it was vanity, then it was just, for why did you give me the strength? I can't live without that money.

38 Razumikhin says to him: "You spoke some strange words yesterday."

39 She says to him later: I am guilty; do not be angry; some time ago; but he wanted to beg forgiveness of her.

40 (And then the proud element and full defense.)

41 The mother; letter from Luzhin about a girl of doubtful reputation; would that he were not here.

42 "The Russian people have always suffered like Christ," says Sonia.

The mother says to Razumikhin later: He wanted to get married once before; he hurt me; and now he wants to marry this one.

Razumikhin is an intermediary.

The next day there is a reconciliation. ~~Can they really?~~ [Razumikhin brings them together] glad. Although he is happy and tender, he is gloomy. Luzhin. They chase Luzhin out; what's to be done, no money. Razumikhin gets some. A society is established. He finds an apartment, live together. He *doesn't want to.*

N.B. N.B. N.B.

Razumikhin insults Sonia [admits it to Sonia].

He separates himself completely from his sister and his mother. Solitude of thought. The inspector. Madness. (Razumikhin supports that.)

Mother and Sonia.

Marmeladov moved to Sonia's; he insults the mother who had come to Sonia's. Mrs. Marmeladov loses her mind. Scene on the street.[43, 44, 45]

He confesses to Razumikhin, who has been persuading him. But why have you been telling me that? But can they really be honest relationships! N.B. Sonia will not leave me [even after hearing my confession], but you will leave. I lied today to the inspector. Thousands of proposals and projects of Razumikhin on how to do it. Let's go home to mother.

N.B. He almost arranged a reconciliation and then aggravated something (Dream, etc.).

Then and again doubts; after all, it's only because of a weak character that I can't bear it. The arithmetic is right but I'm soft. I can't accept Byronesque torments.

---

[43] Arithmetic destroys, but simple faith saves. Everything became unclear. Nothing to believe in, nothing to stand solidly on. Simple faith is after all a prejudice. Believe in the beauty of the Russian element (Sonia).

[44] N.B. From that time on scenes take place in various places; several intrigues. He and Sonia (Sonia's letters to him). His mother against Sonia; Razumikhin is with the daughter; the inspector's; the young man's. And his wandering.

[45] He begins to work in order to live; carries to Mrs. Marmeladova's.

He confesses to Razumikhin, who has been persuading him. But ~~can they really?~~ Why have you told me this? But can they really?

Razumikhin says: go off someplace. And money? Where. And the old woman's? He looked at him.

He doesn't look into the purse even to the very end of trial. (About this in the last chapter)

N.B. N.B. One can be great in humility, says Sonia; she proves it, that is.

Reisler and the girl that stole. (Reisler says to Sonia) it's a pity only that he taught you: kill; Sonia informs Razumikhin; Razumikhin, having passed himself off to Reisler as Sonia's enemy, got Reisler to talk. Doesn't know anything. But Sonia has already got 50 rubles in advance in order to go to Liza Ivanovna where Razumikhin himself advised her to go. Razumikhin breaks everything there at Luisa's and is astonished that Sonia should have sold herself for him. Razumikhin saves everything and defends her before the mother. Comes to him and states that he is guilty before Sonia and her actions and says to him—"Love!" "Do you really think that she can love me?" he exclaims and he then confesses everything to Razumikhin. Sonia and he. "Haven't you suffered?" He kneels down before her. "I love you."

He kneels down before Sonia. "I love you." She says to him; "Give yourself up." "It's clear that you don't love me," he says. She remains quiet. He wanders about. The fire. (He gets a reward.) Mother, sister at the bedside. Reconciliation with everyone. His joy; joyful evening. In the morning at the Mass he bows down to the people—goodbye. "I will come," says Sonia.

N.B. Important. When he says that it is *lacheté,** then suddenly it is shown to him from the outside that it is not from *lacheté* that he can't bear Sbogara. (That comes from Sonechka).

N.B.? "Denounce yourself," says Sonia.

---

* French: "cowardice."

Notebook Two

III

Fragments from Marmeladov's tavern speech—Raskolnikov's plea for pity and his fear of his mother—Raskolnikov's relations with Sonia—Raskolnikov reflects on confession, suicide, and the redemption of his crime by good works—Razumikhin and Zosimov at Raskolnikov's sickbed

The chief incidents, reflections, and scenes of this section are the following: a brief conversation between Razumikhin and Raskolnikov about God and prayer; several fragments from Marmeladov's tavern speech, the entirety of which is found in Section I; a brief conversation in which Raskolnikov taunts Marmeladov about the non-existence of God; a desire plaintively voiced by Raskolnikov that someone take pity on him; fear that his mother will curse him if she finds out about the murder, and fears of being alone with the knowledge of his deed; a repetition of Marmeladov's account (found in Section I) of how he went to beg money of a civil counselor when he knew he would not get it; scattered references to Sonia and Raskolnikov's relations and love; Raskolnikov meets her on the street plying her trade, condemns her for stealing, at one point insults her and then falls on his knees before her; repeated references to Raskolnikov's intentions to redeem his crime by good works; alternative decisions to confess or to kill himself; references to Lizaveta's baby (not in final version) and Raskolnikov's love for the baby. This section ends with a narrative fragment of several pages, a conversation between Razumikhin and Zosimov (called Bakavin here) at Raskolnikov's sickbed about the murder and the suspects. This conversation is to be compared with Part II, Chapter 4, of the final version.

Much of the content of this section has to do with the alternatives Raskolnikov faces after the murder, and various reflections he makes about his motives. The humanitarian motive looms large: Several times Raskolnikov voices his intention to redeem his act by a lifetime of good deeds, silently accomplished for the benefaction of others. On each occasion he rejects the plan, and on one occasion he follows the intention by these words: "Nonsense. Complete nonsense." His alternating desire to do good and his sharp dismissal of the desire are paralleled by a similar alternation of wistful sympathy and contempt for the silent masses. "Why don't they groan?" and "How disgusting they are!" are repeated more than once. At times he considers seriously what one might call a variation of the humanitarian motive: that he did it for his mother and sister. At one point he says: "Poor mother, poor sister. I did it for you." And, "Oh, mother, oh, sister; everything for you, beloved ones." Yet, the relationship with the mother—as the material in Section II demonstrates—is complex. He is afraid, for example, that his mother will curse him if he confesses to her. He fears apparently that his mother will not accept him as he is—the good and the evil—but only as he meets her image of an ideal Raskolnikov. One may even hazard that his motive in part is to test those who love him.

Several fragments from Marmeladov's tavern speech, which appear in this section in new contexts, seem to support this. At one point, for example, Raskolnikov asks for pity in words remarkably similar to those Marmeladov uses. The passage is important: "Oh God, if someone, someone were to take pity on me? But pity for what? For my foolishness, my bestial selfishness, for my wildness and shamelessness, for my failure, for the uselessness of my deeds; rather it's something to spit on, it's horrible and laughable. Who then will take pity? No one? No one? I am a base and vile murderer, laughable and greedy. Yes, precisely, is such a one to be pitied? Is there anyone like that in the whole world? Is there someone to take pity? No one, no one! No one! And yet that is impossible. And my mother? God, what will happen to her? Won't she have to curse me? Me, her womb and her love?"

This passage comes immediately after the fragment of Marmeladov's tavern speech in which he insists eloquently on the fact that his wife Katerina Marmeladova is a lady and he is a pig. The juxtaposition is not without significance, for the notes make clear what is implied in the novel: there is a parallel relationship between Marmeladov and his wife and Raskolnikov and his mother. Katerina, for example, accepts Marmeladov—and then not completely—only when he lives up to her nostalgic and unrealistic memories of her former husband. Marmeladov wants to be himself, and if Katerina will not accept him as he is, he will make her "feel" him by the destructive acts that he commits. The havoc he brings down on her is a distorted way of manifesting his dignity and his freedom; his destructive acts are in part a way of paying her back for her pitiless treatment of him; they are in part a way of establishing a "living," if destructive, relationship with her; and most of all they are a grotesque but nevertheless real way of revolting against her abstract and thus conditional view of his being. The relationship between Raskolnikov and his mother is similar. She too has an abstract and conditional view of her son. Just as Marmeladov must bear the burden of living up to the ideal of Katerina's former husband, so must Raskolnikov bear the burden of living up to his mother's ideal image of him. Both Marmeladov and Raskolnikov attempt to liberate themselves by destruction, by attempting to kill, at least symbolically, what limits them, one by theft and drink and the other by murder. If a Dostoevskian character can hurt in no other way, he will do so by hurting himself. Dostoevsky's characters—Marmeladov and Raskolnikov are examples—are always looking for what dignifies them: love, freedom, life. But such is the character of men and the nature of the world that they do not understand what is true love, freedom, and life, or when they understand are powerless to achieve them, accepting in return distorted imitations of these virtues.

Marmeladov and his family have another important structural function in the novel, which is emphasized in these notes. They represent the "meek ones" for whom Raskolnikov has presumably committed the crime. He is like them in situation, but unlike them because of his greater strength. The meek ones are exemplified by Sonia. This is clear in the novel, but in the notes this is made explicit —as well as his attitude toward them—by the juxtapositions we find in the following passage: "N.B. Afterward before *giving himself up,* about Marmeladov's daughter; Why don't they groan? What is her fate? Pale creature at night . . . She also sacrificed herself. He becomes enraged: Why don't they groan? Why are they quiet, meek? Do they think that it's right to be so treated? . . . He says this to her: 'Well what will happen to the family? You [the daughter] will have enough for a year, for two, and then, then?' He pushes her to hysteria and *to love*. Why don't they groan?"

It may be that Raskolnikov comes to realize—and possibly Dostoevsky also—that the "humanitarian" motive for the crime is only an apparent motive, that the alternating contempt and love he feels for the people depends on whether they are laughing at him or groaning in weakness before him. In the notes we find: "How low and vile the people are . . . No: gather them up in one's arms and then do good for them. But instead to perish before their eyes and to inspire only sneers." Raskolnikov, it seems, comes to realize that he had not committed the crime for them, but in order to tower above them. Similarly, in the variation of the humanitarian motive by which he committed the crime for his mother and sister, one might say that he did not commit the crime for them. Something of this perception is caught in the following fragment, in which Dostoevsky seems to see that Raskolnikov's essential character is not humanitarian, but proud and demonic: "At first there was danger, then fear and illness, and the whole character did not show itself, and then suddenly the [whole] character showed itself in its full demonic strength, and all the reasons and motives for the crime became clear." If Raskolnikov has not lifted up the meek, they—in the person of Sonia—will lift him up to their strength. This is the paradox that the proud, self-willed Raskolnikov must come bitterly to face.

That was an evil spirit; How otherwise could I have overcome all those difficulties? etc.

Zametov said that Razumikhin's birthday

He went (after the quarrel) because his conscience justified him completely and he convinced himself that his life was not ruined at all, not over, and that he was still part of humankind. But *experience,* that is, the visit of Razumikhin showed him the contrary.

The *story* ends here and the *diary* begins.

Very important question which he finally formulates for himself clearly and asks positively: why has my life ended? Grumble: But God does not exist and etc.

I should have done that. *There is no free will, fatalism.*

The door is open (the inspector thinks). That's clever (Bakavin). Zametov confirms this completely and deduces from this that he is a weak and inexperienced man, that it was his first step and that he had had an extraordinary lucky break.

N.B. But Zametov was more interested in making my acquaintance than I was his, especially when he learned that I was on his side; he came himself, dug around in the books, and then when (we . . .) in the tavern. He got me to drink like a pig.

The point is that *my watch.* Is it written on many of them who they belong to?

In getting things cleared up with the landlady: About the fact that the apartment is upstairs and she is downstairs.

A speech made up for my "benefit" apparently, to stir me up, but which almost never succeeds in such cases.

Conversation with Razumikhin.

"I admit, brother, that I liked it very much, Vassia, when you said loudly that you believe in God. It has been rather shameful up to now, you know, to admit this in our group; and yet at night I pray and you know even with the same words that my dead mother taught me when I was three years old. You can find, you know, more learned words for prayer, but the early ones still are better. But Zametov said to me that you are mad."

"I came to you (to Razumikhin) because I thought that I had a right to come."

"For goodness sake you spoke in that way."

"I thought I had the right to talk, but now I have felt."

"Leave me."

Precisely from that moment Razumikhin imagined that he was guilty of murdering the old woman, and beginning with that evening he broke off his acquaintanceship with Zametov.

"And suppose it was I who killed?" He laughed in Zametov's face (spite).

"But admit it, you suspected me."

"What are you talking about, for pity's sake?"

Razumikhin. He pushed Razumikhin away angrily and walked away.

His wanderings begin. He tells about his whole life; all his impulses. Gets stronger, goes to Razumikhin. Conversation at night by a post.

When Razumikhin returned, that is, caught up with him at night: "Listen, Zametov has already told me that he considers you to be mad." Frenzy. Why. The young girl. Memories of childhood impressions.

What about it; maybe I really am mad I thought. Visit to the apartment of the old woman (painters there, spoke with them), and then sort of by chance—the biography of Lizaveta.

And then when I become noble, the benefactor of all, a citizen, I will repent. [He prayed to Christ and then went to bed.]

[The misfortunes of his father, mother.] How nasty people are! Are they worth having me repent before them? No. No, I'm going to remain silent.

My pledge was at the old woman's.

They themselves do things a thousand times more filthy, and yet they hunt me like a rabbit, like an animal. That's all they know. That's the only thing they've learned.

Then a completely unrelated story.

How disgusting people are! And just now the letter from the mother. (That keeps him from becoming embittered.) Heroism. The young girl on the boulevard. (Scoundrel!)

(Dream!)

On Krestovsky Island. Memory and healthy thoughts. Came. Analyzes completely all the circumstances from the beginning and the whole current situation.

"How disgusting people are!"

"But there are good ones, too!"

"I know, I know. Why should I be evil? Crime? About God: Napoleon, etc. They have only that."

Poor mother, poor sister. I did it for you. If I committed a sin, I have decided to take it on myself, just so you would be happy. Not much money; it didn't come off, but it will help me and then I will be your support; I will be honest, but money, money, money above all.

No! Be honest without money. I know, I know those ideas.

But with what contempt. How low and vile people are . . . No: gather them up in one's hands, and then do good for them. But instead to perish before their eyes and inspire only sneers.

Hatred choked me, and I lay down. Memories: horse with a stick (Mitya). The civil servant with a bottle.

He goes out in a frenzy and goes to Razumikhin. Conversation.

The civil servant with a bottle. And am I not suffering? She beats me. And I feel pleasure, for if she did not beat me, I would be very unhappy. She comes from a good family. Daughter. I would go to my daughter, and she would give me money for drink. She lives at a tailor's. Story of the joy when he brought home his wages. About her pride, etc.

The civil servant: "Poverty, yes, is not a vice. Poverty is nothing, but destitution, dear sir,—destitution is a vice. If you're destitute they drag you off to the police station. The worst of scoundrels will feel contempt for your destitution, and he will have the right, for I feel contempt for my own destitution. What do you think? Will many of the destitute, like me, hold out and not begin to feel contempt for themselves? The most noble pride is destroyed. Sir, they sweep out the destitute with a broom.[1] They beat up my wife. What am I supposed to do? And I drink, because I feel contempt for myself."

---

[1] and not just blows only but the end of a stick and not just a stick, but a broom.

N.B. I was astonished that I could get enraged because a carriage driver hit me, as if I were no longer a member of humanity and had lost my rights. Oh, how painful these feelings are!

My wife turned her out (the stepdaughter); but when she came back disgraced, she sat all night at her feet and kissed them, and I lay there and heard everything. I lay there drunk. She is now a registered prostitute.

He entered the house and went down on his knees.

Of General Importance N.B.:

In all these six chapters, he must write, speak, and appear to the reader in part as if not in possession of his senses.

N.B. As he was returning from the name-day party at Razumikhin's, a whole night of terrible and completely clear arguments, and about morning suddenly the girl, Sassia; he embraced her.

The civil servant. Beautiful little pictures.

And when he came to the entry, he got down on his knees. And when he is beaten, he cries out: I like it, dear sir, I like it.

Drown one's self? No guts. N.B. He is crushed by horses; his death at home. More original and shorter. For a candle. The wife cries.

And when I dream, I think. Well, if I were rich, I would bring them money; I would rehabilitate and regenerate my daughter, the children also—for I love them.

N.B. Cry of the young man. Oh, you who have never sinned! (Dream of an earthly paradise.)

Civil Servant. "No one can stand contempt for himself. Oh, dear sir, you think that I am saying this out of pride or spite or out of a desire to justify myself. Oh, dear sir. I know, I know that there are great hearts that are crushed under tons of weight, and bear the burden silently, doing what they must do. I'm not talking of those who have won high rank and built fine homes. I am not speaking of them. I am speaking of the angels of God. And such an angel of the Lord is my daughter, who gave me 30 kopecks today; she is an angel despite her yellow ticket, and so is my wife, yes, my wife. But, dear sir, if I speak of the angels of the Lord, I am not, however, one of those angels. We are the poor, the fallen, the lost. Let it be, let it be, let it be that we are lost! But, dear sir, who will take pity on us? It is necessary, after all, that a man be pitied! Who will take pity on us, on us, on us who are poor, lost, bestialized!

"But my wife, my legal wife! Dear sir: If you see me in this piggish state, then know that she is a lady. Yes, dear sir, a lady! a lady! [I am a scoundrel, but she is a lady] And yet, God, if only she would take pity on me. I know that when she pulls me by the hair, that she pulls only from pity. Yes, yes, it is so! But, God, if only she could pity me without pulling my hair. Sir, dear sir, perhaps I would be myself again. Yes, hmm. [Besides] No, I would not be myself.

"I would drink up everything, everything; I'd drink it all up.[2] I'd sell her last stockings for drink. [And besides I have already drunk up her mohair kerchief,[3] and she caught cold in the winter because of that.] Dear sir, have [you] ever seen a pig, a fat pig, a filthy pig? Well, here I am. (He began to drink again from the bottle.) And yet my daughter took pity on me. Why did she give me 30 kopecks? She knew, you know, that I'd drink them up. And yet, she gave them to me. Why? because she took pity on me. That's how the angels of the Lord pity: they take pity on you whether you are a sinner or not; they cry over you, pamper you, and love you. One can say that the pity is bad, because it serves no purpose. But, it does serve a purpose, for if the 30 kopecks went for drink and for harm and filth, her deed also went to my heart and my suffering. I torture myself and cry, but because of that deed, I live."

The Civil Servant. "I took 30 kopecks from my daughter. And she needs them; she has to look after *grooming* now: dress up, make herself up, show a nice pair of shoes in crossing a puddle. Do you understand, do you understand [what I'm talking about], dear sir?"

"I will take the liberty, dear sir, of beginning a conversation, because even though you don't look important, it is clear that you are an educated man." And then after the conversation: because I saw suffering in your face.

---

[2] My dear sir, do you know that once I sold her stockings for drink, not her shoes (that would have passed for something decent, that is, in the order of things), but stockings, stockings—the same that ladies wear.

[3] made of goat wool, to protect her from the cold, and I drank it up.

N.B. 15 kopecks a day; she can't earn more and then not every day; and one state counselor didn't give her anything for sewing some shirts; he even chased her away with insults.

Sassia comes from Razumikhin and a letter comes from his mother. *Brought* at once a 25-ruble note.

Oh God, if someone, someone were to take pity on me? But pity for what? For my foolishness, my bestial selfishness, for my wildness and shamelessness, for my failure, for the uselessness of my deeds; rather it's something to spit on, it's horrible and laughable.

Who then will take pity? No one? No one? I am a base and vile murderer, laughable and greedy. Yes, precisely, is such a one to be pitied? Is there any one like that in the whole world? Is there someone to take pity? No one, no one! No one! And yet that is impossible.

And my mother? God, what will happen to her? Won't she have to curse me? Me, her womb and her love? Can it be that she will? Can she really? No, it is impossible, impossible . . .

And therefore I shall be *alone* all my life!

Alone when I'm with my wife, alone when with people. Always alone. Perhaps others will bless me; always alone. If my secret were to be known, everyone would immediately turn with horror away from me. And therefore I will be alone for eternity.

Can one live that way? We'll see, we'll see, we'll look it over seriously and then we'll decide.

N.B. We'll examine why I did it, how I decided to do it. There's an evil spirit here. N.B. (And then an analysis of the whole deed begins, of the bitterness and destitution.) The conclusion is that he had to do it; it turns out that I acted logically.

And then begins (. . .) his; about the wife, and children. Why talk? I will repay it with good. *I will immerse myself in good.* Sonia, the daughter of the civil servant. *Veuve Capet.* Dreams of universal happiness. And still it doesn't work out. Finally, rage . . . I am a chicken; I have a stupid heart. Napoleon and so forth.

Kissed her feet (the end). Bowed down to the people. Gave myself up.

With the civil servant.

"Dear sir, did it ever happen that you had to beg for money without any hope of getting it?"

"I don't know, perhaps . . . What do you mean, no hope of getting it?"

"That is, no hope, no hope whatsoever. Look, you know in your heart that this man will not give you anything under any circumstances, that you will drown yourself sooner than get anything from him. And still you go to him to beg, knowing that."

"Why?"

"And suppose there's no one else to go to? Suppose there is no one, no one at all except him? So you go to someone like him. So I went once before my daughter [from the first marriage] went out for the first time [to walk the streets]. Then I went once again. I bowed down to his feet, kissed his shoes, and came back; well, I came back [after kissing his shoes] drunk. [Because, dear sir, when you kiss the shoes of someone else for the first time, a creature like yourself, you will of necessity return home drunk.] That's where the drunkenness came from," he added suddenly. "[But then God knows where it comes from.] There sits a perfumed old man. Why should he give me anything? I will, you know, drink it up; I will not give it back. From compassion? But you know he doesn't feel any compassion; well, after such a visit, you end up drinking.

"We are God's children; we live in hell. There is one, Christ. He took pity on everyone; they laughed at him for this and that, and laugh at him, and 'insulted him.' He will come and will ask where is my daughter who sacrificed herself for her drunken father,[4] for her evil and consumptive stepmother and for the little children?[5] [And he will tell her, come, come: your sins are forgiven because you loved much.] And then after he has judged all, he will say: Come out too [you] drunkards. And we will appear. We will all appear, [all] without shame. He will spread out his crucified hands, open up his arms, and will say: Come unto me all ye that labor and are heavy laden. You are pigs and beasts. But you have suffered. I have seen everything and have judged everything. I saw your cowardly vileness, and saw that you suffered more than those you hurt; and therefore come, and we will fall down . . . all . . . and cry—Lord, may your kingdom come!"

"[N.B. And the strong will say: 'Lord! We did this and that and you accept them. They lived only for their own unhappiness and the

---

[4] the old man

[5] and took pity on the drunkard and was not horrified by his bestiality.

unhappiness of others, and always by their own fault.' 'I know,' he will say; 'but they were humbled too much, even beyond measure, because they were disgusted with themselves. They suffered too much, and that is why I am taking them to my bosom, because not one among them considers himself worthy of that. Come, come all, all, all as brothers.'[6] And then I will embrace my wife and I will get her a crown for her martyrdom. (I will be reconciled and will embrace her in harmony.)]"

"And suppose none of this ever happens; suppose none of this will ever be?"[7]

He looked:

"That is, there isn't any God, and there won't be any Second Coming . . . then . . . then it'll be impossible to live . . . It will be too animal-like . . . then I would throw myself at once into the Neva. But, dear sir, it will come to pass; it is promised, for the living. What, what otherwise would there be for us? Nowhere . . . Whoever is living, even though up to his ears, but only, *if he is really alive,* then he suffers, and consequently he needs Christ, and consequently Christ will come. Lord, what is it you said? Only those who feel no need for Christ, who are barely living and whose soul is like the inorganic stone, do not believe in Christ."

1) What is to be done next.

First he went out and ran to get the purse.

After the talk with Zametov in the inn, and after he had been chased out of the murdered woman's apartment, where he even exposed himself to danger, he was in the gayest of moods. Then the meeting with the civil servant. N.B. In general the meeting with the civil servant makes him more rational. The next morning he is thinking rationally and reflecting.

[N.B. Why, why, can't I be of use? Oh mother, oh sister; everything for you, beloved ones. The old woman, Lizaveta. Why did they turn up?] Meanwhile a letter from his mother. He received (. . .) to Razumikhin's. He returned the money at night. He came home. Sassia. Later in the evening the civil servant is crushed.

---

[6] You are beasts, pigs, and not worth calling at all, but, you, come too!

[7] just because you have to be caressed.

Is man worth that?

Civil Servant. [When they beat him] "For I find pleasure in it, dear sir, I find pleasure in it."

She: Your unfortunate money will be spent on the funeral.

She (to him), when he came to her. "How unhappy you were, but my tears were not flowing then. And now you will make up for it all: if you have taken another's life, then you will give yours in exchange."

N.B. He went to her in this way: First he fell in Hay Market Square, then he went directly to the bureau, then he returned and went to her, whom he had not seen for a long time.

It happened this way with Sassia: He caresses Sassia, and she came to him. (from [the widow] wife) And it was clear that she herself was glad to have a pretext for coming. She said that she is the daughter of Lizaveta [and that she knew Lizaveta]. When he admitted his guilt to her, then suddenly, no Sassia. She came and took her away to her place. He understood.

N.B. Not a word between them about love. This is a *sine qua non.*

N.B. The civil servant says: Much is forgiven to her, because she loved much.

The first meeting in the tavern with the civil servant: I often met him roaming about.

N.B. Near the end, in repentance, when *she* had already rejected him; the rage begins. (*Veuve Capet*)

If to an old man, or to no one, that would be no different from playing. Why am I like that? [Then the Dream]

Filled with rage he meets her plying her trade. A scandal on the street. She had stolen. He confirms it. He went to her. Crying. He came to say goodbye. They say goodbye.

Then he threw himself down on Hay Market Square. Then he gave himself up.

N.B. But after he had insulted her on the street and after he had come to her, he found her in tears and agitated, and she, having forgotten that he had recently insulted her, says: "Don't judge me; she was sick with fever; the children were crying; what was I supposed to do? He called me and I thought that he would give me some money, but he robbed me . . ."

N.B. (No, not there, but before he confesses to her).

She and Bakalin.

Program of conversation at Razumikhin's begins with Razumikhin's account of his troubles to justify the worker.

Somebody else talks about people who don't want to get their hands dirty and how all of us want to get rich quickly.

Others ask the question: Why is it that crimes are committed so stupidly—clues are left and evidence is there for everyone to see?—He begins to talk heatedly about all that he'll do; how he will begin to work on the stock market. Gas. And he goes out trembling with fever. At that point, the conversation under the street lamp. And then he went to add to the money. Tomorrow Sassia. N.B. Something troubles him yet; he looks for reconciliation. He remembers the civil servant. N.B. The Dream.

The definitive theme of the conversation under the street lamp. "Leave me. If you really knew what I have done, you would recoil from me, and I am proud and I don't want to steal your friendship. Goodbye." He added 25 rubles.

Unbearable pride with which *he expounded the problem* (*example on the boulevard*). N.B. Why do they run, why do they hunt the criminal? Are you [yourselves] any better? And Napoleon? The rut, crowd, Andrey Alexsandrovich. Oh, baseness!

So that there is then a *coup de maître*.* At first there was danger, then fear and illness, and his whole character did not show itself, and then suddenly his [whole] character showed itself in its full demonic strength, and all the reasons and motives for the crime become clear.

Not about Gas; someone else talks about Gas.

I've made out a program for myself: [take heart completely], take on fully my studies, work, make boots, learn a trade, or take up the

---

* French: "masterful stroke."

stock market. To Kheruvimov also; look for things to do. Not to be turned away from this for years on end, for decades. Not to beg for anything from people, and not need their friendship or their love. Live without people. Die proudly having paid for a petty [and ridiculous] youthful crime with a mountain of good and useful deeds. Don't take the old woman's money. Nonsense. Complete nonsense. Nothing to be afraid of.

But the development of his love for Marmeladov's daughter bewilders him.

Before that. Conversation with Marmeladov's daughter after the funeral. He finds it a burden that she has taken to visiting him. Why do you come to me? She went away crushed. Insulted her. He wanted to go to her, but suddenly he met her on the way humbled. He goes to console her, tears; no *you can't live without people!* Again new sufferings. He confesses everything. They part. She took Sassia, etc. Again he calms down and approves of himself. *Dream.*

He decided not to visit Sonia. Sassia. Is it possible I can't love her? *Lizaveta's.* In the evening meeting with the crushed Marmeladov.

He goes out and description of St. Petersburg. Farewell to this whole world, sadness. Magnificent description and then suddenly the meeting with the crushed man.

*October 14 (aboard the "Viceroy")**

N.B. Introduce this episode: because of his conversation with Zametov, the visit in that same evening to the apartment of the murdered woman, giving of money to Marmeladov's widow, careless conversations and so forth—he is tracked by the inspector. Interrogation. He gets himself out of the matter proudly and with complete ease.

N.B. N.B. *Change in the program.*

After the scene at his bedside with Razumikhin and Bakalin he decided to run away ~~in the evening.~~ that night. (N.B. Mama sent 40 rubles by way of a merchant and a letter, which he had not yet

---

* In 1865 Dostoevsky was returning from Copenhagen where for ten days he had visited his good friend Baron Vrangel.

opened, but Razumikhin said that Sonia would wait.) In the evening he takes with him only the unopened letter from his mother, but he leaves the money in an open dresser to settle his account with the landlady. He goes to take the purse out from beneath the stone. He counts it on Krestovsky Island. Then he reads the letter from his mother. Then he judges himself. Gets stronger. Analysis of his crime. "No,—no and no! I didn't have the right to kill. But I'm taking it all on myself." Touch on the principal idea, lightly and generally though. Desperate contempt and boldness suddenly arise after the morning on Krestovsky Island. All that is still unhealthy. Scene on the Admiralty Boulevard takes place. Drunkards. All filthy things. (Memories of the horse, of Demianenskoe)* In the evening, scene with Zametov. Visit to the house. Death of Marmeladov. The next morning ~~at Marmeladov's~~. [Sassia. At Marmeladov's.] Accompanies Marmeladov's daughter home. Conversation with her. Evening at Razumikhin's. The next morning, Sassia. Sonia's visit. At their place after the funeral. She is insulted on the street, etc., etc.

N.B. Afterward before *giving himself up*, about Marmeladov's daughter: Why don't they groan? What is her fate? Pale creature at night . . . She also sacrificed herself. He becomes enraged: Why don't they groan? Why are they quiet, meek? Do they think it's right to be so treated? . . . He says this to her: "Well what will happen to the family? You [the daughter] will have enough for a year, for two, and then, then?" He pushes her to hysteria and *to love*. Why don't they groan?

N.B. Scene with B. on Hay Market Square (with the fish).

N.B. Oh, why aren't all happy? Picture of the golden age. It is already carried in our minds and hearts. How it must come, etc.

N.B. But what right have I, I a vile killer, to desire happiness for people and to dream of a golden age?

I want to have that right.

And following on this (this chapter) he goes and gives himself up. He stops by only to say goodbye to her, then he bows down to the people. ~~Denunciation.~~ Confession.

---

* Property where Dostoevsky had passed his childhood.

She sacrificed herself for the family. Lord. Even in the most august sacrifice, there is ugliness [and vileness]. Fate humbles the humbled to the point that even in their noblest sacrifice there is disgrace and ugliness!

Memories appear:

Why when his mother was reading the Bible—Talitha cumi.

N.B. He thinks suddenly in his *last* feverish imaginings how they will talk of him: *Fool,* he couldn't even do that. Kill—he killed, but took only 100 rubles of the money. He becomes afraid. Mother. Sister. He imagines the conversations in the provinces: sister of a murderer. About how they are going to remember him: Oh, the nastiness of it all! No, not for anything! Not for anything!

Prospectus No. 2

He came back at night. Burst out laughing. At night. *Dream.* In the morning, he was himself again; remembered what he did yesterday, but the positive part remained. He went to look at the purse, put it in his pocket, set off for the islands. The incident on Admiralty Boulevard. Oh, vile people. He went to look the money over, and how strange it was: He remembers all the circumstances of the crime and is astonished at them, [about how he wanted to conduct himself, not touch the money, etc.]. No, now one had to more serious! About the crime itself: why reflect on it—all are scoundrels. Are they worth it, are they? I won't spend anything, but there. [Why that dream? Why do they frighten me?] Oh, only you, my poor mother and sister! [About the sister and mother. The incident concerning his sister. I wanted to kill him, but at that time I was busy with love.] Ridiculous love. Reliably and positively. I'll stop by at Razumikhin's: the evening at Razumikhin's. Conversation under the street lamp; the letter from his mother arrives.

[The next day.] Do you really want to tear apart her heart. Can't I really be like Gas? [He knocks at the door of the room.] Child. Oh you lovable creature; [this is Lizaveta's]. About Lizaveta.

(The episode with the drunkard on Krestovsky: don't you think my heart hurts, doesn't it hurt? About the wife. How he respects her and who she is. He took him to the apartment. [I ought to throw myself into the Neva, but being a scoundrel, I go on living.] He gave him money from the purse. Then he returned the money to the purse [under the stone].)

Then he goes to Razumikhin [after the street lamp]: then scoun-

This manuscript page corresponds to pp. 91–93, beginning with the title "Prospectus No. 2" and ending with the phrase "Poor creature." This is a well-worked-over sheet and seems rather messy, but it is clear where the marginal additions are to go.

drel, scoundrel, scoundrel gave back the money, which he got by way of the knife.

He went to the daughter. Like a prostitute. Then the daughter herself came. The daughter helps the mother. Takes the money. Pity for the children. Sassia to her: Auntie [My daughter walks the streets with a yellow passport.]

At this time the episode with the drunkard. To Razumikhin's. The summons comes to his home. Letter from his mother. Added to it under the stone. Mother, sister, the story of the love. Why can't I become a Gas? Why is everything lost? The baby. Who will forbid me to love this baby? Can't I be good? Prayed. Then the *Dream*. The next day, he went. The Widow Capet. In the evening the civil servant's daughter brought to him. And suddenly: I am astonished why I don't pity Lizaveta. Poor creature!

Several notes for 1,500 turned up, but he did not [take them], but took a few [odd] things [the devil knows why]. ~~He didn't succeed and precisely because he was prevented and because she disturbed him.~~ Perhaps he might not have succeeded in [taking] anything, and not because he was prevented, but because he lost his head. [He didn't know what to take.] True, he was disturbed; Lizaveta ~~and not the other~~ came in [she was definitely not supposed to be in, and she couldn't be in, yes], and she happened to have a bundle with her, and the caretaker saw her [go through the gate] with the bundle and go up to her room. That was 10 minutes before they found the murdered woman. That means that the whole business took about 5 minutes or so. The murderer frightened that the door [was] open [and that Lizaveta had entered] closed it [and killed her. Note that he washed the ax.][8] Then [suddenly] Bergshtoltz and Kopilin* ~~came and began~~ appear and begin to knock. ~~Neither one nor the other had ever seen each other before, and they proved it by all kinds of evidence. Despite the stupidity [of all the evidence], they brought them~~

---

* These two are called Kokh and Pestriakov in the final version.

[8] There turned out to be blood in the water—that's what he was busy with. That means he's a prudent man. No, no, not prudent, but just inexperienced. Oh, it's a pity that I can't tell about all of this now. [Well] why do you blame Porfiry for suspecting Bergshtoltz? It was impossible not to worry him and the student [Kotel'n].

~~in [anyway] [and the inspector really made a blunder in suspecting them because the next day in the evening] because [and it was not possible in any other way] there was not any error of the inspector's.~~ But most important the day before yesterday and no later than the morning the earrings which ~~were pawned to the proprietor of the tavern on the eve, pawned~~ had been pawned in the tavern to the peasant Mortirin, pawned indeed on the very evening of the murder ~~at 9 o'clock~~ and by the [very] painter who had been painting there in an empty apartment, were brought to the police station. The earrings were in a small case and [the case was wrapped] in paper and on each similar wrapping the old woman usually wrote the name of the person who pawned the object, and [many of] those objects left in the trunk turned out to be wrapped in such a way with the surnames written on them. The worker confessed [to everything] and presented the wrapping; he had thrown it in the apartment.

["Confessed? that means . . ."] ~~That's a proof then~~

"Precisely, that's not it at all, [does not mean that at all]. [In your opinion, but not in fact.] We are busy with ~~the worker~~ that; he explained everything and told the truth [to the very end].[9] That very object [those very earrings]," Razumikhin went on clearly and solemnly, "that very case ~~with the earrings~~ he found in the empty apartment behind the door; he found it at the same time [almost at the same moment], when upstairs the caretaker, Bergshtoltz, and the student entered and saw the corpses."

~~"Well, and so he's the one who killed."~~ "But what proof does he have?"

"They saw him, saw! That's the point, they saw him! Three witnesses who were going up the stairs almost at the same time saw him. Bergshtoltz and the student [from the very beginning when there was no suspicion of him], showed that he had been there when they had gone up the stairs, one behind the other [and when the apartment was locked. How could he be locked in there and here at the same time? A civil servant [a stranger], who met Bergshtoltz on the stairs, remembers that the worker was there at that time.] And Bergshtoltz even stopped and asked the worker: whose apartment is this? (the empty one which was being painted). ~~He gave as his justification~~

---

[9] Be that as it may, the murderer was one of the customers. That goes without saying! Porfiry has been interrogating them. How did he find them? Some of them, as I've pointed out; they're interrogating the customers? And so?

~~that he entered [only for one] moment, [that in a minute they were calling the caretaker together] and that (. . .) therefore it was impossible in kill in one moment. Also if he had killed and not stolen, and left the trunk open, there was no point in calling the caretaker. Yes, he's not the one; the worker is.~~ He brought forth this question and this conversation with the worker as evidence [at the first evening of the interrogation], [that is, that the worker had seen him. He presented the worker as a witness; at that time there were no suspicions whatsoever of the worker]. As soon as they had gone after the caretaker, the worker had run out of the apartment after Mitka, after the other worker [his comrade whom he painted with] and wildly yelling he fell onto the whole group, on Bergshtoltz, the student, and the caretaker, who were already going upstairs. They gave him a good chewing out, but he went on, nevertheless, looking for Mitka. The point was, therefore, precisely this that the real murderer was able to skip out; hearing that the caretakers were coming, he slipped into the open [wide open] apartment, which just happened to be empty, [because the worker had just run out to catch up with Mitka]. Then he waited until [the caretaker and Bergshtoltz] passed by him [imagine his state at that moment] going upstairs. [And when it was all over], the only trace he left was the lost little box containing the earrings. And the worker, having pommeled Mitka, appeared a moment after, ~~found the thing~~ [looked on the floor], and saw the earrings. ~~Finding them, not delaying any longer~~ [He didn't think very long about it]; he closed the apartment and [of course] went off immediately to the tavern where he pawned them [his find to Mortirin for 2 rubles. The same earrings cost 6 rubles new.] They heard the next day about ~~the search, the peasant Mortirin~~ And when Mortirin heard everything, he thought and thought and then went off [exactly the day before yesterday to the police station] with the earrings, and he gave a full account of the whole affair! [And so you see they got everyone mixed up in the affair.]

["I didn't hear about that.] It's a complicated business!" muttered ~~Zametov~~ Bakavin.

"But [do you know what, Razumikhin], one must note, ~~Mr. Razumikhin~~ that you ~~you like to interest yourself with things~~ are a big bustler scandalmonger.

["Yes, the hell with it. I said something perhaps in heat a little while ago, and you felt insulted, is that it?"]

["Well the devil with you," said Bakavin in a half friendly manner, shook his head, and went out.]

["What, is he angry or something?" yelled Razumikhin.]

"He lived with Lizaveta," Nastasya blurted out as soon as he left.

"What? Him? It's not possible," Razumikhin cried out.

"Him. She did his wash for him. Also he ~~paid little~~ didn't pay her anything for it."

"No, it just isn't true at all!" Razumikhin cried out. "She had someone else. I know."

"Well maybe there [was] a third and perhaps a fourth," Nastasya said laughing. "She was a girl who tried to please. It's not that ~~she herself had to~~ she did it by her own will, but she sort of bore it out of humility. ~~She did not know how to say no.~~ Every mischief-maker had fun with her. But the infant they found was his [the doctor's]."

"What baby?"

"But don't you know? They performed a Caesarean on her. She was six months' pregnant. A boy, born dead."

"Yes . . . I remember . . ." said Razumikhin reflectively. "I didn't know that about Bakavin. [But nevertheless you're lying Nastasya.]" Rakhmetov* whistled. "Besides one doesn't prevent the other, because, you see, Vassia, he's angry at the inspector [at Porfiry, Ivanovich]. They're both courting the Poroshin daughter, almost fighting over her; [they're rivals in everything]. Look, he'll go again today to ~~the Poroshin daughter. Give vent to his spite, because they don't like him there at all. As he is truly~~ the Poroshins to quarrel with him, [vent his malice. But a good fellow, nevertheless . . .] But we've tired you out, Vassia; what a conversation yet! Are you sleeping?"

I silently turned toward the wall.

"Actually I'm a funny guy ~~to be sure a scandalmonger,~~ I get mixed up in everything. Am I really a scandalmonger?" [He said this in a kind of good-natured reflection]; "to be sure I am a gossiper. Bakavin was right when he said that. I'll break that habit," he added in good-natured reflection.[10] "Well, yes, that's enough. Nastenka, do you remember what I was telling [you]. No, no, come over here and take a look. And in the evening. ~~I have to go. Goodbye.~~ Goodbye, Vassia. ~~I have to go.~~ I gave up my things, my money . . . I haven't forgotten

---

* Dostoevsky obviously means Razumikhin here. Rakhmetov, a character in Chernyshevsky's *What Is to Be Done?* may have been on Dostoevsky's mind.

[10] he added seriously.

anything—Goodbye. Nastasya, let's go out. I want to tell you still [another nice] word."

When they left, ~~Nastasya stayed for a moment, wanted to say something, but decided not to and went out.~~ I fell on my back and caught hold of my head.[11]

---

[11] (having suspected everyone . . . I now write from memory)

IV

Raskolnikov returns to his room after the murder—Summons to the police station—Concealment of stolen articles—Visit to Razumikhin—Raskolnikov's dream

In this section we have a long narrative fragment corresponding to the last pages of Part I of the novel and of Chapters 1, 2, and 3 of Part II. The narrative covers Raskolnikov's return to his room after the murder, his frantic efforts to wipe the blood from his clothes and to hide the stolen articles, his summons to the police station, his relief at finding that he is wanted only because of an old debt to his landlady, the return to his room and his hiding of the stolen articles under a large stone, the whiplash he suffers from a carriage driver, the offering he receives of 20 kopecks from a merchant's wife, his visit to Razumikhin and rejection of translation work, the dream in which he sees his landlady beaten by the assistant superintendent, and the bedside scenes in which Razumikhin scurries about feeding and comforting him.

Except for the few pages dealing with his return to his room, which are narrated in the third-person, this fragment is narrated from the "I" point of view, as was the fragment in Section I of these notes.

This fragment follows very closely the final version, but there are a number of changes, some of which seem to be significant. On the whole, the scene at the police station is pared down in the final version; some of the descriptive detail is cut out. On the other hand, Dostoevsky converted the German landlady's Russian to a defective Germanized Russian at a later point, since in the notes he merely states that she speaks in a thick accent. There is also an addition in the final text which perhaps points to Dostoevsky's conscious intent to emphasize a specific effect of the murder upon Raskolnikov. After Raskolnikov learns that the summons has nothing to do with the murder, he establishes a human relationship with the district superintendent, enjoys listening to Lt. Gunpowder's upbraiding of the German landlady, and feels generally relaxed and happy to be talking to and in touch with others. Suddenly, however, he is overwhelmed by a feeling—new to him—of indifference to the people in the room, and to his own life. This sudden conscious indifference to those about him and to his own life is not in the notes even though the narrative is closely followed in the final version. One may hazard that Dostoevsky wished to emphasize the sense of disassociation from life—his own and others—that Raskolnikov suffers as one of the consequences of the murder. This possibility is strengthened by the fact that he adds a similar reflection at a later point in the same fragment as it appears in the novel. After Raskolnikov has hidden the money under a stone, he stops to watch the cupola of the cathedral from the bridge—a panorama he had watched many times—and Dostoevsky tells us that he experiences the sensation of watching his past as if it were at the bottom of some deep chasm. Here, too, as in the police station, Dostoevsky has added a reminder of how Raskolnikov has cut himself off from life.

Another interesting change from notes to novel is to be found in Raskolnikov's dream of the assistant superintendent beating the landlady. Both versions are similar, but Dostoevsky suppresses in the novel the identification that Raskolnikov senses between himself as victim and the landlady as victim. In the novel Raskolnikov's fear is general: "Cold terror gripped his heart; it left him numb and exhausted." But in the notes Dostoevsky is explicit in stating that Raskolnikov feared for himself: "Soon they will come for me [also], I thought, and I raised myself to hook the latch, but then I came to my senses." Even the later (added, because bracketed) "also" points to a step in Dostoevsky's creative process in which he senses the significance of Raskolnikov's fearful sympathy for the landlady. In the same vein Dostoevsky crossed out in the notes the following statements: "Lord, what is it all about—and why did Aleksandr Il'ich come?" And, "Wasn't he asking for me?" The crossings-out and the changes do not indicate that Dostoevsky changed his mind about the symbolic identification of Raskolnikov and the landlady; rather, as much of this section shows, Dostoevsky was suppressing explicit details in order to make the scene speak for itself.

Something of the same tendency toward economy and suppression for dramatic purposes is to be seen in the following change: the scene in which Raskolnikov faints in the police station at the significant moment when a conversation takes place about the murder of the pawnbroker. In the interrogation that follows, the two versions are very close. In both, the assistant superintendent (Lt. Gunpowder or Aleksandr Il'ich) interrogates Raskolnikov about how long he had been ill and whether he had gone out the previous day. But in the notes we have the following additions crossed out by Dostoevsky: the assistant superintendent asks him whether he knew the pawnbroker, when he visited her, and he questions him in detailed fashion about what he pawned at her place. In the juxtapositions of crossed-out and retained material, we can see Dostoevsky at work suppressing details that he felt would distract from the dramatic implication of the scene.

This section is narrated, as is Section I, from an "I" point of view, and the importance of the change to a third-person narration in the final version is great. As is usual in a remembered "I" narration, we have two narrators, the narrator remembering and the narrator acting, a present time and a past time. Such a point of view is characterized by a divisive consciousness which must necessarily be at odds with an intention to immerse the reader in the dramatic action. We can gauge the extent to which such narration separates us from the action because of an interposed analytic consciousness by the following example from the notes: "Oh, how happy I was imagining how they would be struck dumb when they learned that the sick man, who [only yesterday] could hardly move, had already moved to another apartment. Why I imagined that I would get rid of them, rather than attract them even more by just such an act [even though to a new apartment], and perhaps stimulate by this act real suspicions—I can't understand that. But now in thinking it over and weighing all the past, I have come to something of a conviction that during [all these days and especially] that whole evening I wasn't completely in possession of my senses. [Besides] the next day I myself began to suspect that [more or less]. I remember that." Raskolnikov is supposed to be thoroughly engrossed in his plan and to be fixed wholly on his determination to elude his imagined pursuers. But the "I" point of view forces him to provide his own interpretations and, even worse, his own stylistic refinements. Every stylistic refinement wars against the realism of the dramatic action. Even something as innocent as the metaphor in "As quietly as a cat I stole down the stairs and went to Voznesensky Bridge," introduces the other Raskolnikov, the narrator, and emphasizes the distance between us and the action that is going on. Descriptive detail, reflections, and interpretations are, of course, present in the novel also, but—and this is crucial—Raskolnikov is not doing the describing and interpreting. By giving the conceptualizing to the third-person narrator, Dostoevsky permits Raskolnikov to act and think dramatically.

The contrast in effectiveness between the two modes of narration is most acute at those moments when Raskolnikov is in a state of semidelirium. What we get—and it is almost comic—is Raskolnikov's effort to remember what happened to him. In the final version, some of Dostoevsky's finest effects come from gestures and words said in semidelirium. Here is an example from the notes: "My strength was leaving me so quickly that I began to lose consciousness. Remembering now in detail everything that happened there, I see that I have almost forgotten not only how I walked in the streets, but even in what streets. I remember only that I returned [home] by a completely opposite way."

The third-person narration permitted Dostoevsky to be more dramatic, but, that aside, he seemed to move from notes to novel by pruning descriptive detail and conceptualizations of various kinds. The instinct that led him to give up the "I" point of view was the same that led him from conceptualizations to action. When Raskolnikov and the assistant superintendent argue about the time that Raskolnikov was supposed to have come to the police station, Dostoevsky eliminates from the final version the following reflections that we find in the notes: "[I myself did not understand what I was doing. Besides, I never could stand an attack on my rights and on my dignity, not suspecting that (. . .)]" Also, after Raskolnikov talks back to the assistant superintendent by reminding him that he is smoking a cigarette in a government office, we find the following in the notes: "I myself am astonished now how I could then stand on my self-respect." In the final version, Dostoevsky changed this to a dramatic description of what Raskolnikov was experiencing: "Having said this, Raskolnikov experienced inexpressible pleasure." Long before Henry James, Dostoevsky struggled with the refinements of his craft, molding it into an instrument of delicate effectiveness. He had no a priori programs; he knew when drama was needed and he knew when conceptualizations were needed. Most of all, he knew that technique was never an end in itself.

Prospectus No. 1

He went out to rent an apartment. ~~Conversation with the landlady is more complex.~~ He wanted to read *The Voice*. Meeting with Zametov. Challenge and bravado! [Razumikhin invites him to his name-day party.] Breakup with Razumikhin; bravado; (he went to the house and to the apartment). "Look, he's the same one who came." He got hung up on some words. Crazy thing. The landlady comes, asks forgiveness. [I quarreled with Razumikhin.] I came home, decided to remain and not to move. The evening about the daughter. [Dream]

In the morning, money. The scene on the boulevard. Utter conviction that it's all nonsense. Memories of childhood. About mother and sister: No, for you, for you my dear creatures! But people are base. Consoles himself completely. The deed has to be made right. To Razumikhin, for the name-day party; [Razumikhin is a bustler, but he's good]. Letter from his Mother. What, can it be that I want to tear apart her heart. No. I will be worthy!

(I suspect everyone. I am now writing from memory.)

~~Scoundrels, torturers, scandalmongers! scandalmongers! scandalmongers! [why] Why did Zametov tell him about the fainting spell? That means that Zametov suspects that I fell into a faint [precisely] from *that*. [From the very beginning he suspected] knew; [I suspected] that he suspected! [What a] snake! He'll find out; [he'll sniff~~

~~it out!] Razumikhin is a scoundrel. He is spied on, and they use him as a spy, and he doesn't notice . . . [What am I to do! What am I to do now!] Scoundrel! The United States of America! What a cadet corps witticism! Is it really going to continue eternally, eternally! Tomorrow, I'll move from here. Oh, how I hate them all! How I would like to take them all and slaughter them all to the last one. [I'll slaughter] Zametov! May I be cursed. Oh, damned illness . . . I remember very well that I wanted to go and rent an apartment that night [not understanding that it was night then and not day]. Several times I leaped from my bed, shaking off a deep drowsiness [and then grinding my teeth, I would fall again on the bed]. [Oh, how hard those awakenings were.~~] Toward morning in my sleep I kept dreaming of my project to go away, to flee [somehow or other], at first to Finland, and then to America . . .

But meanwhile the sickness was getting over. In three days [when all these moral sufferings, [the sickness] suspiciousness and mistrustfulness had grown to monstrous proportions in me—physically], I began to feel my strength [more and more]. But I pretended; I deceived them [all]. [I was impelled by a kind of animal, beastly cunning: to deceive the hunter and throw the whole pack of dogs off the scent. I thought only of myself and of saving my own skin, and did not suspect, by the way, that there were by no means the kind of suspicions and clues that I ~~I imagined with such terror, imagined~~ exaggerated for myself, and that in essence I was practically in no danger. But the conversation ~~about the crime~~ about the murder, which took place by my bedside between Razumikhin and Bakavin, made me feel an unbearable malice; and what is remarkable still is that during these agonies, this terror, I never thought a single time ~~with the slightest personal compassion~~ about the murder I had committed. Animal fury and the feeling of self-preservation swallowed up all my feelings.] [And so I deceived them all.] I pretended on purpose [for three whole days] to be so weak that apparently I couldn't move. [I did it so that] they would believe me. I practically didn't speak a word with them and especially with Razumikhin. I don't understand: I showed him so much [hate] indifference and rudeness by my looks [during this period] that it seemed he should have thrown me over. As a matter of fact, he seemed to be beginning to take insult inside of himself quietly, and what was more irritating than anything to me was that he [probably] attributed all this to my sick state, [and therefore bore it]. He had apparently given his word that he would get me back on my feet, and be my nurse up to then. ~~That's why I decided.~~ I wanted all the more to confuse them all, so that they would not attribute [my rage] only to my sick state.

On the third day about evening when that damned Bakavin ~~went away~~, who had fallen into the habit of coming over to us to chatter [Oh, God, what terrible blabbers they all are], left, I immediately pretended that I was sleeping. Razumikhin, having given his usual directions [and having expressed all kinds of regret that I would not be able to come to his place tomorrow in the evening for his name-day], left.[1] [I knew that he made up for the time lost with me at night working till four o'clock in the morning.] As soon [as he left] I [quick as a wink] rose, got dressed, and left the courtyard to look for another apartment. I hoped that my money would be enough for the move. [I would rent a corner from some lodgers and furthermore] in a few days I was to receive [some more] from my mother. Oh, how happy I was, imagining how ~~I would confound them all tomorrow~~ they would be struck dumb when they learned that the sick man, who [only yesterday] could hardly move, had already moved to another apartment. Why I imagined that I would get rid of them, rather than attract them even more by just such an act [even though to a new apartment], and perhaps stimulate in them by this act real suspicions—I can't understand that. But now in thinking it over and weighing all the past, I have come to something of a conviction that during [all those days and especially] that whole evening I wasn't completely in possession of my senses. [Besides] the next day I myself began to suspect that [more or less]. I remember that.

As quietly as a cat I stole down the stairs and went to Vosnesensky

---

[1] When they left, I jumped out of bed and later I was even surprised as to where I had got so much strength [run, run]. I began to get ready, but after five minutes I slumped down and began to sob with rage. Rage, unbearable rage. Oh, how I could have slaughtered them all; for two whole days I had been like a crazy person, and strangely there was only the feeling of wanting to pretend, to deceive them all, and to flee. I'm not going to tell any more about one feeling —madness. Deceive and go away, and I laughed maliciously at how I would deceive them. None of this was rational, but sort of childish. I found one sensation attractive: they'll come and I'll not be there. I ran away suddenly. On the fourth day that took a more rational form in me. The thought came [I could somehow or other weigh things] that I had nowhere to run to after all, and it would be better to rent an apartment, a corner, and not let out a whisper where for a whole month I would sit locked up. Then no one would come to torment me and no one would find me and it would be like that forever. I have to remark that my health was really returning and then later I became so happy when I dressed down Zametov and Bakavin.

Bridge. I wanted to rent something somewhere a little farther off near the Fontanka.* It was about eight o'clock; on the corner of Sadovaya and Vosnesensky streets, I came upon a hotel and since I knew they had the newspapers, I went in to read what they said in the paper ~~(in *The Voice*) or in *St. Petersburg*~~ [under the rubric of current events] about the murder of the old woman. When I was still ~~lying~~ home ~~before the sickness~~ I thirsted to read about it, but [so as not to awaken suspicion] I was afraid to ask Razumikhin to get me the papers. As soon as I entered and asked for a glass of tea and the newspaper *The Voice,* I saw suddenly [as if on purpose] Zametov in the other room sitting with some kind of very stout gentleman. A bottle of champagne was in front of them. The gentleman was treating. But that wasn't all: I was completely convinced from the first look that Zametov saw me, but didn't want to show that he had seen me. I decided on purpose not to leave; I lit up a cigarette and sat with my back to Zametov, closer to the door. When he left he couldn't miss bumping into me. Would he want to recognize me or not, I thought.

There was already a second article in the paper ~~*The Voice*~~ with allusions to the first. I asked for the number with the first article. They looked for it and brought it. I was not afraid that Zametov would see that I was reading it. On the contrary, I even wanted him to notice [that I was reading about it], and I asked [for the earlier number] partly for that reason. I don't know why I felt impelled to take the risk with such bravado, but I felt precisely the need to risk it. Perhaps from spite, from animal spite, which is not rational.

In the newspaper.

(Prospectus conversation with Zametov)

Nervous (. . .)

"Yes, I am reading about the crime in the newspapers."

"Besides this newspaper is known . . . Here is something also about the Pope. Voltaire's *Candide*. About Fontenelle. Besides you are not a literary man."

I looked at him ironically.

"[Besides] the other novels are more profitable. Boy you are elegant. Who was feeding you champagne?"

"True, we drank some."

---

* One of the main canals of St. Petersburg.

"Well, he treated, of course. Razumikhin is crazy about you; he says that you know all the secluded spots."

"What a ruffian he is."

"It's true that he's a ruffian, but you're in luck. You profit from everything."

"Why do you think so?"

"Come on, old man, it would be a pretty thing to get your hand on that pile. [sure, suddenly, get rich] For example, suppose you were to lay your hands on the old woman's pile. Pretty nice. You could lend it out for interest."

"It would get out, you know." (a defiant look)

"What would get out? That depends on how you do it. Take the guy who changed a *counterfeit* 5 per cent note. He didn't count up and so awakened suspicion. He should have held up the note to the light, etc. The same thing here. Walk around without socks for a couple of years, and then bring out the money. How about that?"

"You can't guard yourself against it. There it is (. . .) killed. [With something. Yes, you know, you make me simply tremble. What a guy!]"

"I wouldn't have done it that way. Don't you really know?"

"I'll bet [that you] think now that I'll tell you what I don't know. Well, no, I do know. I pawned things at her place. What would you think if I were the one that snatched her money and put it under a stone. Suppose it were me."

"What are you saying?"

"Admit it, after all, that you did think that it was me. But why, but (. . .)" He stopped (. . .) Razumikhin burst out laughing as he entered.

Zametov affirms (N.B. after) that he had no thought, neither before nor in the office, but that *there was something like that* (but from that evening on the suspicion passed away completely).

Why are you all ears already? But I know really why you are all ears. What kind of head is that anyway? I'll explain it to you further.

In the streets. [How did I have enough strength for that!] My strength was leaving me so quickly that I began to lose consciousness. Remembering now in detail everything that happened there, I see that I have almost forgotten not only how I walked in the streets, but even in what streets. I remember only that I returned [home] by a completely opposite way. ~~My strength and my memory were leaving~~

~~me with extraordinary speed.~~ [I still remember that minute when I managed to get to V. Prospect, but after that I remember only badly. I remember as if in a dream someone hailing me close by: What do you know; he's drunk. I must have been very pale or was swaying.] I became myself again when I went through the gate of our house; no one was there. [But I was in such a state as to be past fear and taking precautions . . .] I had already started up the stairs, but [suddenly] I remembered the ax. ~~I don't understand how I could even for a single moment forget about it; [it was after all necessary]. It tortured me now. It was the last pressing difficulty I had to take care of.~~ [I had to put it back, and that was of first importance, and yet I was so exhausted I had forgotten about that. Oh God ~~what torments they were!~~ how difficult it all was, and it was only a miracle that it was all accomplished, that I passed through all those terrors then without being noticed.] ~~I went down~~ Coming down again through the gate I saw that the door to the caretaker's room was ajar but not locked. Therefore the caretaker was either there or somewhere close by in the yard. But I had so lost by then the capacity to reason and control myself that I walked up directly to the door and went down [the usual] three steps [into the caretaker's place] and opened the door. What I would have said to the caretaker if he had asked me: "What do you want?" [I would have said nothing; I would not have been able to say anything, and would have betrayed myself by my strange look.] But the caretaker was not there. I took out the ax and put it in its former place under the bench, covering it with a log, so that it lay as before. I remember as in a dream that I was even glad and satisfied when I was finished with the ax. Then I went out, closed the door, and went home. I met no one, not a single soul [right up to the apartment itself]. The landlady's door was closed. Entering [my room] I immediately threw myself on the bed. I didn't fall asleep, but fell into unconsciousness ~~and something in the deepest unconsciousness~~ or semi-unconsciousness, because if at that time anyone had entered my room, I would have leaped up at once [and cried out]. Scraps and fragments of thoughts swarmed in my head [a whole storm of them]. I don't remember a single one . . .

[I continue.] Finally I realized that I had a fever and I turned over. Chill.

Chapter 2

N.B. Completely unneeded and unexpected details must leap out at every moment in the middle of the story.

16 June. The day before yesterday at night ~~something impelled me to begin~~ I began ~~to write down~~ the description and I remained sitting for four hours. ~~This will be a report . . . What kind? For whom? Besides.~~ This will be a document . . . These pages of mine will [never] be found. ~~About that I can be completely safe.~~ The sill of my window can be lifted out and no one knows that. It's been like that for a long time, and I've known about it for a long time. If need be it can be lifted and put back in such a way that if someone else moves it, he will not be able to lift it. He won't even think of it. I hid everything there under the window sill. I took out two bricks from it . . . ~~If I had begun to record from the 10th, on the next day after the 9th, then I would have written nothing, because I couldn't remember anything in order. For three days it was as if everything around me was swirling. But now everything is so clear that . . .~~

Nastasya has just been in with some cabbage soup for me. She was not able to bring it during the day. She keeps it a secret from the landlady. I had my supper and returned the plate to her myself. Nastasya doesn't say anything to me. ~~She evidently has pity . . . But about that. But about that. I told her everything about that so that no one would suspect me . . . But in order. Because I want to write everything down in order. But I [am going] to continue.~~ She also seems to be dissatisfied with something. ~~But no one suspects anything about that.~~

I stopped [then] at that point [having replaced the ax in the caretaker's shop and having dragged myself home]. I fell on the bed and lay there unconscious. I apparently lay there a very long time.

It ~~often~~ happened ~~with me~~ that I would sort of awaken from time to time and at those minutes I noticed that it had been night for a long time, [but I didn't think of getting up]. Finally ~~suddenly I hear~~ I came to almost completely, and I noticed that ~~it had begun to get light completely again, even though the sun had practically not set~~ [it had become] light already. I was lying on my back on my couch, still numb from the sleep and unconsciousness. Frightful, desperate yells from the street drifted up to me vaguely, [yells I heard every night under my window at three o'clock]. [Well] the drunks were coming out of the taverns [already], I thought, at three o'clock. ~~That took place at three o'clock every night here. I thought~~ I thought and suddenly I jumped up, as if someone had torn me from the couch. What? Three o'clock! I ~~leaped up~~ sat down on the couch, and then I remembered everything, everything! [Suddenly, in one instant] I remembered everything.

A ~~instant~~ minute later I leaped from the couch in terrible fright.[2] I was seized with cold. But the cold was from the fever which had begun long ago [in my sleep] and which I had already felt . . . [As soon as I got up] I began to shiver suddenly so much that my teeth almost fell out, and everything, everything in me began to tremble. I ~~leaped toward the door and~~ opened the door and began to listen. ~~like a wild animal I thought~~ [But] Everyone was completely asleep [in our house]. ~~It was three o'clock in the morning.~~ I looked around me and around everything in the room with ~~astonishment and terror~~ astonishment and I did not understand: how I could have not hooked the door [when I came in yesterday] and threw myself on the couch not only not undressing, but even without putting away my hat, because it had slid off and was lying there on the floor near the same place where the pillow was. If someone had entered, what would he have thought? [that I] was drunk?—But . . . suddenly I leaped toward the window. ~~My window is small, but~~ There was enough light, and I began ~~like a madman~~ to look myself all over, all my clothes: are there any traces? ~~No~~ But it was impossible to see. Trembling from the chills I ~~pulled~~ began to take everything off and to look them over. [I turned everything over, to the last thread, to the last shred; and not trusting myself, because I felt that I couldn't possibly focus enough attention, I looked over and turned over everything three times.] ~~With trembling hands I [looked over] turned over [every part] everything. But there was nothing on the clothes~~. [But ~~thank God~~ there wasn't anything, no traces at all] except there where the trousers had frayed on the bottom and hung like a fringe. [Thank God, thank God! I said to myself.[3] I was really happy.] There were [sort of, a couple] of spots of blood on the fringe. [The trousers' fringe must have got soaked and the blood had dried.] I seized my ~~scissors, knife, pen knife~~ pen knife and cut off the whole fringe. ~~I looked over the flaps.~~ There was [nothing] else anywhere. Then I suddenly remembered [thank God] the purse and all the things which I had taken from the trunk; they were all still in [my] pocket! I had not thought to take them out and hide them. ~~But suppose they were to find me with them?~~ Immediately I began to

---

[2] It seemed that I was being burned.

[3] whispered to myself. I remember that I

take them all out and throw them on the table. ~~It was sort of strange for me [to look again] at those things. I remember only that it was somehow very strange.~~ [Besides, I was not then myself from the fever and the dizzy spells.] I took everything out, and even turned the pockets inside out to make sure that there was not [something] there yet; I took that pile and carried it over to the corner where ~~I had long ago already [just in case] prepared [I noticed one] a place.~~ I had noticed a [certain] spot. The wallpaper was torn there and I began to shove everything into that hole under the wallpaper.[4] I found it strange to look at that pile, and I hurried in order not to have to look at it.] The place was not noticeable [because it was dark], but the place was stupidly [chosen]. [Even though my head was swirling, I knew that.] I had not counted on bringing objects back and therefore had not prepared a place.] ~~I counted at first only on money.~~ [I had thought there would be only money], and I would have found a way somehow to hide money. [That was clear.] What had to be done? [Tomorrow I had to find a place for everything, I thought.] [In a kind of exhaustion and perplexity, I sat down.] I sat on the couch. As soon as I sat down ~~quickly the cold seized, at once~~ the chills shook me unbearably. Mechanically I dragged my warm coat from the chair [nearby], which was completely in rags, and covered myself with it, and a sleepy delirium seized hold of me.

But ~~agitation, worry took over and I~~ suddenly [as if someone had again grabbed hold of me] I again ~~I leaped up, leaped up again and again~~ leaped up and threw [everything from me] and again began to examine my clothes. [How I could fall asleep again, and not even put away my clothes, oh my God, and yet that was what I did! That's the way it was.] I had not taken off the sling under my armpit. ~~It never occurred to me to take it off even~~ [I had forgotten and not even thought of it. Can it be that my reason had forsaken me, I thought.] But suppose there is a search and they begin to examine me? I pulled out the sling, and having unrolled it, I began to tear it into pieces, ~~destroyed everything to the last thread~~ and then I threw all the pieces under the bed. Pieces of linen could not [under any circumstances]

---

[4] and I was glad that I was shoving all that, but my God, I thought, is that really hidden, is that really the way that things are hidden? Then I remembered that there was blood on the purse. But it is in my pocket, joy. Good, that means I'm still thinking clearly.

provoke suspicion. I was standing in the middle of the room with strained attention, because I [still] could not in any way gather together my full memory. I started to look all around the floor and everywhere to see whether or not I had left anything yet? Harder than anything was my impression that I had sort of been abandoned, ~~that God had left me and was taking away my reason~~ that my memory also was leaving me. I wanted to gather together all my thoughts and examine everything, take all precautions [and to calculate everything for my safety] and I couldn't; I did not know how to. How is it that I could have missed the sling when I was examining my clothes? Isn't there something else yet? I looked dumbly around me, straining my attention.[5] The thought came to me that perhaps my clothes had many spots of blood and that it only seemed that there weren't any, because I was so weak, confused, and was thinking badly [so that I couldn't even guess that my reason was getting mixed up and had left me]. Suddenly I noticed again threads of that fringe which I had cut off from the trousers. [They were lying on the floor, cut off and not put away.] [Lord how could I have just thrown them there!] Where could I put them? I can't put them under the bed, in the stove? [But they will certainly go there first of all.] They'll start digging around and find it at once. At that moment a ray of sunlight lighted up my left boot; I looked at my sock, which peered through the boot, and I saw what looked like spots. I rushed to take off my boots. To be sure, spots [of blood]. [I must have spotted it when I put the boot down in the puddle.] I looked over the boots also, but there was nothing to be seen on the boots. But what, what was to be done with all those spots ~~of blood~~? Wash them? No it would be better to go out somewhere and throw everything away, everything . . . Yes, better to throw everything away! I said, ~~and I saw that I was again already on the couch.~~ [again sitting down on the couch from exhaustion.] [I was depressed by a strange dejection from the fact that I was not even capable of hiding the objects and from the fact that the feverish chills had begun again.] But [then] I could no longer get up; ~~and pulled the coat on me again, could not throw away~~ [I was frightfully tormented by the thought that I had to get up and act again, examine, put away, hide.] And for a long time, perhaps for a couple of hours, everything seemed to me [as if in delirium] that it was

[5] I don't see them because I'm thinking badly; I'm confused and my mind has blanked out.

necessary to throw everything away, [go] somewhere and throw everything away. [But I didn't get up.] ~~finally completely. Then I sort of dropped off.~~ When I[6] managed to put my coat on—I don't remember. ~~Then I awoke and already much, much time had gone by. Suddenly I heard something. The next day~~[7] [I was awakened very late by an extraordinary knocking at my door. At first it even seemed to me that they were breaking it down.] They were knocking at my door; [then I felt that I]. [When I heard it, I guessed at once that I] was completely feverish and perhaps delirious. ~~And I knew why long ago and realized that I was in a fever, even though I was unconscious.~~ I felt that even in my sleep. The knocking continued. ~~And suddenly I again remembered everything and a terrible freight seized me.~~ [I leaped up and sat down.]

"Open up! Are you dead or something? What's he still doing snoozing!" yelled Nastasya. "He snoozes all day long like a dog. Got nothing better to do."

"Maybe he's not home," said the caretaker.

"And who put the hook on the door? [Hah, locking himself in now! Afraid they're going to rob him?] Open up! Get up!"

I ~~began to get up, tried to understand something at least, at least to reflect upon something, at least to grab hold of something, to find help. These two voices. Why two? And when was it necessary . . . What do they want? Suddenly, I felt as if I had been transfixed. Why them?~~

Lord, when was it Nastasya's habit to awaken me, and why the caretaker? When has the caretaker come to see me? Why do they want me? Lord. It's them. Them! Oh, Lord. What is it! Does it mean, I thought, in terror.

I got up [bent forward and] unhooked the door. My whole room was only three steps wide and you could take off the hook while sitting on the bed. So it was: Nastasya and the caretaker, big as life! Nastasya sort of looked me over strangely. I cast a defiant [though vacant from sleep and delirium] [and desperate] look at the caretaker. Without saying anything he handed me a grey, folded paper, sealed with bottled sealing wax. ~~Ominous sign.~~

---

[6] When I managed this time, when I pulled it on again.

[7] Wrapped up in the greatcoat. Another voice said, "Bah, caretaker, what's the matter?" I leaped up.

"[From the Police], a summons ~~for you. To the bureau~~ from the station," [said the caretaker].

"To the police?" I said . . . "Why?"

"[And how am I supposed to know?] [They want you, so go.]" He looked at me strangely, [then looked around] and turned to go away.

"Are you by any chance sick?" Nastasya said suddenly, keeping her eyes fixed on me. [The caretaker [also] for a minute turned his head.] "Look, he's all feverish." I didn't answer and held on to the paper without opening it.

~~I started to let down my feet from the couch.~~ "Look, don't," repeated Nastasya, "look don't get up," she added seeing me letting down my legs from the couch. "If you are sick, then don't go. . . . What do you have in your hands?"

I looked and I saw that I had in my hands the pieces of the fringe I had cut off and yesterday's sock [and the pieces (. . .)] [They had remained in my hand.] I had slept with them that way: Later, thinking about this I remembered that half awakening in my fever, I would tightly, tightly squeeze them in my hands and then go back to sleep.

"[Get that, he's gathered up some rags and sleeps with them as if with a treasure." And Nastasya burst out laughing; she was given to laughter.]

I immediately shoved all that under my coat and ~~looked and not understanding anything~~ stared [intently, intently] at Nastasya. ~~Sock, I said, looking at it fearfully. But it's nothing.~~ [Although I couldn't tell absolutely, I sort of felt that they don't talk that way to a man they've come to arrest. But the police!]

"You ought to have some tea, want some? I'll bring it."

"No, I'm going at once, I'll go," I said.

"[Go ahead], but you won't make it down the stairs."

"Yes, I will: I'm going . . ."

"As you wish," she turned around [and went down].

I grabbed the sock and [began to examine it]. There was a spot, [but] it was not noticeable; it was all dirty and smeared [yesterday already]. Nastasya would not notice it even if she examined it. ~~And this . . . Lord! I unsealed it, rushed to and then it seemed to me strangely~~ [Mechanically] I unsealed the paper [which had been brought] [unsealed it] and read. [I read it for a long time and finally I understood.] This was an ordinary summons from the police station asking me to appear today at 9:30 in the bureau of the district police station.

I felt sick at heart. Five minutes went by in this way. [Maybe] it's cunning; [maybe] they want to entice me by cunning. [What kind of business could I possibly have with them] flashed through my mind. However, why the summons? ~~Why didn't they themselves come, I thought. Strange, I continued. If they have any suspicion, then . . .~~ No, I'll go, I'll go. [I'll go myself.] Lord, I [threw myself down on my knees to pray, but I leaped up and] began ~~to put on my shoes~~ to get dressed. I'll put the sock on, I thought, and it will get even dirtier and smeared and the traces will disappear. But as soon as I put it on, I immediately pulled it off. Realizing that I didn't have another, I put ~~the same one~~ it on again. Besides the fear of the impending visit to the district station was swallowing up every other feeling. [They are using cunning.] I was also very dizzy and my head was hurting from the fever.

It was very hard for me when I took my hat and went out swaying down the stairs. On the stairs I remembered that I was leaving the things there in the hole in the wall [and I paused], but then such a sense of despair took hold of me that I waved my hand and went on: What happens, happens. [I felt crushed by so much anguish, and I felt so little capacity to preserve and defend myself.]

[The faster they find out the better! I said to myself.]

They saw [it] yesterday when I passed by the station after the deed.[8] [It's cunning! I thought, and went out into the street.] ~~Yes, yes, cunning.~~

The heat was terrible, stuffiness, crowds, plaster from the scaffolding, sand, dust, stench from the shops [and particularly from the taverns], shouting hucksters and drunkards, who were falling down on the street at every moment, despite the fact that it was a weekday and still early. The sun brightly flooded over me and everything around me so that it was hard to see and everything swirled dizzily. I had the usual sensation of someone with a fever who had stepped out onto the street. [It seemed to me that my head would burst like a bomb.] ~~I looked around at everything greedily and I tried to grab at something with my thinking. Otherwise I~~ I went along swaying,[9] and hurrying and probably bumping into ~~those I met~~ people passing

---

[8] I am walking on blood

[9] I walked swaying; a deep inner terror continued and ate up all my sensations; several steps.

by. ~~If I could only find out quickly. What happens, happens. A deep inner terror continued to swallow up all my sensations.~~ If I'm asked, I'll say yes [I thought], no I'll say no! [no, no, no] All that ~~flew through my mind.~~ was passing in my mind when I came to the bureau . . . ~~I don't know why but my heart sank again completely.~~ I was trembling all over and my heart sank from what faced me.

The Police Bureau was about four hundred steps from my place. I knew where ~~our bureau~~ it was to be found, but I'd never been in it. Going in under the arch, I saw a peasant [from some province] coming down the stairs with a book of some kind in his hands. That means that [the bureau is] up these stairs. And I began [also] climbing up. ~~I don't know what I'll say, I thought.~~ [Whatever comes up I'll speak. I'll go in and fall down at their feet and I'll tell everything.] The bureau had just been moved ~~to the new apartment on the fourth floor. I already knew that from Nastasya.~~ to this building. The stairs were narrow, dirty, [and] covered completely with slop water. All the ~~doors~~ kitchens of all the apartments on all four floors opened up ~~every minute~~ onto these stairs [and stayed open like that almost all day long]. Caretakers with books under their arms, people with errands, and various [men and women] and visitors were going up and down the narrow stairs. ~~The stuffiness was terrible even on the stairs~~ On the fourth floor on the left the door to the bureau was wide open; I walked in—and stopped in the vestibule. Peasants of some kind were standing around there waiting.[10] [The air was bad enough on the stairs, but here even worse the smell of wet paint pierced your nostrils.] But having waited a bit, I decided to move on to the next room. [All the rooms were small.] Clerks of some kind were sitting [and writing] there, dressed hardly better than me. I turned to one of them:

"What do you want?"

I showed him the summons from the station.

"Are you a student?" He asked[11] having read the summons.

"I'm a student."

[He looked me over curiously.]

"Go on to the clerk there," and he[12] pointed with his finger to the very last room.

I went into this room. It was small, cramped and crowded with *the public,* with people, a lot better dressed than in the other rooms.

---

[10] About the fringe, about how I could be such a fool.

[11] having looked at

[12] smoke a cigarette.

There were [even] two ladies there. One was in mourning and poorly dressed; she was sitting at a table across from a clerk and was signing something at his dictation. The other woman, very stout, crimson red [small spots] imposing, dressed rather splendidly[13] was standing ~~modestly~~ to one side and was waiting for something. There were still two others there in rather worn-out coats, a merchant [in a short coat] completely impregnated with the smell of a saloon and wearing a black [unbelievably dirty satin vest,] and some kind of foreigner [and someone else yet but I don't know who], don't remember. People were scurrying about the four rooms, some were coming in, others were going out. I handed my summons to the clerk; he glanced at me, said "in a minute" [wait] and continued to busy himself with the lady. ~~I took heart. If it were anything serious they would not meet you that way.~~ Surely it's not that passed through my thoughts. Little by little I ~~took heart, thoughts became clearer, I~~ [began to look around], sort of began to wait. ~~I stood there and looked around greedily, but my thoughts were very scattered, and I couldn't make them focus on anything.~~ I stood a long time waiting. [Some things struck my attention sharply to the smallest detail and interested me; I paid no attention to other things at all.] The clerk* stimulated my [particular] attention very much. [I wanted to pierce him to the core, to tell something by his face.] He was a young man [about twenty-two] with a happy countenance, dressed in fashion, like a fop, his hair parted to the back of his head, carefully done and slicked down; he had numberless rings on his white sparkling fingers and [gold] chains for his watch and lorgnette. He exchanged a few words in French with the foreigner. ~~He seems to be good, I thought.~~ [No, he certainly is not going to talk about that, I thought]; ~~everything interested me terribly~~ [and with all the effort I could summon I looked into [his] face trying to make clear what it was and what he had on his mind regarding me].

"Louise Ivanova, you should sit down," the clerk said cursorily to the dressed-up crimson-red lady, who seemed to be afraid to sit down.[14]

"*Ich danke*," she said quietly, sitting down on a chair with a silken stir [and looking around her]. [I turned around and began to exam-

---

* Zametov.

[13] dressed rather splendidly with a brooch on her breast as big as a saucer

[14] I also looked at the lady. She was a splendidly dressed, a florid woman with a brooch as big as a medal.

ine her intently.] Her dress was [pale blue trimmed with white lace] and looked like a balloon. It spread itself out around the chair and took up almost half the room. She sat [evidently timid about the fact that she was taking up half the room, even though] smiling, but sort of timidly waiting.[15]

The woman in mourning had finished and had begun to get up. ~~And perhaps that's their way of setting the trap, I thought; they make out that it's nothing and then bang! And suppose they're searching the apartment now!~~ Suddenly an officer came in somewhat noisily and swaggering a great deal [and sort of specially swinging his shoulders with every step], threw his cap [trimmed with a cockade on a table and sat down in a chair] and sat at a table. The splendidly dressed lady leaped up from her place; [on seeing him and she began to curtsey, but the officer didn't pay her the slightest bit of attention and she no longer sat down in his presence.] He was a sub-lieutenant, the assistant of the district police commissioner.* He looked at me askance with a certain indignation. My suit was really in bad shape. And it was doubtlessly me too, disheveled, sweaty and feverish.

"What are you here for?" he yelled, seeing that I wasn't cowering before his thundering look. [That yell heartened me partly. "It means that [nothing] is known]."

"I was asked to come . . . summoned . . ." I answered trembling a little, [and suddenly I was seized with indignation. His insolent bearing (. . .) and I myself am now astonished.]

"It has to do with the recovery of money. . . . [from him] from the student," said the clerk. "Come here, here:" he said to me, giving me a notebook and showing me the place on one sheet. "Read."

[What kind of money? I thought. It's not at all therefore about the other matter.]

"And what time were you ordered to come?" cried the sub-lieutenant, [still ready to pitch into me; ~~because it seems~~ he was very touchy]. ~~perhaps precisely because I was a student and because one cannot use the familiar form of address with me~~ "It says 9 o'clock, and it's already going on 12 o'clock." [I was very much not to his liking.]

---

* Referred to in the rest of this scene as Aleksandr Il'ich and as Lt. Gunpowder. In the Garnett translation he is referred to as Ilya Petrovitch; in Magarshack's translation, as the assistant superintendent.

[15] As soon as she turned around, you could smell the perfume.

"They brought it to me only a quarter of an hour ago," I answered him sharply loudly. "And it's quite enough that I've come being in a fever. You should have sent it earlier. You write 9 and they bring it at 11."

"Don't yell [sir!]"

"It's you who are yelling and I'm speaking quietly. Please know that I'm a student, and I will not permit [you] to be discourteous to me."

[I myself did not understand what I was doing. Besides I never could stand an attack on my rights and on my dignity, not suspecting that (. . .)]

The lieutenant so lost his temper that he leaped to his feet trembling with rage.

"You will be quiet! You are in an official chamber. You will kindly refrain from being coarse, sir."

"You too are in an official office, and look you're smoking a cigarette."[16]

"You are not, therefore, showing us [the proper respect]," ~~You are showing a lack of respect to the whole public, do you understand?~~ I said. ~~I myself am astonished now how I could then stand on my self-respect.~~

The clerk,[17] [who was also smoking], looked at us with a smile. ~~I do not understand how I could talk [in that way].~~ I was trembling all over with indignation. The lieutenant was visibly taken aback.

"[That] is not your business," [he yelled disturbed, and [really] unnaturally loud in order to cover up his emotion]. "Here, be good enough to give the reply which is being demanded of you. Show him [Aleks Ivan–]," he yelled to the clerk. "[Complaints about you. You're not paying the money you owe . . . There's a bright fellow for you." ~~That [clerk] opening up the book again showed me the place with his hand. I was trembling all over from indignation. I am astonished now how I could then [in such a fright] still stand on my self-respect. However, I read; however,~~ I took the paper[18] [and

---

16 Yes, I was trembling in indignation and nothing could distract me; I even forgot everything. To be sure I was still saying it all from old habit [but all the same how could I] not yet understand anything. My God, did I think that I could [really], that I had the right to breathe freely, and that everything had been already taken off my chest, only because all the traces had been hidden?

17 Clerk was a clever and roguish lad

18 I was trembling with astonishment.

began to read]. [But I was no longer listening. I read the paper greedily.] I read it once, a second time, and I still didn't understand it.

"What is it?" I asked the clerk.

"They want money from you, for the note: You must either pay up with all the costs and fines, etc., or declare when you will be able to pay, and at the same time declare your willingness not to leave the city until you pay, and not sell or hide your property."

"But, if you please; I don't owe anything, anything."

"Well, that's your business. But we've had presented to us [a legal demand] on your note, signed by you and made out to the widow of the collegiate assessor Zarnitsina nine months ago for seventy-five rubles."

"But she's my landlady."

"Well, so what [that she's your landlady?]" The clerk looked at me with a condescending smile [and] pity and in addition with a certain triumph, as you'd look at a recruit under fire for the first time. ["How," he seemed to say, "do you feel now?"] But joy and good spirits were flowing into my soul and sort of flowing out into all my veins, ~~It had nothing to do with that, with that; therefore, and the hell with the note.~~[19] ~~What do I care about a note!~~ [despite the fact that it had so astonished me, I thought]. And so ~~[suddenly] it became pleasant to me to discuss things [with this good] clerk and I even wanted [suddenly] to drag out the conversation with him further, talk to him in more detail, more familiarly. My whole spirit became sort of softened.~~ [I looked at the clerk with pleasure and in a friendly manner.][20] [That was pure] animal ~~cowardly~~ [instinctive] joy of self-preservation. [I breathed deeply.] ~~Please, please, think of yourself in my situation, I began like an actor preparing myself [from gentleness] for a very eloquent explanation.~~ [But at that minute] suddenly thunder and lightning struck us.

It was really something like thunder and lightning.

"And you, you creature you," the lieutenant, [still] very much shaken by my lack of respect, burning up all over [turning to the splendidly dressed lady] evidently venting his anger and wanting to

---

[19] The note not only did not worry me but I hardly paid any attention to it.

[20] I listened and understood and answered mechanically. My mind was filled with something else, something else. I will not lie if I say there was a minute, no only a single instant, of uncontrollable happiness.

hold up his self-respect in the presence of other people, [wounded by my reproach about smoking]. "What did you have at your place [an orgy?] [heh?] [a disgrace again?] You're responsible for fights, drunkenness all over the street. Do you want [to try out] a cell? [I told you, you know, I warned you once already, you ~~bitch~~ wench, [you witch, that I'm not letting you go the next time] and you have again, etc., you worthless wench]."

The paper which the clerk was handing me even fell out of my hands, and I looked wild-eyed at the splendidly dressed lady, who was being so unceremoniously raked over. [I remember only that it even gave me a great] certain pleasure. "Il'ya Petrovich . . ." began the clerk in a concerned manner, but he decided to wait because it was already impossible to restrain the lieutenant, except perhaps by pulling him by the arms.

The splendidly dressed lady was shaking all over. ~~but assuming an unusually amiable and dignified air~~ All at once, and strangely, despite the most scurrilous words, her air became suddenly unusually friendly, extremely attentive and [even] the more scurrilous the names became, the more bewitching and amiable that smile became that she turned toward the menacing lieutenant, [as if all those curses gave her some kind of a pleasure]. She kept shifting in place and continually kept curtseying, waiting until she would finally be permitted to put in her word.

"There weren't any fights or commotion at my place, Captain, sir ~~and the further she went on the more and more excited she became.~~ [and no scandal]," she began suddenly to jabber like (. . .) with a German accent even though she spoke fluently in Russian. "They came about three o'clock, Captain, sir; I'll give you a full account [Captain], but I'm not to blame, and the girls are not to blame, because I run a proper house [Captain, sir, and the behavior is always proper] and I myself never [never] want any kind of ~~big~~ scandal. And they were drunk, and then they asked for three bottles of champagne, and then one [got up, on his feet] and began to play on the piano ~~with his fists~~ with his feet. That simply is not done [in a honorable house] and he wrecked the piano entirely [entirely]. [These are not proper manners and I told him] that. I said this wasn't polite. [And he said that he always gives a concert like that in public, and then he took a bottle and began to push one of the girls from behind with the bottle] and he hit me with all his might on the cheek. ~~Another drunken [guest] took a bottle and began to push one of the girls from behind with the bottle.~~

And then when I began to call the caretaker and Karl came, he took Karl and blackened his eye and did the same thing ~~with his fist~~ to Henrietta, and hit me again [three times] in the cheek. And that is not good manners in an honorable house, Captain, sir. ~~And I am not to blame for anything because I run an honorable house.~~ [And I was yelling and crying, Captain, sir.] He then opened the window on the canal and began to squeal like a little pig, and that's a disgrace. How can you permit someone to squeal like a little pig out of a window: hooi, hooi. ~~And what kind of customer is that? I myself, Captain, even though I am the proprietor, and he said that he had to do it.~~ That's a disgrace. A guest cannot be permitted to act like that; because ~~Officer, sir, even though I am the proprietor and can do what I want in the house~~ I myself [the proprietor] would never permit myself anything like that [in my own house, Captain, sir]; no one up to then had ever squealed like a pig out of my window. And Karl was pulling him away from the window from behind by the coat, and it's true [Captain] that Karl tore his coat. And then he began to yell that he had to have 15 rubles as a fine. ~~And he said he would break all the mirrors.~~ And I myself Captain gave [brought out] 12 rubles. ~~I gave for his coat, I paid for his coat~~ And what an improper guest, Captain! He took the money, and then in the very center of the room in front of all the girls, he did a dirty thing. "I," he says, "[always like to do that and] I will write a satire on you. I'll print it in the newspaper because I can write anything about anyone in the newspapers."

"He was a ~~littérateur~~ writer then?"

"Oh, Captain, sir, what a dishonorable customer, Captain, when in a honorable house and in front of all the girls, in the very, in the center, on the floor."

"O.K., O.K.! You're talking through your hat now. An honorable house, all right. [In the center? All right old witch, so be it," he said to her more gently.] "I told you before, told [three times I've spoken to you already]. If there's a scandal at your place even one more time [most respectable] Louise Ivanovna, ~~I'll give you an honorable house.~~ I'll make it hot for you, as they say in high society. So, a littérateur, a writer took 12 rubles for his coat! . . ." ["Il'ya Petrovich . . ." the clerk called [again] quietly. The lieutenant glanced quickly at him. The clerk nodded to him slightly. "The affair is clear.] There are your writers for you!" (And he threw me a menacing-mocking look.) "The day before yesterday [another] incident of that kind took place in a tavern: [he had dinner and didn't want to pay: 'otherwise] I'll write,' he said, 'a satire about you.' [Another one also a week ago] on board ship dressed down a respectable family of a civil counselor accompanied by his wife and daughter with the foulest words. [Three days ago] some officers had a versemaker thrown out of a confectionary. There are your writers, littérateurs, students, heralds for you. Pfew! ~~An educated crowd! What philosophers!~~ And you, ~~jabberer,~~ why didn't you appear earlier," he cried turning on a sort of ~~peasant~~ bourgeois in a short coat and a silk [black, dirty] vest, "and you go I'll give you an honorable house. In the very middle! . . ."

Louise Ivanovna curtsied [hurriedly] in all directions amiably and in a dignified fashion, and continued curtseying all the way until she reached the door. But in the door she bumped into [from behind and again jumped] a distinguished-looking officer [with a fresh, open face] and with splendid pitch-black handle-bar mustache. That was the district chief himself [Nikodim Fomich]. Louise Ivanovna hurried to curtsey almost to the floor and with quick little steps, skipping, ran out of his presence.

"Uproar again, [again] thunder and lightning! Storm and hurricane!" said Nikodim Fomich amiably and in a friendly manner to Aleksandr Il'ich. "Once again you've got yourself all worked up again, all steamed up again. I heard you all the way from the stairs."

"Well, so what," Aleksandr Il'ich said, crossing the room with papers of some kind to his table, shifting his shoulders [with every step] and clearly showing off in an affected manner. "Look [take a look please] a gentleman writer." He pointed to me, "a former student, former [that is, student]; he doesn't pay, signs notes, refuses to move, continual complaints about the likes of him, and he had the nerve to take offense at my smoking a cigarette. He himself acts disgracefully. Take a good look at him, please. He is a pretty sight!"

"Poverty is not a vice! You are really a keg of powder, old boy. It's well known! Something certainly rubbed you the wrong way and you couldn't restrain yourself," continued Nikodim Fomich, turning to me in a friendly manner,—"but it's all a mistake. I assure you that he is a most honorable, honorable man,[21] but a veritable keg of powder, [powder; he exploded]. He takes fire, explodes, burns out, and no! and then everything is over [and as a consequence—one] thing only is left [gold] [nobility] a full heart! ~~Hussar, hussar,~~

[21] well-developed man

~~old hussar!~~ But he's honorable, honorable! Everyone in the regiment knew him as a lieutenant-gunpowder!"

"And what a regiment [that was]," said Aleksandr Il'ich, very satisfied that he had been nicely praised and had his vanity tickled [energetically shifting his shoulder]. As for me I [suddenly felt myself in a sort of enthusiastic, ~~in a blissful expansive~~ state: in a mood to say to them all something very agreeable].[22]

"If you please, Captain," I began [I was ready to beg forgiveness of them even, if I was . . . in anything]. "I am a poor, sick student, weighed down with poverty." (I said it in that way: weighed down) "I have given up my studies, because I can't support myself now. But I will receive some money. I have a mother and a sister in S——y Province. They will send me some. And I will pay everything up. I have lessons I can give. I will find a way, and pay for everything. My landlady is a good woman, but she has got so angry at the fact that I lost the lessons I was giving and have not paid rent for four months that she isn't giving me anything to eat for dinner. I don't understand completely what this note is all about. She is demanding payment from me on some note; what can I pay her?"[23]

"Well, you, after all," began the clerk. "You signed the note ~~a year ago~~ [and therefore obligated yourself to pay]" noted the clerk.

"Permit me to explain[24] to you," I continued, turning not to him but to Nikodim Fomich and trying also with all my force to address Aleksandr Il'ich, ~~Even though he was foraging about, he was listening to me.~~ although he pretended to be rummaging about in his papers and disdainfully was not paying any attention to me. "Permit me to explain that I have been living at her place for more than two years, since I first came from the provinces and before . . . well, why not admit this . . . from the very beginning . . . I . . . I promised to marry her daughter. True, I was not in love, but at the same time I assure you that I was not being forced. I had promised by my own free will . . . And then my landlady extended a lot of credit to me. I was leading a different life then; I was thoughtless . . ."

~~But all these details, he began~~ "What details!"[25] snorted Aleksandr Il'ich . . . [Intimacies]

---

[22] I wanted terribly to reconcile myself with them all, and in order to,—a single word.

[23] "That's not our affair," he remarked.

[24] Permit me, all the same, I interrupted quickly

[25] You are not being asked to give such intimate details, my dear sir.

"Permit me," I interrupted. "A year ago her daughter died from typhus. [I've already said that I was definitely not in love, but only thoughtless.] I remained as I was a lodger at my landlady's; when she moved to her present apartment, she said to me—and she said it in a friendly manner and with tears in her eyes—that she had complete faith in me . . . but would I be willing to sign a note for 75 rubles—the sum of my debts to her, according to her calculations. Permit me: she said that as soon as I signed [that note] she would again extend to me all the credit I wanted and that never, never, never,—these are her own words,—would she use the note until I myself settled it. ~~She said that I was eternally dear to her as the fiancé of her [departed] daughter~~ She said this with tears in her eyes . . . And I admit that I was touched and signed, even though I admit again that I was not at all, not at all particularly in love with her daughter, but simply out of thoughtlessness . . . And now look, when I've lost the lessons I was giving and I don't have anything, in addition to stopping my dinners because I owe her for four months, she is even demanding payment on the note. What do you think of that! Excuse me but that is, that is . . . what can I say now?"

"All these [touching ~~intimacies~~ details] my dear sir [absolutely] do not concern us," [disdainfully interrupted Aleksandr Il'ich, "and you should have kept them to yourself."] You have to give an answer and sign a commitment, and as for the fact that you were in love, all ~~your misfortunes there~~ those tragic episodes do not concern us [at all].

"Well now you're really too rough . . ." murmured Nikodim Fomich looking at me with compassion. Besides he immediately went up to the table of Aleksandr Il'ich, sat down, and began to sign something.

"Write," the clerk said [to me].

"What am I supposed to write?"

"I'll dictate it [for you]" . . . It seemed to me that he spoke [to me] much more carelessly and disdainfully since my confession. ~~How could I bother myself then with those stupidities? But I was so happy, so happy with all that humiliation, like salvation.~~

"But you aren't capable of writing; the pen is falling out of your hands," the clerk said looking at me with curiosity. ~~You are feverish.~~ "You [really] are ~~very~~ sick."

~~My head hurts and is dizzy I said; I threw down the pen, put my elbows on the table and~~ "Yes . . . I am dizzy," I answered, "Go on with the dictation."

He began to dictate the usual declaration, that is, that I can't pay, ~~Well, at least in a year~~ that I promise then not to leave the city, nor sell my property, nor give it away.

"But you know I don't have any property."

"Well, it's only the form."

"What am I supposed to do? ~~What am I supposed to do? Tell me, she'll put me in prison, you know~~. What's she going to do, have me sent to prison?" I asked, continuing to write.

"Maybe she won't send you," the clerk murmured indifferently examining my signature; "you may somehow get together, ~~in the meantime~~ there's still a couple of days left." ~~It is impossible to delay any longer.~~

[But I was no longer listening.] I threw the pen down, put both elbows on the table, and squeezed my head with my arms. [My head was burning up.] ~~"[What hurts] you," asked the clerk. "My head hurts, it's turning . . . And really."~~ My head hurt so much it was as if someone were driving a nail into it;[26] I wanted to get up, but suddenly I felt myself frozen in place. Nikodim Fomich was recounting something heatedly and his words reached me.

"It can't be . . . They [ought] to free them immediately. In the first place, everything contradicts it: Judge for yourself; why would they call the caretaker? If they had done it, why give themselves up? ~~And secondly [the students] saw them at the archway with three friends [as they were going in]; the caretakers saw them and [he] asked the caretakers about lodging there; all three friends are witness to the fact that he was with them in the tavern.~~ As for Povalishchev,* before he went up to the old woman, he spent a half hour with the jeweler below, and he went up to the old woman's exactly at quarter to eight. Consider now."

"But wait a minute, how is it that they say that they knocked and the door was locked, and three minutes later when they came back with the caretakers, it was open."

"That's it exactly. ~~At the time~~ He ~~the murderer~~ was sitting there. The student left Povalishchev waiting to guard in front of the door. If Povalishchev had not gone away to hurry up the caretaker, they

* Called Kokh in the final version.

[26] I did not regret the failure or her baseness. It was another feeling of anguish —it seemed to me that if they were my brothers [to narrate] then I couldn't have spoken any longer and I would have felt the same way.

would have caught the murderer. But he [left] just then [and the murderer] in that ~~time when they went away~~ interval managed to get down the stairs and slip by them [somehow]."

"But no one saw him?"

~~Well, he got out somehow, slipped past. And that's not all, take this circumstance into consideration, that there was along this very staircase an empty apartment left wide open; the worker who was painting it didn't lock it when he went to a tavern [perhaps exactly at the same second when the fellow worker] with the intention of [coming back] later to lock it up. Precisely at that time when they were coming up the staircase, the murderer was waiting in this apartment behind the door, and then he slipped by and disappeared. The affair is clear! The affair is clear! [Look (. . .)]~~ "How see him there; that building is a veritable Noah's Ark; there must be 100 lodgers there," the clerk remarked getting up from his seat.

I got up, swayed, and found my hat on the floor with difficulty and ~~half dead~~ made my way to the door . . . I don't remember anything more.

When I came to, I saw that I was sitting on a chair, that I was being supported from the right by the gentleman in the greasy vest, that someone was standing on my left side with a small yellow glass with [with yellow warm] water in his hands and that Nikodim Fomich was looking at me in a rather worried way. I got up and swayed.

"What's the matter with you, are you sick?" Nikodim Fomich asked sharply but with a certain pity.

"Yes . . ." I answered, looking around me.

"When he was signing the paper, he could hardly hold the pen in his hands," the clerk remarked, sitting down at his place and going to work on his papers.

"Have you been sick for a long time?" Aleksandr Il'ich yelled, standing at his desk and leafing through his papers. He most likely had been examining me when I was unconscious and went off to the side when I came to.

"[Since] yesterday," I murmured.

~~"Did you go out yesterday [evening]?"~~ "Didn't you go out yesterday," continued Aleksandr Il'ich.

"I went out."

"May I ask where you went?"

"Walking." ~~My head hurt.~~

"Hmmm." ~~"Did you know the old woman?" he asked suddenly, fixing a menacing and questioning look on me . . .~~

"But he can hardly stand on his feet, and you . . ." ~~"Why are you asking that?"~~ Nikodim Fomich remarked. ~~"Permit me, permit me . . . Did you know her or not?"~~

~~"No, [that is] not very much. I pawned a watch there three weeks ago," I added suddenly with a kind of bold desperation.~~

~~"Watch? You had a watch? [What kind of watch]? We'll find out about that. Silver. What kind of watch and how much did you pawn it for?"~~

~~"It was silver and I got two rubles," I answered insolently looking him straight into his eyes. "Besides, may I ask why you are interrogating me?"~~

~~"Of course . . . A man can hardly stand on his feet . . ." Nikodim Fomich murmured again, but. "And do you know that that old woman and her sister were killed yesterday evening about eight o'clock . . . No one knows by whom." No. No? No . . . [nothing].~~

"It doesn't matter . . ." Il'ia Petrovich* said in a sort of special way. Nikodim Fomich seemed to want to say something yet, but he decided better after glancing at the clerk who was looking at him intently.

It was all very strange.

"Well, very good, ~~go on, nothing more is needed~~," Aleksandr Petrovich concluded, ~~it seemed to me as if in reflection~~. ["You can go."] ~~I started toward the door; I wanted to turn around at the door and begin again: "But permit me" . . . But at that very minute Aleksandr Il'ich yelled after me. "So you saw her three weeks ago?" "Yes, about three weeks," I answered . . . "O.K."~~

I went out. I heard how a lively conversation ~~in a whisper~~ began [suddenly] as soon as I left. Nikodim Fomich's voice was louder than anyone else's. In a minute I was already making my way down the stairs. And ~~I already~~ I had come to completely. ~~I understood what they were talking about.~~

"There's going to be a search, a search right away," I repeated, trembling and freezing with terror. "They've guessed.[27] That scoundrel the helper [Il'ya Petrovich] guessed.

And suppose the search has already taken place, now ~~in my ab-~~

---

* Dostoevsky obviously means Aleksandr Il'ich here, and has inadvertently changed his name and patronymic. He is called Il'ia Petrovich in the novel.

[27] Scoundrel, scoundrel, how could you so quickly, so meanly jump from one feeling to another; no you don't have long to live.

~~sence. What if . . . No, no [can it be] they would not release me? . . . I came up to.~~ [while I was] in the police station, I thought, going down the stairs, what . . . [Suppose . . . I come upon them just now in my place?]

But here's my building. ~~I was already mounting the stairs.~~ And here's my room. Nothing happened; probably no one even looked in; ~~everything remained as it was~~ everything is untouched. [Even] Nastasya didn't touch anything. [Besides] she stopped making my room long ago. [The dust was undisturbed.] I breathed a sigh of relief.

[Consequently] Neither yesterday nor today [yet] did they have any suspicions of me . . . ~~even astonishing that~~ [I made an effort to reason.]

But that Aleksandr Il'ich has awakened suspicions in them [now], whether from foolishness or from spite; and most likely they will begin to . . . keep me under surveillance [and perhaps also visit. Perhaps even at once. And that is very, very, very probable.] But, my God, my God [how I humbled myself. Quick, quick save myself, quickly, immediately, Lord!] Where, where will I put all those objects now, where? [I sat on the bed and suddenly a strange sensation took possession of me.]

Hide the traces. I must do that.[28]

It's absolutely necessary ~~to hide them~~ to take them someplace, immediately, immediately ~~take them away before.~~ without delay, before they have a chance to begin . . . [And how on earth was I able to leave all this without paying attention.] I felt that I needed all my faculties now to think through my situation, all (my) strength, so as to save myself.[29]

I rushed to the corner, shoved my hand under the wallpaper and began to draw out all the objects and shove them into my pockets.[30] [If I'm not mistaken] there were eight pieces altogether. [I didn't examine them, but only remember it that way.] [I made note of this

---

[28] But, nevertheless, I had a presentiment that the situation was running away from me and that after a little while I would be mute, weak, bereft of reason and defenseless.

[29] Where to go? It is dreary all over the city; I went down to the banks of the Neva. I looked into the purse. Put it under a stone. I looked in on a friend. Translations. Three rubles, in a tavern. I came home. [Lay down. Noise.] Nastasya's account. (At night) That's blood on you. I bought boots, pants, and a hat. Newspapers. Great joy.

[30] in that hole? God, give me reason, reason Lord, reason!

mechanically, after counting them; it seems that there were exactly two,] two small boxes, [I remember that for sure: certainly [something with] small earrings of some sort; (I didn't look them over)]; [then still sort of] ~~two~~ four small jewelry cases; one [sort of to judge by touching] little chain was wrapped up simply in newspaper. I had ~~not yet examined a single one of the objects.~~ [It seems] that there was also a bundle of some kind ~~and another of that kind~~ [but it may be that I'm mistaken, for everything at that time was dancing before my eyes]. I shoved everything into different pockets, so that they wouldn't bulge. I took the purse and put it in the side pocket of the coat. [I remember] the purse [as if it were before me]: round, [green] suede [with a steel border] and [on one side] spotted thickly with blood. I hadn't opened it yet [even once], [and] I had no thought of opening it now. ~~I didn't examine it [earlier] yesterday.~~ My pants pocket is therefore stained with blood also, I thought. ~~Then putting on my hat, I left at once carefully, hurrying along.~~ Then I ~~went out~~ hurried out of the room as usual not locking it; indeed the door itself could not be locked from the outside; the key had long been lost. ~~Certainly they had not managed yet to give the order to have me put under surveillance, I thought, and I will beat them to it. I didn't meet the caretaker. They have already, to be sure, summoned the caretaker to the district police station, I thought, going out of the archway. He wasn't around, really. It's very possible that they've already summoned him to the district station, I thought, [for questioning]. They're going to have me followed, doubtlessly . . .~~

I walked quickly and firmly and I felt that they would follow.[31] But where to? Nowhere, I though; [my head]; some sort of artificial strength was welling up in me. I rushed ahead. I felt that at least my thoughts seemed to become clearer and more distinct, doubtlessly because it turned out that I had been summoned not because of that . . . and even though it was perhaps unnatural, I felt arise in me suddenly a physical strength from that strain. The first terror had left since the matter in the police station had turned out better than I thought. [I was afraid that I would be pursued]; I was completely broken, but I was in possession of my consciousness [now]. I was fully conscious that [my mind was growing dim, and I was getting weak. I had to, therefore, take care of things while I still had left even a little reason. I was afraid that within a half hour, a quarter hour, an order

---

31 "Oh give, give me reason for this last deed, but there" . . .

would already be given to put me under surveillance. I had to get it done, get it done. I had to succeed in burying all the traces up to now]. ~~And although I was weak~~ [This time] I was [practically] not swaying and stumbling as before. The point is that I had [already] long ago, by this morning, already during the night decided [to throw] all those objects somewhere in a canal or [throw] them in the Neva or simply shove them somewhere under somebody's staircase and—and I had made up my mind to be finished with everything.

But it was necessary to go somewhere a little farther. But where?[32] Several times I had looked over the stairs going to the [Catherine] Canal. But ~~below~~ everywhere near the stairs there were either rafts, or boats, or ~~50 steps away on the opposite side~~ windows on the wharves from which you could see everything: [notice a suspicious man stopping and throwing something into the water. No, it was ~~impossible to throw it into the canal~~ impossible to throw it into the water. All the more because all the passers-by were looking so curiously at me, as if they had nothing else to do but look at me. Finally, I surmised it would be better to go to the Neva; fewer people there.] I had not noticed and I was astonished that I had roamed about for half an hour, that I even knew that I had to go farther, and yet I didn't think of these things consciously and didn't decide to go to the Neva. [It took me so long, so long to think of that.] I was thinking with difficulty. I went on V—— Prospect. While walking suddenly another thought came to me.

[Suddenly] the thought flashed through my mind to go somewhere ~~a little farther~~ far away, somewhere like Krestovsky or Petrovsky Island and [there] in an isolated place [in the forest] bury everything under a tree [and make a note of the tree]. Reflecting on this and thinking it through [as well as I could, that is, making an extraordinary effort to come to at least some kind of conclusion], I found the thought to be very attractive and directly I set off in the direction of Vasilevsky Island, not taking into account that perhaps I would not get there because I was so weak and hungry from the previous day. And when I had already gone about a quarter of a verst, I said to myself: It's good that I'm going far away, because if I had continued to roam about the canal near my place [they would certainly ~~they would notice me. Besides it's very possible that I had at that moment~~

---

[32] Half hour gone by already, and perhaps more.

~~a very wild countenance, and my face was distorted with sickness and . . . and perhaps I even frightened everyone. But perhaps [I was imagining much of this. That day I was imagining an awful lot that never existed. But I continue.]~~ have searched me out].

I was not meant to get to Krestovsky Island, and I certainly would not have reached it. This is what happened: Coming out of V— Prospect onto Marynsky Square, suddenly I saw on the left the entrance to a yard completely surrounded by blank walls. Deep in the yard there were sheds of some kind and a pile of ~~firewood~~ logs. Farther yet in the back was an old wooden construction, apparently for workmen; it was some kind of carriage-repair or locksmith shop, I don't know. In the back there was a lot of coal in the dirty yard, and everything [around] was dirty and black from the coal. There's a place to throw everything away flashed through my mind; throw it away and have it over with. With such thoughts I entered the yard and as soon as I passed through the gate, which was made of dark boards, and opened wide [on the street] I saw on the left a wooden fence, which began ~~almost~~ at the gate itself and went on for about 20 steps, and then curved off to the left. Immediately to the right of the gate the rear ~~brick~~ blank, and unpainted wall of the adjoining four-story building stretched out. As soon as you passed through the gate there was ~~right by the gate~~ a [wooden] gutter (the kind you find everywhere for buildings where there are many workers, coachmen, and artisans). As it is in all such places [someone] had written [as is expected] in chalk over the gutter on the fence: It is forbidden to stop here.

Despite that, it was just such a place; [but that's the way it's done always]. Therefore, it was quite a break for I would not be suspicious in entering, and stopping [at the gutter]. I looked around—there was no one. Good [exactly!] now to throw everything, everything at once all in a pile and run.

[I looked around once again and] and I already had my hand in my pocket, when suddenly I saw a large stone weighing about thirty-five pounds against the wall itself between the gate and the gutter (where the whole space was about a yard or two wide). This wall lay directly against the street wall, [which was made of stone] and beyond was the street, where on the sidewalk one could hear the coming and going of the passers-by, who were always very numerous here. But none [of them] could see me here, unless one of them were to come to the gutter [which was a real possibility and for that reason I had to hurry]. No one from the yard seemed to be about. It was a matter of a minute. ~~I thought~~ I grabbed hold of the stone and without [much] trouble[33] rolled it[34] away. There was a hole under it, ~~under it as was to be expected, there was formed.~~ as to be expected, which the stone had ~~naturally~~ made under itself. I ~~looked around and~~ rushed to take everything quickly out of my pocket, throwing it into the hole. The purse ended up on the very top, but understandably the hole was only half filled. Then I lifted the stone, and with one turn rolled it back on its former side, and it lay precisely as it had lain before, looking perhaps just a bit higher. I managed to push it with my foot a couple of times. It'll settle down by itself, flashed through my mind. Then I left by the gate and went off in the direction of Marynsky Square. No one, no one noticed me! A deep joy possessed me. Enough! All the traces had been hidden. And who, who would ever think of looking under that stone? And who would ever think of turning the stone over? It's been lying[35] there perhaps twenty years. [I felt so happy I even laughed.] [And suppose they find it, what will they have? Who will think of me?] And I ~~almost~~ even laughed [quietly and joyfully] at this thought. ~~Complete, fully complete security! Oh my God. I~~ I took a long and deep breath of fresh air. ~~Walking past Isakievsky church I went~~ It was very hot and dusty and close. ~~And walking on in a minute my chest began to pain so that more than once I crossed myself.~~ My chest hurt. I went next onto Senate Square.[36, 37] There's always a wind there, especially near the monument. It is a gloomy and oppressive place. Why is it that I've never found anything in the whole world sadder and more oppressive than the sight of this large square? ~~I don't remember how it affected me then; but I did not look at it then.~~ Now I looked at it strangely and soon I sank completely into torpor; I was distracted. ~~The joy had gone away and I felt that my thoughts were scattering, fleeing, that I had a hard time latching onto~~ My thoughts were scattered. I came to Nikolaevsky Bridge and only there realized clearly that I was going

---

[33] twisted it around with difficulty

[34] turned it over

[35] lying there fifty years.

[36] Truly I remember that I seemed to laugh. Yes I remember that I was laughing while walking on the square.

[37] I went farther and farther, there was Vasilyevsky Island and Nicholas Bridge; was it a mood or something on the admiralty?

to Razumikhin's, my former friend, who like me had also been expelled. [A week ago I had decided to go to him because of a very necessary matter, but now when I put the purse under the stone, the matter became even more necessary.] It is very curious as to why I went to him; ~~because it was not Razumikhin that I needed.~~ I thought of going to him half an hour ago when I decided to go to Krestovsky Island.[38]

Why go to Razumikhin's? So that later if they track me, accuse me, and interrogate me: where [and why] [was it so necessary] for you to go away [for a whole day] from the apartment, when everyone saw that you were sick and had had a fainting spell?—then I can say: I was [really very] hungry, and I went to see a friend to borrow some money, and my friend lives [far] away on Vasilyevsky, at the Small Neva,* and understandably the friend will later be a witness that I really did come to him to borrow money, and that consequently there was nothing suspicious in my long absence. ~~And the strangest of all was that all that was born in my head without any systematic reasoning, [but sort of suddenly and] sort of suddenly all by itself, I became conscious of all the motives and reasoning as to why I was going only when I found myself on Nikolaevsky Bridge. I thought it all up therefore mostly by instinct, and I astonished myself by it: [how painfully] it seems that the reason becomes muddled and the faculties and all strength of man desert him, but his instinct of self-preservation continues to live and work and may appear almost unconsciously under the guise of a kind of animal cunning. It must be similar to the way an animal makes his way when it is tracked and a whole pack of dogs gives chase to him.~~ I am simply at a loss to understand (don't understand) how I was able to think of that in my situation, because my memory, reason, and strength had completely, completely left me, and only at times, for minutes was I able to reason.[39] [I even did not notice how I had thought all this up, especially since I positively was not in condition to reason about anything then.] ~~Besides [it was only now that I] on Nikolaevsky Bridge thought and realized that I was going to Razumikhin. Then crossing over the~~

---

* One of the branches of the Neva River at its mouth.

[38] and it appeared strange to me—how basely I had talked a short time ago? It doesn't matter—was I on another planet?

[39] cunning to go to Razumikhin's.

~~whole first line and because of extraordinary [weakness almost not] . . .~~

For example I did not notice at all that I had crossed the whole endless [and boring way] of the right side of the Small Neva, and I didn't even feel any fatigue from such a crossing; that always happens when a man is fatigued beyond measure and his forces are spent.

When I climbed up to the fourth floor of Razumikhin's place, a very strange thing happened to me, which I don't quite know how to put in words [well].*

Razumikhin was home in his little hovel, and he himself opened the door. He was working, writing. We had not been very close friends—former comrades [but rather good ones]. Now, I had not seen him for five months. Having decided to go to him, I had not thought [at all] about the fact [that] [I would consequently have to face him shortly, ~~and I will say~~ and facing him was something very different from simply thinking to myself about meeting him]. [It was disgusting that I had come and it became suddenly unbelievably clear that I had nothing to say to him.] [In short I can say that I can't understand this sensation, but it seemed to me that I should not have come at all. ~~And though the matter was necessary~~ And at the same time I felt that now I ought not to have [perhaps] any practical affairs at all.] That is, I had not thought of it ~~that I had nothing to speak with him about, that I felt I couldn't be with him for some reason~~ but if there is [now] for me on earth something [especially] hard [and impossible] then it is to talk and have relations . . . with other [people, as before. I don't know how, in short, to express exactly what I felt then, but I know it]. And as soon as I entered ~~that appeared to me even as completely impossible~~ I suddenly felt all that for the first time. And [the consciousness of all that] was an instant of the most oppressive longing for perhaps all that last month, in which I went through so much endless torture.

"What's the matter with you," N.B. he yelled in astonishment looking me all over. "Is it really that bad?" He looked over my clothes. "Well, brother, you've outdone us [all]." [Razumikhin was dressed

* Dostoevsky has encircled the following paragraphs with the words "As concisely as possible," beginning with the words "When I climbed . . ." of this paragraph and ending with the words ". . . which was in worse condition than my own" on p. 135.

practically in rags, but, nevertheless, better than me.][40] "Sit down," and when I slumped down on the oilcloth-covered couch, which was in worse condition than my own, he noticed only that I was sick.

"But, you are real sick, and seriously." He began to feel my pulse. I wrenched out my hand.

"Don't," I said, "I've come . . .[41] [I came to you because I don't know anyone besides you, who could begin to help]. Look, here's what: I don't have any lessons to give at all . . . I wanted. But then I don't need any lessons [now]."

~~He was silent a moment~~ "It seems that you [you know, brother, that you're] delirious," he said after being silent.[42]

"No. Goodbye!" Got ~~to go home. I took my hat and~~ I got up from the couch.

"But, hold on, hold on! [what a character!]"

"You don't have to ~~not worth talking~~," I repeated wrenching my hand away.

"But listen to me, and then do as you wish (he always talked with abbreviations) Look: I don't have any lessons, and the hell with them but I know a bookseller at the second-hand market, Kheruvimov. [He's really better than giving lessons, in fact he's a lesson in himself.] He's publishing little editions, and now is putting out little books on natural science. Look, here are two sheets of a German text, the silliest rubbish you could imagine [briefly the book examines whether woman is a human being or not, and solemnly proves that she is a human being].[43] I'm translating it; he'll make six sheets out of these two, put it out with a magnificent title covering half a page,

---

[40] Razumikhin was as always: good, tall, lean, unshaven, black hair, and with large eyes like teaspoons. He was not stupid and at times he would make a row, and he had the reputation of being a bruiser. One night, in the company of others he knocked down a very tall policeman with one blow. Razumikhin was remarkable in this also that he could go without eating for an unknown length of time and could suffer extraordinary cold as if it were nothing. Once he did not heat his room for a whole winter and said that it was even better that way for sleeping.

[41] You are more honest and better than anyone else. But I see now that I can't give any lessons. So, it's not necessary. Goodbye. Not necessary. But brother people don't act that way. Look Razumikhin, you say that I'm crazy. Good God, brother, there are many crazier.

[42] I looked at him and I even felt strange myself: why had I come?

[43] is woman a human being or not?

and sell it for a half a ruble and the enterprise will prosper.[44] I'm getting six rubles for each sheet [that means 12 in all] and I took six rubles in advance. I'll translate it and there'll be other translations ~~he is readying [something]~~ [about whales]. He's tireless, want to translate the second sheet? If you want it, well take it right now, and take three rubles, since I took an advance on the whole translation, and consequently that's what your share comes to. [Besides, you'll be helping me, even doing me a service. I know the orthography very badly, you know; I don't know anything about German. ~~True—I think that I've invented much of it~~. For the most part I invent it as I go along, I swear it! It's better all the way around, it seems to me; the book wins out, I swear it. Well, want it or not?]"

I took the German sheets silently, articles taken out of some kind of ~~special dictionary~~ journal, took the three rubles and without saying a word, I walked out; ~~Went out, without saying a word, and now gives it back and goes away~~ but after reading the first line, I turned around, went back up the stairs to Razumikhin's and put back the German sheets and the three rubles on the table, and walked out [without saying a word].

"What's the matter with you, are you crazy?" yelled the stunned Razumikhin. ["Why did you come then?"]

"Not necessary . . . translations . . ." I said, already going down the stairs.[45]

"Hey, V . . . [What the devil do you want?]. Where do you live?" He yelled down at me. But I didn't answer and went home by the same way.

["Well the devil with you!" came down the stairs.]

[I walked probably sunk in thought][46] and on Nikolaevsky Bridge

---

[44] and it'll work

[45] You are more sincere than the rest; I'm a scoundrel; I'll come another time. Listen, you know, perhaps you have not eaten for three days, don't hide it; let's assume that I had decided everything.

[46] Why did you throw away 20 kopecks without thinking it over, but I would throw them away after thinking it over, after thinking it over. Lord, am I delirious or not? Here's the Neva that's flowing. A little while ago I wanted to throw all the objects into the Neva, into the canal, and the purse also and the purse. Why did you kill after that if you are throwing away the spoils? Yesterday, you wanted those spoils. Wanted? Yes and today into the canal. But maybe that was done unconsciously, from fear. But consciously with your reason, in possession of all your faculties—how would you have acted? Rationally, too, into the canal. Right? Do you remember that you are sick? You are crazy [now]. You are delirious? Delirious, but remember that you have not yet opened the purse and have not looked into it. [Nó] Maybe I didn't think of it.

I came to and this is what happened: A driver [of a carriage] gave me a good whack across the back with his whip, because I had almost fallen at the feet of his horses, despite the fact that he had, it seems, yelled out to me many times.[47] The whip's blow made me so furious that, having jumped to the railings, I angrily ground and [gnashed] my teeth. ~~All around, as to be expected with wild laughter, as to be expected. But as soon as I realized what the point was [then the rage in me immediately disappeared. It seemed to me that it was no longer worth while concerning myself with that]. The thought came to me instantly that it would have been a lot better [perhaps even good] if the carriage had crushed me [completely].~~

[But in that same instant, when][48] I stood at the railing and ~~suddenly~~ senselessly looked after the carriage, suddenly I sensed that someone was putting money into my hands: "Take it little father in the name of Christ." I look: a merchant's wife, [certainly a merchant's wife] middle-aged with her daughter. I took it and they passed on. By my dress they could very well take me for a beggar, for a genuine street grubber for pennies. I was indebted to the blow of the whip certainly for the twenty-kopeck piece. The blow had awakened their pity for me.[49]

I squeezed the twenty-kopeck piece [in my hands], went on for about 20 steps and [I remember] I turned toward the Neva: [in the direction of the Palace*].[50] The day was sizzling and clear; the sky was clear and the water was almost blue, which is true of the Neva only rarely. The cupola of the cathedral, which looks better precisely from this spot [from the bridge], several steps from the Nikolaevsky

---

* Reference to the Czar's Winter Palace.

[47] the blow of the whip helped me come out of the unconscious state into which I was falling every moment, but as soon as I came to the spite went away at once, and I was even sort of astonished that I could get angry because the matter had nothing to do with that. Yesterday, I wanted the spoils and today with a new nature you decided that you do not want. I'm sick, I'm crazy, nonsense, I'm sick I don't understand anything. This

[48] living, though dead now, but (. . .) talking and relating (. . . . . .) It's because of these that you are unhappy (. . .)

[49] A little while ago with the lieutenant. What baseness! And I, I took part in the argument, in the yelling. Granted—it's an old habit, but afterwards, afterwards—that (. . .) from (. . .) from baseness. No, it's not worth living if you have to live with the realization of yourself as so base. And now what kind of self am I going to have to live with?

[50] Coming to the place where I had stood a little while ago, suddenly, I stopped, I don't know why.

chapel, than from any other point, shone so—and through the clear air you could distinguish clearly even the [smallest] ornament. [I remembered suddenly, the thought flashed that] when I attended the University, I habitually returned ~~from the University~~ [home, it so happened] this way, and perhaps several hundred times I had examined intently all that truly splendid panorama. ~~[I began to laugh.] At the best moments, when the sky was pure and clear and in the worst moments when the panorama was gloomy, sad, and rainy, each time the same impression was formed in me by itself, without any effort; the impression was: despite this unexampled splendor and this astonishing river, this whole view was worth nothing.~~[51] I even got the habit of fixing it in my mind for two minutes,[52] precisely from this place,[53] and yet the view has a [complete] coldness [and deadness] about it.[54] This is a quality that destroys everything [kills everything], turns everything into nothing.[55] An inexplicable cold blows from it. The spirit of muteness [every time] and silence, the spirit—"mute and dumb"[56] is poured over all this panorama [oppressing my heart].[57] I can't express myself but I know that my impression was not at all what is known as abstract, intellectual, and reasoned out, but completely immediate. I haven't seen Venice or the Golden

---

[51] It seemed suddenly strange to me now to stand on this place, as if I could no longer stand on the former place.

[52] I even liked to stand here marveling each time at my impression.

[53] but the Neva seemed to me suddenly so far away; all that seemed to me somewhere deep under my feet, somewhere in the infinite distance. I stood there a long time and finally remembered the 20-kopeck piece; I loosened my grip on it, looked at it and silently, and let it fall into the water.

[54] A terribly long time ago—terror—but now suddenly it was as if thirty years had already passed and I had arrived from somewhere, from the southern hemisphere perhaps and was astonished.

[55] I remembered now that every time the same impression oppressed me with a kind of undefined sadness and I remembered and smiled at the fact that I had such impressions [and then] it seemed strange to me that I was preparing myself somehow not to have any thoughts at all any longer—not because it was strange that I could have such interests, but because it was impossible for me to have them about this or about other things; that everything was a matter of indifference to me, that everything for me was (. . .) that it was no longer my thoughts, but someone else's, alien

[56] It always seemed to me to be something dumb and silent, something negative. . .

[57] [And so] suddenly, I remembered now all those former impressions, and I felt strange.

Horn, but certainly there life has long since died, even though the stones still talk, still "howl" even now.

And so now when I stopped there out of habit, suddenly the same [painful] sensation which oppressed my chest at Razumihkin's half an hour ago, the same sensation oppressed my heart here. Because suddenly it seemed to me that there was no reason for me [any longer] to stop [here or anywhere] and it was a matter of indifference to me what kind of impression this view made.[58] Now, I had something else to concern me, something else but all those, all those former sensations and interests and people were far away from me, as if on another planet.[59, 60] I was standing bent over the railings and I felt in my hand the coin that had been given to me and I relaxed my ~~hand~~ palm, looked at it [attentively] and ~~completely consciously I let go of it; I threw it even though remembering completely what I~~ was ~~doing.~~ [then] let it drop into the water. And then I went home by the former road. When I got back to my place, it was already late; it was evening.[61] [Consequently, I was returning at five or six o'clock and I don't know in what condition I had been all that time.] I took off my clothes and trembling all over, no longer from the fever but from weakness [like a driven horse, which I had seen in my childhood] I lay down on the couch and drew over myself my coat. I kept my socks on. I took them off and threw them into a corner. Then my mind went completely blank. I didn't think of anything.

When it was fully dusk I was awakened by a terrible cry, and at dusk my room [in summer] is almost completely dark. I opened my eyes. God, what a scream! I had never heard such unnatural sounds, such yelling, grinding of teeth, sobs, curses, and blows. I couldn't imagine such savageness, such frenzy. In terror I got up and sat on the couch. I wasn't trembling; I was simply paralyzed, in torment. But the fighting, yells, screams, and curses became worse and worse. And then to my indescribable astonishment I suddenly distinguished the voice of my landlady; she was yelling, screaming [and pleading] quickly—quickly, pronouncing the words in such a way that it was impossible to make them out, begging for something, probably beg-

---

[58] and what does it matter to me what kind of impression is produced by that view?

[59] as if I had flown off to another planet.

[60] I decided that I could no longer rise, and that I was longing for truth.

[61] To get drunk. A dark memory, thrown out of the tavern

ging for the beating to stop, because she was being mercilessly beaten, at first in the apartment—and then they dragged her out on the stairs. The voice of the person beating her became so terrible from rage and frenzy that all he could do is wheeze; nevertheless, I made out that it was ~~no one else~~ but Aleksandr Il'ich[62] who was beating her, and he must have been beating her with his boots, with his hands. He trampled her; and grabbing her by the hair he slammed her head against the staircase. There was no other way he could have beat her to judge by the squeals and desperate cries of the poor woman. A large crowd had apparently collected. Many voices on all the stairs were heard; people were coming in, knocking, shutting doors; everyone came running. What is it all about, I thought, why [is he beating her], why? Fear like ice penetrated me to the core. It seemed to me that my mind was getting muddled, and yet I heard all that clearly, clearly. [Soon they will come for me [also] I thought, and I raised myself to hook the latch, but then I came to my senses.] Finally, after about 10 minutes all that din began gradually to quiet down. The landlady was groaning and moaning, and Aleksandr Il'ich, still evidently menacing and cursing her, began to retreat. I even heard his footsteps. I heard also how the landlady, going back to her room, locked herself in. Then little by little people went away on the stairs, [and back to their apartments] quarreling and exclaiming, raising their voices to yells and at times lowering them to a whisper. There must have been many of them; the whole house had come running. Lord, what is it all about—and why did Aleksandr Il'ich come? ~~Wasn't he asking for me?~~ And can it be that all this is possible? How could he dare beat her.[63, 64]

I finally lay down again, but I could no longer ~~fall asleep~~ close my eyes. I think I lay there about half an hour [tormented by astonish-

---

[62] And, nevertheless, he talked—talked—quickly something of the sort, but in such a way that it was impossible to understand.

[63] And you think that something is left for you in life?

[64] Isn't it monstrous that just a little while ago I meddled in the affair with the girl. Isn't everything a matter of indifference to you? let them perish, wallow in vice. Save whom? Is it up to you to save? Why are you so eager to meddle in life? But is life closed to me? Is it that I. You are a murderer. I know, but I consciously, I (. . .) did it. But why is it that you haven't even glanced into the purse? You took fright. No, I'll look into it later. It was simply prudence. But how it is that you wanted to throw it into the Neva? It means that you wanted to give it all up. You couldn't stand up to the act then.

ment and a sensation of horror in a way I had never before known]. Suddenly ~~darkness~~ light. I see before me Nastasya with a candle and a plate of soup. She looked at me and saw that I was sleeping. She began to lay out the bread, a dish, and a wooden[65] spoon on the table.

"You probably haven't eaten since yesterday; ~~Eat! What's the matter? What a guy!~~ you roamed around the whole day, and yet you're ~~shaking~~ ravaged by a [fever]."

"Nastasya, why were they beating the landlady?"

"The landlady? Who was beating the landlady?"

"The landlady, a short time ago, half an hour ago, Aleksandr Il'ich, [inspector] the assistant. ~~of the district . . . I recognized him by his voice.~~ Why did he beat her up so? And how is it that she permitted it?"

Nastasya examined me in silence [intently] [and looked at me severely for a long time]. I became afraid.

"It is the blood!" she answered quietly and gloomily.

"Blood! Whose blood! What kind of blood?" ~~Looking at her with fear~~ I barely got this out and my face became distorted all over in a sickly fashion.

"It's the blood [that is crying out] coursing in you. That's why you're seeing things; [it's terror]. ~~You're seeing things while you're awake.~~ No one was beating the landlady . . . and no one is going to beat her," she added.

A yet greater terror seized me.

"But I wasn't sleeping; I was sitting on my bed," I said after a long silence. ["But Aleksandr Il'ich did come here, didn't he?"]

"No one came here. [That] is the blood in you crying out. When the blood begins to congeal, [then you begin to see things. Here, eat! Well, are you going to?" I didn't answer, and silently again lay down on my bundle.

[In place of a pillow I usually put a bundle consisting of all my linen under my head, and that's the way I slept. I hadn't had a pillow for a long time.]

It ~~was so frightening that I think that~~ I happened that [my hair stood up on my head]. Nastasya continued to stand over me.

"Give me something to drink . . . Nastasya," I said at last.

Without saying a word she went downstairs and seemed to return very quickly, but I was no longer thinking clearly. I remembered

---

[65] tin

only [that I drank] one swallow of water and [then] and then lost consciousness.[66, 67]

[It's not that.] ~~However, all that time~~ I was already completely unconscious: I remember much which flashed through my mind or went through it in a different way from the way it was in reality. At times it seemed to me that there was a very large crowd gathering about me and that they wanted to take me [somewhere] and carry me off, and that they quarreled and argued over me. At other times I was completely alone and everyone had abandoned me ~~and no one will come to me and no one wants to come.~~ and even were afraid of me and only once in a while the door would open and from the door they would threaten me. ~~They would make fun of me with their fists or their tongues.~~ [They cursed me or laughed at me. They seemed to do the last more and more often.] I remember Nastasya near me often. I saw still another man, someone I knew very well, but who precisely, I could not for the world remember, and I was miserable from that, tossed about, and sobbed. I strained my thoughts to remember who it was but I couldn't. [I asked; they answered me but I couldn't remember.] At moments it seemed to me that I had been lying there about a year already; at other moments that ~~all that happened only yesterday.~~ the same day was still going on. At times a terrible fear began to torment me [and what was most strange, not at all about that; I remember that very well; but it seemed that some man tried to track me down with a bulldog and was holding him hidden behind the door, quietly or something of this sort]. But what I was afraid of [precisely]—~~I was not aware at all~~. I didn't know and I forgot completely about that, but I would dart away and try to leave, [run away] but someone would hold me back by force and I would again fall asleep. Finally, I awoke completely.

It must have been [after dinner] at five o'clock.[68] At that time there was usually a ray of sunshine in my place. Nastasya and some man were standing over me, looking me over with great curiosity and with some kind of care. [I had never seen him.] He was young [still a lad] dressed in a Russian caftan and a small beard. By his appearance he looked like a worker. The landlady ~~She stood in the back of~~

---

[66] You ought to be beaten for that, but I reasoned that hunger too can cause that and I forgave.

[67] N.B. We get together here every day in the inn.

[68] about four o'clock in the afternoon.

~~the room~~. peered out of the half-opened door. I looked at all of them [intently] with wide-opened eyes, then raised myself a bit.

"Nastasya, who is that ~~with you~~?" I asked pointing to the lad.

"Well, how do you like that, he's come to!" she said.

"He's come to," answered the worker like an echo. The landlady hurried immediately to efface herself [and she closed the door].

"Who are you?" ~~What do you want? I asked~~ I asked the worker.

"Well, I've come, on business, that is . . . He began ~~and he wanted to go away~~ but at that minute suddenly the door opened and Razumikhin entered bending his head [bending down very much because he was very tall].

"A veritable [sea] cabin!" he yelled. "You call this an apartment! ~~They take money for it. So what?~~ Well, it [seems] you've come to?"

"He just came to," said Nastasya.

"He just came to . . ." added the worker.

"And who are you may I ask?" Razumikhin asked [forgetting all of us and suddenly] turning to him. "I am as you see Vrazumikhin; not Razumikhin as I'm called, but Vrazumikhin, a student, of noble birth, and he is my friend. But you. Who are you?"

"I work for the merchant Sherstobitov, and I'm here on an errand."

"Be good enough to sit down," Razumikhin commanded. "It's a good thing that you've come to; it's the fifth day, my dear man. You haven't eaten or drunk. I brought Bakavin[69] two times to see you. He looked you over and said it was nothing from the very beginning, that it was trifles, a nervous [foolishness of some kind] and [that] you've been eating badly that [they didn't give you enough beer and horse-radish] and that's why you've got sick, but that you would come to soon and that you'd be all right. Good for him. [Bakavin knows how to cure.] He pegged it right! Well, I'm not keeping you," he said ~~suddenly~~ turning again to the worker [of the merchant] Sherstobitov. "Would you mind explaining your business? Notice that this is the second time that they've sent someone from Sherstobitov's; only last time it was not he who came [but another . . .], and we had it out with the other."

"Who came then before you?"

"That [must have been the day before yesterday. Precisely] Aleksey Petrovich, our chief worker."

---

[69] Zosimov.

"Well, he's a little more sensible than you, don't you think?"

"Yes, he's more reliable."

"Well now, what will it be? [But as far as I see, you're O.K.]"

"[Well ~~I was sent~~ I'm here from] Semen Semenych, whom you had the opportunity to know more than once," began the worker turning directly to me. "If you are already in full possession of your senses, I'm to give you 10 rubles, since Semen Semenych has received a notice to this effect from Tolstonogov from Penza. Do you know him?"

"I know the merchant Tolstonogov." "~~You see he's reasonable.~~ [Listen, he knows Tolstonogov! [He's in full possession of his senses then.]" [Razumikhin yelled out.] "[I said that a little while ago just for the heck of it.] [Besides you seem to be a clever fellow.] I've just begun to notice it. But continue. It's pleasant to hear intelligent talk.]"

"It's Tolstonogov himself. [Andron Ivanovich] and on the request of your mother, he has transmitted to you money more than once; he did not refuse this time and has asked Semen Semenych to give you 10 rubles from your mother, in expectation of better times, since your mother is not ~~completely~~ still well off, [but their affairs, it seems, have been put in order]. Semen Ivanovich will arrange things with Andron Ivanych as he did formerly . . ."

"Well, what do you think, is he in full possession of his memory or not," Razumikhin interrupted him, pointing to me.

"As far as I'm concerned, it's all right. Only [look], I need a receipt."

"He'll scribble it. What do you have there, a register of some kind?"

"Yes, here is a register."

"Give it here. ~~He took the pen and immediately wrote~~ Well, Vassiuk* draw yourself up. I'll help you up; here's a pen for you and sign it. ~~Jot down your name~~ And it's money received; because, brother, it's money we need more than anything [frightfully]. [More than syrup!]"

"Not necessary . . ." I said, pushing away the pen.

"What isn't necessary?"[70]

---

* Diminutive of Vasilii; another variant of Raskolnikov's name.

70 "Because their affairs changed. Do you know Ivan Kuzmich? Well here's a letter about how their affairs changed, and how they themselves are going to write to you—but as for [precise] details I haven't heard anything."

"I'm not going to sign."

"The devil take it, what are we going to do without a receipt?"

"The money's not necessary."

"Well you're lying brother. ~~He's raving~~ He's begun that again, don't worry. I see that you are a rational man . . . look, we'll . . . make him see the light."

"But I can drop by another time."

"No, no, no [you are a rational man] Well! [Vasil'.]" He began to direct my hand.

"Leave me alone, I'll do it myself" . . . and I signed.

The worker paid out the money and went away.

"Well now, Vassia, don't you want to eat?"

"I do," I answered.

"Do you have any soup?"

"Yes," answered Nastasya, who had been standing all that time nearby.

"[Potato and rice soup.]"

"I know it by heart. Bring the soup [with barley] and bring some tea also."

"I'll bring it."

She returned in two minutes with the soup and said that she would bring the tea quickly.

There were two spoons and two dishes for the soup. [The tablecloth was clean.] The spoons were silver [the landlady's]. A salt cellar appeared near Razumikhin and also a whole service with mustard, etc. There was some beef in the soup.

"It wouldn't be bad, Nastasya dear, if Sofia Timofeevna were to give us two bottles of beer. We'd have a drink."

"Oh, you're quick for that," said Nastasya, and she went off to take care of the order.

I still could not completely take in all that. ~~What's the point?~~ Meanwhile, Razumikhin sat down nearer to me on the couch itself [awkwardly like a bear], took hold of my head with his left hand [despite the fact that I felt myself much stronger than he thought], and with his right hand began to lift the spoon of soup to me, blowing several times beforehand so that I wouldn't burn myself. But the soup was scarcely warm. I drank one spoonful greedily, then another, and with the third began to refuse, ~~by the fourth I [couldn't] didn't want to swallow anything at all.~~ but Razumikhin forced me to drink it. At that moment Nastasya entered carrying two bottles of beer.

"Do you see, Nastasya, only three spoonfuls![71] Do you call that being very hungry! Do you want any tea?"

"I want some tea."

"Bring some tea quickly, Nastasya [still]. ~~Perhaps we'll also drink three spoonfuls.~~ And here's the beer!" He began to seat himself at the table and draw [to himself] the pot of soup and the beef. He began to eat as if he had not eaten for three days.

"I've been dining here every day, brother,"[72] he said[73] as well as he could, with his mouth crammed with meat, winking at me with his left eye. Do you think it's charged to you? ~~Don't worry~~ Not at all. They won't charge it to you. Do you think that I'm going to pay for these two bottles of beer? Not at all. It's Sonechka, your landlady, who's treating us as a sign of her pleasure.[74] Well, here's Nastasya with the tea. Nastasya, you want some beer?"

"Oh, bother, go to the devil."

"How about some tea?"

"Tea, O.K."

"Sit down [at the table]—and pour yourself some. Wait, I'll do it for you." He saw to it immediately; then he poured still another cup, stopped eating, sat down again on the couch as he had done before and lifted up and held my head with his left hand. [Despite the fact that I assured him that I wasn't that weak] he began to feed me with a spoon, continually blowing on the spoon.[75] In this way I was forced to drink ~~ten even though I did not want to at all~~ spoonfuls and then I fell back on the pillows.[76] [There really was a pillow under my head. Before I always rolled my clothes, which I took off

---

[71] You ought to be beaten.

[72] I have my dinner here every day, brother. Do you think that I pay for this beer?

[73] winking

[74] Not bad at all, brother, that is, even very, very, very much in order.

[75] despite the fact that he could very well sit himself down on the sofa without anyone else's help, and felt himself strong enough not only to direct his hands, but perhaps even to walk. But a strange thought suddenly occurred to him: to hide [from everyone]. Since he was much stronger than they thought, he would pretend to be weak and helpless as before and learn first: What is happening around him? Why is Razumikhin here, what happened? How many days have passed; is something known, etc. (For the time) he decided rather to remain quiet and to listen. Having drunk a spoonful, he fell back on the pillows; he noticed that there was a pillow under him.

[76] I made up a plan myself filled with rage against Razumikhin.

for the night, into a ball] I [decided rather] to keep quiet and I listened avidly. Much was strange for me. My memory had come back to me completely, even though my head was turning a bit.[77] [I wanted to find out everything and fix it in my mind.][78]

"Sonechka must send us some raspberry jam today. To make [him] a drink," said Razumikhin, sitting down and taking to the soup and beer again.

"And where is she going to get raspberries for you?" asked Nastasya.

"In a store, my friend, in a store. [She'll get the raspberries in a store, my friend.] You see, there's a story in it all. When you took off from my place in such a scandalous fashion and didn't tell me where your apartment was, I decided to look you up and within an hour [on the very same day] I started my search.[79] I really walked and walked, asked and asked; I toiled 24 hours and imagine it, I found your name in the Bureau of Addresses. You're registered there."[80]

"Registered?" ~~I asked with curiosity . . .~~ [Raskolnikov cried out, unable to restrain himself.][81]

"Very much so, and yet look they couldn't find ~~some kind of~~ General Kobelev there at all while I was there. It's too long to relate. As soon as I arrived here, I immediately learned all about your affairs. Learned everything, brother, everything; I know everything; look she knows everything also; I got acquainted with Nikodim Fomich and with the caretaker and with Mr. Zametov—the secretary [in this district] and finally I got acquainted with Sonechka. [That crowned everything.] She knows all about you also."

"Flatterer," Nastasya murmured, biting into a piece of sugar and sucking in some tea from the saucer.

"You ought to put sugar in your tea, Nastasya Nikiforovna."

---

[77] He felt himself a lot stronger than, for example, Razumikhin supposed, but from a curious cunning, it occurred to him to hide his strength [not speak about it] and fool all of them. Like an animal in a cage.

[78] I saw you when I was delirious and couldn't make out at all who you were. . . What did I speak of in my delirium?

[79] to give you a thrashing, pardon me, but then I thought it over

[80] I went to your former apartment; I don't remember the number very well; I knew only that Kharlamov; well I looked for Kharlamov, but the building was not Kharlamov's but Fogel's; I just found that out.

[81] I babbled a lot to you.

"What a jackass you are!" Nastasya suddenly cried out, doubling over with laughter. "I'm not Nikiforovna, but Petrovna," she added when she stopped laughing.

"I'll make a note of it," Razumikhin answered. "Well, look, brother, so as not to waste words, I wanted at first to throw out an electric ray so as to ~~have them burned~~ burn out all the prejudices here. But Sonechka won out. Brother I did not expect at all that she would be so . . . comely. What do you think?"

~~Yes, she's all right . . . I murmured, thirsting to hear more.~~ "Very much so. Not bad at all, at all; even very, very much as one would want her."

"What an animal!" grumbled Nastasya, who was apparently indescribably pleased by this conversation.

"What was bad, brother, was that from the very beginning you didn't know how to go about the business," continued Razumikhin. "[You have to deal with her differently! She has, as you know, an extremely unpredictable character. It's almost . . .] How, for example, did you bring things to the point that she had the nerve not to send your dinner to you? Or, for example, that note! Were you crazy to go around signing notes? Or, for example, that marriage proposal when the daughter was alive. She's a sensitive chord though; excuse me but you'll tell me about it later," [he added with a very serious face, as serious as he could make it]. "What do you think, [Vassia]? Is Sonia nuts or not?" ~~"No, she's not nuts, I murmured again. (But) And I also think that she does not seem to be crazy . . . But, you know, she's not intelligent either . . . What do you think?"~~[82]

[82] Do you find her to be crazy? No. I don't either; she's sort of not foolish, but at the same time, you know, not intelligent. Well, yes, Well, yes. She's perhaps not intelligent as a woman ought to be.

V

Razumikhin at Raskolnikov's sickbed—How the landlady gave Raskolnikov's note to a bill collector—Razumikhin dresses Raskolnikov—Razumikhin and Zosimov speculate about the murderer

Apart from a few pages of diverse short fragments, this section is composed of several extended narratives, which correspond to Part II, Chapters 3 and 4, of the final version. As such they follow on the fragment in Section IV of the notes. The narratives contain these scenes: Razumikhin's explanation at Raskolnikov's bedside of how the landlady came to give his note to Chebarov, an unscrupulous bill collector; Razumikhin's return with a bundle of used clothing for Raskolnikov; Razumikhin's lively and humorous explanation of how he came to buy each article of clothing; the virtually forced reclothing of Raskolnikov; and a conversation between Razumikhin and Bakavin (Zosimov) in which they speculate on the credibility of the painter Nikolay's guilt in the murder of the woman. This conversation should be compared with pages 93–95 of these notes, where a version of the scene first appears. The two versions differ and both differ from the version in the novel itself. The most significant addition in the final version is Razumikhin's dismissal of the painter's guilt for psychological reasons. Nikolay, according to Razumikhin, could not possibly have committed the murder and romped and rolled playfully with his fellow worker a few minutes later. In the earlier version of this scene in the notes, Razumikhin seems to accept the confession of the painter as the real thing. In the version that follows Nikolay is not even mentioned, and the students who had almost trapped Raskolnikov in the apartment are the ones who are suspected by the police. Their names in the final version are Koch and Pestriakov; here the names are Bergshtoltz and Kopilin. In the final version the tavernkeeper who brings the earrings to the police is called Dushkin; in the notes, Mortirin. In the early version of the scene the painter is unnamed in the notes, but his fellow worker is called, as in the final version, Mitka.

This section is more about Razumikhin than it is about Raskolnikov. As in the novel, Razumikhin is cheerful, efficient, easily excited, and tirelessly energetic and good-natured. He is a little more of a buffoon and much more of a flirt in the notes. He feels his charm with Pashenka, Raskolnikov's landlady, and much more is made of his effect on the landlady and on the maid, Nastasya. Details that border on the risqué appear in the notes and are omitted in the final version. An example: "Impossible to pinch her; I'll tell you that confidentially; it all slips out of your fingers." As in the novel Razumikhin appears to be the norm of healthy adjustment to life; what is insuperable to Raskolnikov, he handles effectively and easily. Like Raskolnikov he is a poor student crushed by circumstances and an unjust society; but unlike Raskolnikov he is not filled with rage and resentment against these circumstances and society. He is living proof that Raskolnikov tells lies to himself when he explains his lot and motives to himself.

The relations between Raskolnikov and Razumikhin are at times subtly different in this section of the notes. Razumikhin is more intimately solicitous of Raskolnikov's welfare, and Raskolnikov is more irritated with his concern: "As to the fact that Razumikhin looked me up, saved me, doctored me at his expense, brought a doctor, spent his own time with me, arranged my affairs and did his very best to comfort and amuse me—all that only tormented me and enraged me. I waited for his return with cold fury." In the scene in the novel in which Razumikhin forces Raskolnikov to try on the used clothes he has bought, Dostoevsky softens Raskolnikov's hostility toward Razumikhin. In the notes Raskolnikov is in rage and disgust at Razumikhin; in the novel he is sullen and resentful but remains for the most part silent. In the novel when Nastasya and Razumikhin change his shirt by force, we are told that Raskolnikov sank back on his pillow and for a few minutes did not say anything; in the notes, we get the following: "I was in a rage; I fell back on the pillow and fell into tears of rage." In general, one may say that Dostoevsky considerably reduced the whole scene in the final version: Razumikhin's witty account of how he came to buy each article of clothing, his anecdotes, his sense of fun.

Dostoevsky may have a symbolic intention in Razumikhin's reclothing of Raskolnikov. The clothes are paid for by his mother's money and bought and fussed over by Razumikhin, the well-integrated student. The clothes may be a symbolic—for Raskolnikov, a forced—re-entry into society. Razumikhin's cheery insistence that the castoff second-hand clothing is just the thing to rehabilitate Raskolnikov and Raskolnikov's rage against the reclothing seem to support this interpretation. Razumikhin also makes a great deal of the guarantee that comes with the old clothes. Some of the details that support this interpretation are lost—and one wonders if wisely—in the final version.

Plan

After the Dream

Razumikhin came; all three days in rage. On the third day I went myself; the landlady on the staircase; I roam about Petersburg; meetings; *Eccentric escapades*. Wench, old goat. Meeting with Zametov. Inn, conversation [in fear (?) *Calf*]. Razumikhin comes in. I want to move. Leave me alone! The Devil with you.

Recovered. Cold fury, calculation. Why so much nerves? He takes out the purse. Remembers how it was. Letter from his mother. The whole account and all the motives of the murder. He got completely well and went off to Razumikhin. There is a gathering there; Zametov and Bakavin are present. Conversation. Gas.

Sufferings and questions—Sassia—Episodes. *The Widow Capet*. Christ, the barricade. We are an unfinished generation. The last convulsions. Confession.

This manuscript page corresponds to pp. 153–54, beginning with the sentence "The fringe is not noticeable in the stove." and ending with the words ". . . mother will buy your freedom." This is a full and complicated page: drawings, calligraphy, and notes are written both across and sideways. Even the vertical notes, however, are parallel and neatly written. The content is diverse, halting, and uncertain, reflected perhaps graphically in the restless appearance of the page.

Flashes of memories of what he saw in childhood. The horse that was beaten in childhood, the calf that had been butchered, the courier.

The fringe is not noticeable in the stove. I laughed: How could I have been sad about that yesterday?

Everything began as if anew. (Impression) The fringe in the pocket.

Remarks:

1) I didn't look into the purse.
2) I gave it up so easily: Why did I do the murder?
3) How easily was such a hard deed accomplished.

Razumikhin: But I'm really doing nasty work. Working for Kheru-vimov; isn't that nasty work?

Conversation at the students' place. Company. *About Gas.*

He isolated himself, the devil take it; he became gloomy, went to see Razumikhin. Gas. Razumikhin comes to see *him* the next day: *I killed;* Razumikhin leaves him alone.

N.B.—N.B. Plan.

I went down the stairs. The landlady came in and began to excuse herself. I didn't think of going in to see her. I didn't answer anything. He wants another apartment. Does it make any difference? I began to return the money. She refused. I won't rent another apartment. Razumikhin dressed me down and went away. I've busied myself enough with you.

I'll come again. (. . .) and Bakavin came.

Ah! If only you knew how good it would be if you went away.

"Well, what's the matter?"

"Leave me be, leave me!"

"The devil knows what's wrong with you."

Have it all pass more quickly. The event first and then the distortion of his own psychology begins, because only now does he come to.

1. All that after the meeting with Zametov in the inn and the articles in *Voice* and the stories of Nastasya and all the references. Completely. . . . *He got the purse.* N.B.

2. He got the purse. I put that purse there then so as never to take it, and now I take it myself.

N.B. *Important.* After the sickness, a kind of cruelty and complete justification of himself, and when that was shaken, the letter from his mother.

Within an hour he came with his clothes. The meeting with Zametov—why are you with Zametov. We're investigating the matter of the painter.

Account of the murder. Another beer. Nastasya is here also. *How he fell into a faint* when

With Zametov. You fainted when they began to talk about the murder.

The point is that she has decided to chase you out because you are not paying, and while waiting she has put the note in circulation because she knows that your mother will buy your freedom.

["The most unexpected of characters, brother, I repeat to you," continued Razumikhin, understanding completely that Raskolnikov does not want to talk to him, and that Raskolnikov himself saw it in his face, but was not embarrassed or (. . .)]

["No, ~~and I also think. Not a fool, and not intelligent~~ she is not a fool . . ." answered Raskolnikov, bored but saying it in order to keep up his end of the conversation.]

"As is fitting for a ruddy and fleshy woman. She'll see forty soon, but she speaks of 36 and has the right to that. [Impossible to pinch her; I'll tell you that confidentially; it all slips out of your fingers.] Well, brother, the whole affair came about in this way: seeing that you were [no longer a student] and that you had sold your suit and given up giving lessons, and seeing that with the death of her daughter she had no obligation to support you like a relative, [she suddenly took fright since you, on your side, did not keep up your former relationship], and she got the idea to kick you out of the apartment.[1] She had nourished that intention for a long time, but she regretted losing the note. You yourself had assured her that your mother would pay it."

"I said that only because I was base . . ."[2] I said. My mother is

---

[1] We have, so to speak, only an emblem of something, but of what neither she nor I know.

[2] not containing his (rage) this time, said Raskolnikov.

practically begging for a living in Penza . . . I lied so as to keep the apartment."

"Well, that made sense . . .[3] Only the point is that the collegiate assessor Chebarov turned up. Sonechka would never have figured out anything without him. [She's very much of a prude.] Chebarov busies himself with affairs [that is, with little affairs]; he's got a job also. He writes satirical verse also; he tracks down [social] vices, ~~rails at~~ uproots prejudices; he rises to noble indignation about the three fish on which the earth rests;* he rails at cornetists playing with special valves. He gets from three to seven rubles a week for that [from a journalist], well, money. All they want is a bit of money one way or another; you see, there's a lot of them around now (. . .). They're businessmen and they make business out of [noble indignation], but more often they manage affairs[4] of all kinds, litigations, [they lend out money, and run taverns under another's name] and among affairs, something like yours.[5] Sonechka has a note [for example] for 75 115. Question: Is there any hope of realizing it? There is, so to speak, there is a certain mother who will not eat for a year, so as to put aside 75 rubles [in a year and a half] from her pension of 120 rubles. She'll borrow ahead on it; the sister-governess will put a rope around her neck in order to rescue her brother. Why bother yourself? I've learned everything about you, [and I speak of it because I like you; I understand everything]. You were like a brother to Sonechka, and were frank with her. [That's where the trouble lay!] She would not have thought up that by herself [for your situation]. [She's an earthy girl], but Chebarov was recommended to her.[6] [And by the way] it was ~~the businessman~~ he who thought up [the machination for her], because—believe me—the worst scoundrels for fleecing others are the virtuously indignant.[7] [They make business

---

* A popular legend. Dostoevsky here is apparently pointing to false indignation.

[3] Perhaps [the landlady] became angry at you because you didn't want to [know how to] approach her in the right way. Terrible really how sensitive they are to insult if you don't know how to handle them.

[4] There is, brother, such sharks in the world, which swim in the sea. There are all kinds of people in the world, brother Vassia. But that doesn't concern us; we are good people.

[5] But the chief thing—act and among other things this way.

[6] She got to know Chebarov in connection with another matter.

[7] like another satirical man of the three-fished sort.

out of it.] Take careful note [for the future] if [for example] you get in debt to a three-fished scoundrel ~~who doesn't go further than three fishes, he knows what's what.~~ [even if he only has his hand in it], then he'll try immediately to send you off to Tarasov's home.* That's the way they work. They call it a positive approach and a contempt for prejudice. [Contempt for debt, but not for debts, if you owe them something.] Well, Chebarov is precisely one of the three-fished operators [that is, one of those who doesn't know anything beyond the three fishes].[8] He sniffed around and for 10 rubles decided to manage the affair. He didn't intend buying your note from Sonechka; but they arranged it on paper to appear[9] that he was the proprietor [bought it, so to speak] because you see Sonechka [is really too sensitive]. ~~well, he began to demand from you. I . . .~~ She felt ashamed [to be dragging the fiancé of her daughter to Tarasov, and so she hired a whale to swallow you]. I learned about the whole business in a friendly fashion from Zametov. We were together at Louise's. [Do you remember Louise? Do you know Louise? She's a fine person. We would meet together there in company practically every night.] [Afterward] I went to Chebarov; do you believe it I went at all hours, once five times, left notes for him for three days about such and such an affair. [He was never there]; from morning to night and even at one o'clock at night he's at his country home; he has a country home and horses. If I had managed to get to him, I would have let loose [a ray] of electricity; well [at this time I] and Sonechka had come to agreement; I ordered her to bring the business to an end, swearing to her that you will pay. I, brother, acted as a guarantor for you. [Do you hear?] Well, she then ~~wrote~~ ordered Chebarov to terminate the affair, and gave him 10 rubles for his trouble. ~~In that way for 10 rubles they [serve] as sharks; they hire sharks, executioners, jailers.~~ He was satisfied [because he had given himself to the matter with ardor]; what [literary] fire he had invested in the matter. I read his request for a search warrant. 'I consider it my duty to add that N.B. N.B. he intends to leave the capital city of St. Petersburg.' And he lied; how could [N.B.] you have left for anywhere? Well, ~~he, so to~~

---

* A prison for debtors.

[8] which he described in a satire

[9] As if Iulenka had sold it to him; that's how they arranged it. (*Ed.*: Iulenka is the name of the landlady; she is more frequently called Sonia.)

~~speak, denounced~~ to be sure, he's a businessman.[10] Well, if you're thinking of slipping away, the denunciation is at the police station: watch out. ~~Be on your guard, he might slip away. But brother Vassia: He has a carriage and a country house and [fame] a beautiful reputation: he rejects the three fishes. Well, the mother sends us the last crumb . . . Well, those 10 rubles, those 10 rubles on the table beg to go visiting.~~ He's publishing Klopshtok* of 20 years ago. I found this out from Kheruvimov.

"Isn't that right, Nastasiushka? [Look, the nine rubles are now lying there and they are begging to come to me.] And only now do I see, Vassia, that I'm a fool. I wanted to amuse you, give you some comfort with my prattle, and it seems that I've driven you to rage." ~~What's the matter, Vassia? Nothing, I answered.~~

"[It doesn't matter . . . I answered]," turning away, and in a minute I asked: "Was it you that I saw in my delirium by my side and didn't recognize?" [Raskolnikov asked, silent for a minute and not turning around].

"He even drove me into a frenzy. I came by once to see you with Zametov."

"With Zametov? with the clerk? ~~My heart trembled.~~ Why?[11] He wanted to get to know [you] . . . [wanted to himself]. He's a good fellow . . . I was with him at Louise's; we talked a lot about you—now we're friends. Otherwise, how would I have learned anything about you?"

"Did I talk in my delirium? What did I say?" He (I) asked [as if I didn't belong to myself] striving to get up from the bed.

"Look at him. What did you say in your delirium! [Look, don't get up.] It's common knowledge what people say in a delirium. ~~All trifles.~~ [Well, brother,] now brother, time to get back to work . . ."

"Well, what did I say? . . ."

"What did you say? Oh, Lord, he's bent on knowing! Are you afraid you let out some secret? Don't worry: Nothing was said about the countess. But you said a lot about ~~dogs~~ a bulldog of some kind, about a caretaker, about Aleksandr Il'ich, and Nikodim Fomich.

---

* Frederick Klopstock, German poet (1724–1823), out of fashion at this time.

[10] I, brother, if you want, am against three-fishes; but, you know they make business out of this three-fishedness, and outside of three fishes you'll get nothing else out of them. [amuse you]

[11] Why should you be worried?

They made quite an impression on you then apparently. And in addition you were terribly interested in your own sock, complained about it. Give me my sock from my foot, that's all. Zametov himself would look [expressly for your socks] in every corner, and would give you this rubbish with his own washed and perfumed hands [with rings]. Only then would you quiet down and you would hold this rubbish in your hands for days on end . . . [And how! It was impossible to take it away from you.] It's probably now somewhere under your covers. [And what's more you asked for some fringe from your pants. Zametov asked you for a long time: what kind of fringe?]" I didn't answer but grew quiet. ~~Zametov looked for the socks and~~ Zametov [he came to my place] examined the socks. I felt with my hand; there was one sock [even now] near me. I squeezed it tightly in my hand . . .

"Well, back to work," continued Razumikhin. "The point is that I'm going to take something from [your thirty] rubles with your permission, [for I see that they are asking to be taken] and I'll return quickly.[12] And you, Nastenka, if he needs anything, don't leave him. And make sure that he has some jam. [Raspberry by all means.] And besides I'll drop by Sonechka's myself."

[N.B. "I'll send Zosimov. But, I'll come by myself."]

"He calls her Sonechka. Oh, you, pretty mug," said Nastasya ~~obviously extremely pleased with Razumikhin.~~ [as soon as he went out; obviously completely taken by Razumikhin for a long time already]. I was quiet. She turned around; at first she opened the door, so as to listen, and then went downstairs. She was very interested in knowing how he would handle Sonechka . . . [Finally, he remained alone.]

[As soon as she went out, I immediately pulled out the sock, the same one for the left foot, and began to examine it intently under the light: is ~~blood~~ anything noticeable? But the sock had been so worn, black and dirty, and then I had so rubbed it into the ~~dust~~ ground [and wet it] that it was impossible to see with the naked eye that it had had blood on it. On the contrary, the whole tip of the sock [and particularly the sole of it] consisted of one big dark brown spot. I grew calm. ~~But all the same something tortured me.~~ Zametov couldn't discern anything, but nevertheless it was curious that he had come by and managed already to make friends with Razumikhin. ~~Lord, when will this end then? . . . And what else will there be? I was~~

---

[12] In the evening I'll bring you an account of it; that brother is necessary.

~~coldly angry, had had enough of Razumikhin and I silently raged against Zametov~~.

What made me angrier than anything was that I felt so weak, helpless, and under the protection of Razumikhin.[13] I [suddenly] almost began to hate him.[14] Now he won't leave me until I get well, and I am still so weak that [very likely] I'm not rational enough and I'll say something careless. ~~I am even afraid for my head, I'm afraid that a healthy~~ Better ~~only to suffer~~ to remain completely silent. Oh, may they be cursed! I don't want to be with them; I want to be alone! [Alone,—that's what I want. I was seized by irritation and fever.] What are they to me? As to the fact that Razumikhin looked me up, saved me, doctored me at his expense, brought a doctor, spent his own time with me, arranged my affairs and did his very best to comfort and amuse me—all that only tormented me and enraged me. I waited for his return with cold fury. In the meantime my head was hurting very much and everything was going completely round and round. I covered my eyes. Nastasya opened the door with a squeak, entered, looked around and thinking that I had fallen asleep went out again. ~~I hated her, and was in rage precisely because she does not say anything. Look at her, I thought, she won't say anything but has long since heard everything. For a long time before all this, I had counted on her telling me news and gossip. I was so irritated that I didn't think of my poor mother and of what she had sent~~.

~~And where did my poor mother get the money? I didn't even think of her. Oh, not, did not think! think! I tortured myself. But they, they are all around me. They'll destroy me. Oh, why am I sick? Run away somewhere!~~

~~Run away from them, I thought, and this idea so inflamed me that I rose from the bed and from weakness fell down again on my pillow~~.

---

[13] He opened one eye a bit, and without showing that he had awakened, he saw Razumikhin, who opened the door wide and stood on the threshold, uncertain as to whether to come in or not. Raskolnikov opened his eyes.

[14] I am healthy, I'm completely healthy. It's wrong of you to want to make out that I'm sick. Have you been here long, Razumikhin? Yes, I've come by twice already. Zametov, etc. No, but before, were you here a long time the first time? But I told you about it a short time ago. Raskolnikov fell into reflection; as in a dream he remembers, but where did you get the money? The letter? I remember the merchant's worker. Thank you: Well, thank God, now I see that you're in your right senses. But a while ago, my God, I even began to get angry with you. Rodya! I have a little party at my place tonight. I've moved. Why don't you come over? Raskolnikov remained silent. Zosimov (still some irritation).

In an hour and a half about dusk[15] Razumikhin's [loud and ringing voice] was heard on the stairs. [I had dozed off. His voice made me start.] He opened the door, but seeing that my eyes were shut, he stopped [silent on the threshold]. [Then] I ~~opened my eyes and looked around~~ looked at him.

"Oh, you're not sleeping; well here I am. [Nastasya bring up everything," he yelled down. "I'll give you a full account, shortly. You did well to nap!] He had a package in his arms and his air was solemn.[16]

I looked at him coldly.

"It's a good thing to sleep, and I, brother Vassia, am leaving you till tomorrow. [Sleep, it's good for you.] I stopped in on Bakavin [on the way]; he's coming to look in on you. But in the meanwhile [until Bakavin comes] let's look at what I bought. Here's Nastasiushka; she'll keep us company." Nastasya was already in the room. It seemed that she couldn't keep away from Razumikhin.

"Well, first of all," he ~~began~~ continued unwrapping a package, "First—a cap. Let's try it on."[17] He walked up to me, lifted me up a little ~~he embraced me, grabbed my head with his left arm.~~ and got ready to try the hat on.

I pushed him away with distaste. "[Not necessary] Tomorrow . . ." I said.

"No, really, brother, Vassia, don't resist. Tomorrow will be too late, and besides I'll not be able to sleep all night from worry that I bought a hat without knowing your size, simply by chance. Perfect!" he yelled triumphantly, "exact fit! [Now I'll go to sleep peacefully!] That, brother Vassia, is the chief thing," he continued taking off the cap and looking at it with pleasure. "Head dress ~~that's the important thing, just like a philosophy.~~ [speaking generally] very definitely helps one's success in high society. [There's a whole philosophy of life here.] An extraordinary casquette," he continued admiring it with great seriousness. "Well, Nastenka, look here are two hats: this

---

[15] He awoke; he had already slept six hours and awoke about evening. Having opened the door, Razumikhin was standing on the threshold and was looking in very attentively.

[16] Raskolnikov got up astonished, "Who is it! What time is it," he yelled. "You've slept six good hours already. How do you feel?"

[17] I pushed him away with distaste. Tomorrow. No brother, I won't get any peace, bought it by sight without knowing the size.

Palmerston [he got my old round mutilated hat from the corner, which for some unknown reason he called a Palmerston] and put it side by side with [the newly bought] cap on the table—this Palmerston or this elegant acquisition?[18] You know, Vassia, we'll donate this [round hat] to an academic museum and we'll say that this is a bird's nest from Zanzibar and that the eggs broke on the way.[19] Well ~~down to business~~ [continuing]. Evaluate it, Vassia. What do you think I paid for the cap? Nastasiushka!" He turned to her, seeing that I remained silent.

"[Well] You paid 20 kopecks," answered Nastasya, also ~~admiring~~ examining the cap.

"Twenty kopecks, you fool! Sixty. Do you really think ~~you can find~~ that in these days ~~in the nineteenth century such~~ you can [buy a cap for twenty kopecks]? And yet with the guarantee that if you wear out this one [by next year] they'll ~~stand behind~~ give you another [hat], [I swear it]. Now, let's proceed to the United States.* What do you think of these trousers? I warn you: I'm proud of these trousers." And he spread out before us gray, [perfectly decent, but worn also] cotton trousers.

"Not a hole, nor a spot, but used a bit.[20] A vest like that, of the same color as fashion dictates, also worn a bit, [but, after all, that's even better: softer, sort of more tender to the touch]. You see, Vassia, in order to make a career in the world, it's enough to follow the season, in my opinion. Now, it's the summer season, and everything—the trousers and the vest—are summery. In autumn, to be sure all [this] will fall apart, [like the Babylonian monarchy, though not from luxury, but from inner disharmony]; but by then in the first place, the season will demand a warmer material, and in the second place, some thoroughly respectable pieces will still be left for us in the winter for wrapping your feet. ~~Now what do you think, how much!~~ Well, how much. Guess!"

He looked ~~around at me~~ on victoriously [rather] at Nastasya [than at me; my cold and even angry look apparently disconcerted him].

---

* A play on words: *shtany,* trousers; *shtaty,* states.

[18] Nastasya put the package down in front of him, and he began solemly to unwrap it, slyly looking at Raskolnikov, solemnly unwrapping. "That, brother, was very close to my heart," he began untying. "Well, let's begin with the top. In the first place, you see, they sell only at jewelers."

[19] He was so happy I was talking to him.

[20] I don't deny, but almost better than not having been used.

"A ruble [twenty-five] in silver neither more nor less for the trousers and vest. That's really giving it ~~completely free, completely free~~ away [and on top of that] also with the guarantee:[21] if you wear it out—[and you have the right] you can ask for others [in this same store] whatever you choose [from the best of English wool that there is. They'll give it to you for nothing]. Well now [let's go] on to the boots. Look, Vassia, they are worn, but what do you think, they'll last for about three months. They will last that long. I selected them with care. [I'm a specialist in boots and I'm proud of it.] [This pair] has been used [only] a week and the workmanship is foreign: ~~The secretary wore them~~ The secretary at the English embassy dropped them off at the bazaar. [He was in great need of money.] Price—one ruble and that includes delivery. A good buy."

"But maybe they won't fit him," said Nastasya.

"And what is this?" and he [triumphantly] pulled out of his pocket my boot, dirty, with a horrible hole, and completely covered with dry mud.

"I was walking along with my provision and like a naturalist was able to construct the whole skeleton from a single bone; in Fomin's store they reconstructed the actual size for me by this wreck, and what's more they insisted in putting their reputation behind it, and a naturalist ~~perhaps will lie~~ will sooner be wrong than Fomin."

"Now, Vassia, [comes the intimate article]. You don't have any shirts. [I know that one to be worth nothing.] Here you are, two linen shirts,[22] used to be sure, but ~~still expensive~~ they're all the stronger for the use: a ruble and half for the pair, the unmentionables[23] free, thrown into the bargain, [only] one pair, and enough for you, because brother the unmentionables are things hidden from [high] society. Well now, a ruble and a half and a ruble—two and a half, and a ruble 25 kopecks, and [yet also] sixty kopecks—the total, total—four rubles and thirty kopecks and five rubles and seventy kopecks in change and here they are. [He put the money on the table.] [And in addition] the whole costume, from head to feet, because, in my opinion, your coat can still serve and even has ~~something~~

[21] who bought it once can always get it free next year

[22] with a fashionable top. Because, brother, because good linen gets stronger the more you wear it. That's well known.

[23] two pieces: one paid for and the other free.

~~still special about it~~ [a kind of particularly noble aspect]. Now, as to socks, etc. The devil with them. Why need them? [You'll take care of this matter yourself.] I advise you to wash the shirt you have; and since it's been in shreds a long time already, tear it up for foot wrappings. There's enough for two pairs not to mention that this is [everywhere] ~~particularly~~ now in fashion [in fashion even among women]. Well, let me change your shirt."

"Not necessary . . . not necessary." I waved him away.[24]

"Impossible, Vassia, you've worn it so long, sweated in it so much, etc., etc., that it's quite possible that your sickness will last three days more from it. Come on, come on! Nastenka, don't be embarrassed, but rather help. Like that."

And he changed my linen by force. [Nastasya took [the old] shirt to wash it.] I was in a rage; ~~I don't know why.~~ I fell back on the pillow and fell into tears of rage.

"Now, now, now what is it! What a guy!" cried out Razumikhin [changing his artificial and buffoonish tone and looking at me even with reproach].

"I don't need a nurse; [I don't need benefactors and comforters]. Leave me alone, leave me," I said wheezing and crying.

[Razumikhin looked at me with sincere sorrow.

"Why, why must you," I said with spiteful venom, "Why are you talking to me?"] "~~Like a nurse you want to amuse me with various tricks, jokes. But you don't know how. What jokes! About high society, about Palmerston . . . you can't do anything right; . . . nothing goes well for you." I laughed maliciously.~~

[At that minute] the door opened and Bakavin entered. He was a doctor, at the moment without a practice, a skilful doctor ~~black beard, black eyes, swarthy face, dressed in black~~ [blond, with large but colorless eyes] with a sarcastic smile, [tall and puffy]. ~~I had heard of him and seen him before.~~ I had met him before. [I always found it particularly difficult to get along with him.]

"Well," he said, looking into my face intently and seating himself on my bed.

"Look, he's still in a bad mood, decided to cry because we changed his linen."[25]

---

[24] "Please leave it all all, leave, leave," Raskolnikov waved. "I don't want to. Tell me: Where did you get the money for [all this]?"

[25] He doesn't want to change his linen.

"Understandable."

He felt my pulse and my head.

"Does your head still pain?"

"I [I'm healthy, I'm completely all right!" Raskolnikov said persistently and with irritation, lifting himself up.]

"Hmm, it doesn't matter. Very good. Good. Has he eaten anything?"[26]

"Has he been told and asked what he wants to eat?"

"Yes . . . [We can give him something.] Soup, tea . . . as much as he wants. He knows how much he needs. He mustn't have, of course, mushrooms or cucumbers [beef also now] and we'll see what he needs to have tomorrow, [not to speak of the medicine]."[27, 28]

"Tomorrow evening I'm going to take him walking!" yelled Razumikhin. ~~That's decided.~~[29] "Look his clothes are all ready, I'll take him to the Iusupov Gardens and then to the Palais de Cristal."[30]

"Well, [I would] [not] move him tomorrow, ~~It will be impossible.~~[31] Zosimov said apathetically. "Perhaps a little . . . if the weather."[32]

---

[26] Tomorrow I'll look to whatever is necessary. What is the use of the medicine; away with it; away with everything. It's clearly not satisfactory.

[27] Pestriakov the student in this story. An officer, one natural scientist, one teacher, one boy, but besides the devil take it; it doesn't matter. Zametov will be there. Ah, brother Rodia, how I'd like him. . . Well, it doesn't matter.

[28] I'm well, I'm well, and I won't permit anyone to order. I can walk.

[29] I don't understand

[30] I'm well

[31] One mustn't move him. One must still (. . .)

[32] If you could come to me today, I'll be home. I can walk now. I'll go wherever I want. . . if I decide to.

"Who will be there?"

Zosimov kept silent.

"Ah, what a nuisance!" Razumikhin yelled. "I'm having a housewarming, two steps and he'd be there. Will you be there? You promised, you know"; he turned suddenly to Zosimov.

"Well, I don't know, perhaps, who'll be there?"

"Well, everyone from around here; true, for two months I had no guests and then suddenly a whole crowd."

"Who?"

"A postmaster who is spending his life in the provinces somewhere; he's living on a pension now. A pathetic soul, always quiet, but I like him very much, that is, once every five years. Everyone from around here, contemporaries, except for an old uncle, an antique, 65 years of age; he came to St. Petersburg on business a week ago.

"You see one way or another. And all the others. Porfiry Stepanovich, the inspector, your friend. But surely you won't come perhaps because you quarreled."

"What a bother, and the day after tomorrow?"

"And the day after tomorrow."

"What a nuisance, and just as I wanted to bring him and Zametov together. He knows all the spots and is at home everywhere."

"Corners perhaps, but outside of corners what can you or he ~~he pointed at me~~ have in common with Zametov." Bakavin asked, ~~questioning sarcastically~~ pointing to me and [sort of specially] twisting his lips into an accusatory smile.

"Oh, you, all of you, you and your principles. Nonsense! And I like every [good] man. [A good man—that's my principle.] But to tell the truth [I do have] a small matter to see Zametov about."

"It would be interesting to know what about," continued Bakavin. ~~Well, I told you or didn't I?~~

"As for the painter, that is, the dyer? We'll get him out ~~of his trouble~~, but that's not the problem; [they'll let him go without us]. The matter is now [completely, completely] clear, and ~~we'll work it over some more.~~ we'll [simply] give it some steam."

"What dyer?"

"But I already told you. [Oh, no?] No, but I didn't tell you; I told you only the beginning of the affair. [Look] about the murder of the old woman; well, the painter turned up [later] in the affair."

"Well, I heard about the murder before you . . . [I even read about it in the newspapers]. [I'm particularly interested in the affair.]" ~~What does it matter to you? The inspector and I~~

"They butchered Lizaveta also," ~~They murdered, she blurted out.~~ Nastasya suddenly interrupted turning straight toward me.

"What Lizaveta?" I muttered, no longer being able to keep quiet.

"But Lizaveta Petrovna, the peddler. Don't you know her? She used to come around here down below. She even mended your shirt, the very one on your back."

"This shirt," ~~She mended that?~~ [barely audible] I repeated after her.

"What did you think! Did you think that I mended it? I can't mend with a fine needle. Look at this, she put in pieces in five places," she murmured looking over the shirt. "[You've got some shirt!] You still owe her 10 kopecks for mending; you haven't paid it yet . . . [and she was murdered pregnant; they used to beat her for nothing, and whoever wanted to could outrage her]." ~~I knew her and she mended my linen. She's an idiot. The old woman beat her when she was pregnant. I saw it myself. Pregnant, pregnant, sixth~~

"[Well] who was it, the painter?" Bakavin interrupted turning to Razumikhin.[33, 34, 35]

"Well, they charged him with murder without much ado." ~~And look at the painter. They began very simply to suspect him in the act. What kind of evidence?~~

"[Is there any evidence?] But . . . but how can that be? [Once again] has new evidence turned up?" [Bakavin asked, obviously wanting to worm something out of him.]

"What kinds of proofs, the devil take it! And besides what is really a proof or not. That's what has to be shown. At first they suspected [those two, what are there names] Bergshtoltz and Kopilin, the student. [Boy, that was crazy!] [Even though he is a stranger, it gets my bile up.] By the way, Vassia, you know about that business [also]? Without your being aware of it ~~while you were lying here [alongside us, not far away] the murder took place.~~ [a murder took place. What is remarkable is that murders and things like these occur more and more often]. That is, you were still able to get out then, well, that's right, it was when you went to the station . . . [what's the matter with me!], but you yourself heard [about it]. [They were telling about it in your presence, and you fell into a dead faint there.] That was still before your sickness."[36]

~~It's Zametov, I thought~~ I turned away ~~toward the wall~~ remaining silent. I couldn't look at them [and I was barely breathing].

"Well?"

"Well Bergshtoltz,—that stout guy and Kopilin[37] gave the best of

---

[33] And what's it to you? Like that. . . Ah, I understand. about Porfiry Filipich. And what's Porfiry Filipich to me?

I heard that you and Porfiry almost had a fight about this matter. Silence. What a funny fellow you are Razumikhin, always bustling round, he added, grimacing. And why are you interested, as you yourself said a short time ago. Well, for a good deed. . . . Now, now, enough. . .

[34] Bakavin remarks: it turns out that they made up this whole affair together, that is Bergshtolts and the student and the worker did the murder together, and then made up this whole comedy. Now imagine that they really stopped with that. Fortunately, there was a witness. What kind of news are you (making up)? Yes, news. Bakavin got up.

[35] No argument with Bakavin: very simply he relates the affair clearly and briefly.

[36] On the eve you were at my place, before you fell in a faint; they told me that he fell in a faint there. [What, you fell in a faint! Lord!]

[37] Pestriakov—he'll be at my place today.

explanations. [But you've heard about it from Porfiry. Filipich.] First of all, why would they kill for sport, and then immediately bring up the caretaker. The door, they say . . . was open. [They went] to tell the caretaker that the door was locked from the inside, and they came and found the door unlocked. That's the fact that's a stumbling block; [that confused them]."

~~"I know all that already," said Bakavin.~~ "[And] I know Bergshtoltz," Bakavin said. "He used to buy pledges from the old lady ~~at her place~~ that were past due. ~~and sold them to the jeweler below.~~ [He's a scoundrel, ~~I know. A scoundrel but not guilty~~ and this is the way it works with us; since he's a scoundrel and bought up past due pledges, that means he was most certainly the murderer. How could he come to that conclusion? He's a little braggart."

"I know that you almost had a fight with Porfiry at Poroshin's. It's true that Porfiry is proud but he has talent, and he'll make an [excellent] inspector. Now with the reform we need practical people like him."

"Well now, what further?" Bakavin interrupted with irritation]. ~~Both of them, him and the student.~~ "[Well both of them, the student and Bergshtoltz, managed to get away immediately.] Dozens of witnesses saw them in the next half hour. A witness for every minute. Yes [all that's known to me] and furthermore the caretakers saw both of them as they first entered. First Bergshtoltz and then the student." ~~The student came to redeem [pawn] an object on time. In the three minutes more or less [that he was there], it was impossible to do the murder, not even taking into account that both corpses were [still] warm when the caretakers came up. Consequently, at that time when these gentlemen were knocking at the door, the murderer was sitting there. [They were both telling the truth that the door was locked.] They came upon him, were in his way, and he would have been trapped like a rat really, if Bergshtoltz had not got bored waiting for the student and fool that he was had not also gone off to look for the caretaker. The murderer lifted the hook, opened the door, and there he was. I know all those suppositions.~~

"Do they think then that the murderer hid in the empty apartment when they were passing by? [I know all that, all that theory," Bakavin added ironically.]

"Absolutely," [Razumikin cried out heatedly, as if anticipating objections]; "otherwise they would have met him."

~~All the same this smacks of oversubtlety somehow.~~ "[All that's pretty complicated," muttered Bakavin, screwing up his mouth, "cunningly smacking of a subtlety.] It would be better to be more direct, and clear." ~~How well they manage, the inspector thinks; I know the inspector, that inspector is a bit of a braggart in psychology!~~[38]

"[Boy, Bakavin, what a guy you are!" with heated reproach [and with pain] yelled Razumikhin. "You're a peerless fellow and the noblest of men but you're choking with hate. Because you live in the same building and because you're enemies, the devil knows why, you feel you have to contradict and refuse to accept what's obvious! As far as I'm concerned Porfiry has hit it right on the nose.]"

"[You see he has had], from the very first, this question which he can't resolve: were Lizaveta and the old woman together [in the apartment]?" [Bakavin said coolly], "Did the murderer kill them both or did he kill each separately?"

"Separately, separately!" Razumikhin yelled getting hot under the collar. "That's exactly the point, separately; the most remote suppositions are based on that now."

"Separately, that means that he began to beat the old woman, and didn't close the door? [Because the other woman entered afterward. Because otherwise why would he let her in? He would have also [taken fright] and hid himself, as he did when Bergshtoltz came.]"

"That's the point, this [open door turns out] to be the most precious fact, and the whole case rests on it."

~~He was a complete stranger and was so frightened that he forgot about the door. Yes, we've already heard about it, psychological studies, subtle.~~ "Subtle . . ."

"Not at all subtle. What a guy you are Bakavin! when you don't like someone, you're ready to tear him apart. Because you and Porfiry are running after the same woman, must you . . ."

"Cut it out, talking such rot," Bakavin said calmly but turning pale.

~~[Nonsense!] But the facts? He yelled with all his force. Razumikhin got unbelievably hot under the collar; he was beside himself. He was always that way! Bakavin was somewhat apathetic, even sort of sluggish, and it seemed to me even then that he sort of wanted to~~

---

[38] There's psychology to be considered here; one must consider psychological findings, but they look only at the bare fact. With enthusiasm the whole world reveals their thick, base, hardened slime. This is what I'm fighting against, the new men. [It will see me through.] Don't accuse Porfiry; you don't understand him; he keeps quiet. But the worker (. . .)

~~find out something~~. "But the facts! ~~Facts. Wait a minute! Listen then! What was the state of things from the very beginning?~~ [The facts show that it isn't rot, that it's not simple theory.][39] All that has been reconstructed, and it [all] doubtlessly happened in that way. The murderer, first of all, whoever he was, was an inexperienced person."

"But [the inspector] Semenov said that he was very clever and experienced [clever, a sly one]."

"He's lying there. [He lied on that point! and besides he said that only at the beginning, but now he agrees] that he's definitely clumsy and inexperienced and that this was precisely the first time he had done anything of the sort. He lost his head ~~took fright~~ to the point of even forgetting to close the door. [And this, this is the truth of the point, the basis of everything. That's psychology. What are you laughing at?] All he knew how to do was murder, because he didn't even know how to grab the money. There were some 5 per cent notes in that very trunk."

---

[39] Suddenly a most unexpected fact reveals everything. The peasant Pushkin, the owner of a tavern, brings an object in two days later.

VI

Dostoevsky's letter to Katkov, for the first time outlining the plot of "Crime and Punishment"

What follows is a rough draft of Dostoevsky's famous letter to Katkov outlining his first thoughts on *Crime and Punishment.* The letter was written from Wiesbaden where Dostoevsky, having impoverished himself with reckless gambling, was the virtual prisoner of his German landlord. The enormous significance of the letter as his first statement of intention speaks for itself. One might point out, however, that the motive for the crime, which gives Dostoevsky so much trouble in these notes, is put forth here simply as the desire to trade one useless life for his mother's happiness and his sister's moral salvation. We have here also Raskolnikov's "arithmetical" intention to pay back the crime by a lifetime of good deeds. There is evidence in these notes that Dostoevsky first conceived of the motive in this simple way, and that the creative process itself brought him—at times impatiently—to the recognition of the almost impenetrable net of motives that finally entangles Raskolnikov's deed. One might also point to the typical plaint of Dostoevsky—a whiner by nature—that the proper conditions to ply his craft have never been granted him. His repeated complaints on this point have led many critics to accuse him of carelessness in technique and craft, a grievously erroneous deduction as these notes prove so persistently and to which the novel so eloquently gives the lie.

Some of Dostoevsky's most cherished convictions about crime are first voiced in this letter. We have to remind ourselves that *Crime and Punishment* is Dostoevsky's first work about crime, and that this letter is really his first explicit statement on crime. Dostoevsky is already convinced—to judge by this letter—that judicial processes and legal punishment are both irrelevant and ineffective. Moral law, and not fear of punishment, brings the criminal to confession. Indeed,

Ivan Karamazov's ecclesiastical article, which is discussed in the Elder Zosima's cell, voices in more detailed fashion the same sentiments, just as the mysterious stranger who confesses his crime to the Elder Zosima acts out the principles expressed in Ivan's article and in Dostoevsky's letter. Touched on here, also, is Dostoevsky's long-held conviction that ideas and beliefs necessarily lead to action, that a belief is the beginning of action, and that one cannot hold on to beliefs without having such beliefs influence both character and action. Later, he will build these sentiments into the structure of *The Possessed*. We might note, finally, what is not included in this first conception of the novel. The superman motive is missing, as well as any reference to Sonia, Svidrigyalov, or Marmeladov. Raskolnikov commits the crime to help his mother and sister, and he comes to confess because of his nature and his need to suffer. These notebooks are themselves eloquent testimony to the fact that Dostoevsky himself came to realize that such an explanation of the young man's motives was inadequate.

From a letter to M. N. Katkov

M. N.

May I count on publishing my novel in your journal, *The Russian Messenger?*

I've been writing it here in Wiesbaden for the past two months, and I'm [now] finishing it. It will be about five to six printer's pages long. I've got about two week's work still left, and perhaps a little more. In any case, I can say for sure that I will send it off to the editors of *The Russian Messenger* no later than a month from now.

The idea of the novel [as much as I can tell] cannot possibly go against the ~~thoughts~~ tenor of your journal; on the contrary. This is a psychological account of a crime. [The action takes place at the present time, in this year.] A young man expelled from the university, a petty bourgeois by background, living in the most extreme poverty, decides out of lightheadedness and instability of thinking to extricate himself from his deplorable situation with one bold stroke. He has become obsessed with badly thought out ideas which happen to be in the air. He decides to kill an old woman, the wife of a titular counselor, a moneylender. She is a crazy, deaf, sick old woman; [she greedily charges exorbitant interest]; she is evil and lives on the blood and flesh of others, and torments her younger sister. "She is not good for anything," "Why does she live?" "Does anyone need her?" etc. These questions unhinge the mind of the young man. He decides to kill her, to rob her, in order to make his mother happy, who is living in the provinces, and to save his sister, who is living as a companion to some gentry, from [the sensuous] advances of the head of this gentry family, advances that threaten her with ruin. Then he plans to finish his studies, go abroad and [then] [be] honest, and firmly immovable [in] the fulfilment of his "humanitarian duty toward mankind" for the rest of his life. [By which of course] "he will make up" for the slight crime, if you can call an act done to an old, deaf, crazy, evil and sick woman, who [doesn't know herself why she is living] and who in a month perhaps would die anyway, a crime.

Despite the fact that crimes of this kind are done with great difficulty, that is, the criminals [almost always] leave clues that are crudely apparent, traces, etc. [and they leave a great deal to chance, which almost always trips them up], he is able to do the deed, completely by chance, quickly and successfully.

A month goes by from the time of the deed to the final catastrophe. [There are no suspicions of him nor can there be.] Then the psychological process of the crime unfolds. Unresolved questions arise before the murderer, unsuspected and unexpected feelings torment his heart. The truth of God and the law of nature take their own, and he finally feels forced to give himself up, [forced] in order to be once again part of humankind, even if it means perishing in prison. The feeling of isolation and separation from humanity which he felt immediately after committing the crime wear him down. [The law of truth and human nature have their effect (. . .) the convictions.] [The criminal] decides to take suffering on himself in order [even without being forced] to redeem his act. [However, it is hard for me to explain in full my thought.][1] [In addition] I hint at this thought in the novel, that [legal] punishment for a crime frightens a criminal much less than we think [the lawmakers in part] because the criminal himself [morally] demands it.

---

[1] I (. . .) give it now the artistic form in which it has formed itself, but form

I have seen this even among the most uneducated people [in cases of pure chance]. I wanted to express this precisely in an educated man, a man of the new generation, so that my thought would be clearer, more easily understood, and more apparent. Certain events, which have happened in the most recent past, have convinced me that my subject is not at all eccentric, [precisely because the murderer is an educated and even a well-disposed man]. I was told last year of a student in Moscow, who had been expelled from the university after some trouble in school, who decided to rob the post and to kill the mailman. There are still many traces in our newspapers of extraordinary instability in our ideas, which inspires horrible deeds. [That seminary student, for example, who met the girl, by agreement with her in a shed, and killed her and whom they arrested within an hour eating his breakfast, etc.] In short I am convinced that my subject matter is in part justified by our times.

To be sure, in my analysis of the ~~thoughts~~ idea of my novel, I have neglected the whole structure of events. I'll answer for its interest, but I don't take it upon myself to judge its artistic realization. I've had to write too many [much too many] bad things, trying to meet a deadline, etc. [However], I haven't written this piece in a hurry or in heat. I'm going to try, if only for myself, to finish it as best I can.

VII

Raskolnikov and Porfiry—Dunia's break with Luzhin

This section contains, along with fragmental material of a diverse nature, schematic summaries of two scenes: the conversation Raskolnikov has with Porfiry at Razumikhin's apartment (Part III, Chapter 5, in the novel) and the scene at which Dunia breaks with Luzhin in the presence of Raskolnikov (Part IV, Chapter 2). These are not fully worked out scenes but rough sketches of intention. As such they have interest in suggesting how Dostoevsky first conceived the scenes. Dostoevsky will sketch out what will be paragraphs by single words, and a paragraph of single words will be a foreshortened version of a chapter. In such schematic sketching, certain words and phrases will stand out, such as Raskolnikov's determination not to accept his sister's sacrifice in marrying Luzhin.

In the conversation between Porfiry and Raskolnikov, no explicit reference is made to the important distinction Raskolnikov makes between ordinary and extraordinary men, although there is a reference to Napoleon and his lack of squeamishness toward murder. In the novel itself much of the scene is taken up with Raskolnikov's article and his division of men into ordinary and extraordinary types. There are brief references to this division in the third notebook (pp. 226, 228), suggesting that the fully worked out conception of the superman, above law and the dictates of conscience, came late in the creative process.

Porfiry and the duel carried on with Raskolnikov take up a good part of the finished version of the novel. Like Svidrigaylov, Porfiry seems to have developed late in the process of the writing of the novel. Except for the small fragment in this section, most of the notes about him, and there are many, are to be found in the third notebook. In the notes and in the novel he is clever, bright, keen in his observations of human nature, and humane in his understanding.

Despite his inexhaustible patience, his efforts come to nothing. Dostoevsky has given us a formidable antagonist for Raskolnikov in order to strengthen his contention that legal justice is ineffective. What we have of the relationship between Porfiry and Raskolnikov in this section is consistent with that of the final version. Indeed, Porfiry voices what will be his finest perception: that Raskolnikov will not hold out, that his nature will lead him to confession.

Notes for the "Confession"

N.B. Yes, go and declare it: they'll call it stupid; he killed without motive; he took 280 rubles and 20 rubles of objects. If I had stolen 15,000 or killed and robbed Kraevsky,* then they would not laugh [they then would see my goal and would believe that I had great plans]. But now I even have to suffer laughter and contempt: the little fool, they'll say, he killed for nothing. He imagined that he would make everyone happy and himself secure with 200. They won't believe in my plan, when I explain it. I can't even avoid the vilest disgrace.

Oh, I'm a scoundrel; I'm a scoundrel! I call them base and disgusting, but I crave their good opinion! I'm not good for anything, for anything! Life has [still] not given me anything.

N.B. (I thought that I would find 5,000 at her place.)

N.B. (The daughter of the functionary, in passing, present her just a bit more originally. A simple and downtrodden creature. Or rather dirty and drunk carrying a fish. He kisses her feet.)

[Biggest worries are about this: what must he do? He tries to translate, but cannot. Akistov disgusts him. He gets acquainted with the sister of A—v. Write a comedy.]

---

* Editor of *Otechestvennye zapiski* (*Notes of the Fatherland*), a famous journal (1839–84) in which many noted writers appeared, including Belinski, Herzen, Lermontov, and Koltsov.

Current References

Bakalin, about the sickness. Razumikhin [they started to talk about the murder]. Suddenly Luzhin enters, conversation with *him;* has difficulty talking about the younger generation. The other continues to talk about the murder to Bakalin;[1] Luzhin listens and waits; the account of the murder gives him a motive for starting a conversation about the disorder that is arising, about the young generation. His outbursts are according to your theory. "Is it true that you do good deeds?" (Luzhin himself had let this slip.) "Your mother is an enthusiastic woman." "And wouldn't you like to be thrown out?" "What's the matter with you? What's wrong!" (When Luzhin leaves) he chases them out, sleeps in the evening, goes out like a *madman,*[2] prayer N.B. (The sister sent it, but she asked that no one say that she sent it.)

Aristov and his story. He comes to him: Why don't you own up that you did it? At Diusso's.* Naïvely. He sells his sister to a dandy from K— Boulevard. He beats his sister and takes everything away from her. He buys counterfeit notes. Reisler. Luzhin uses him. Beats his mother. The sister leaves for Moscow with Kokh. In class we teased a certain teacher.

"How disgusting it all is, how base!" he says. "Rule over them!"

He walks in to see Razumikhin at 11 o'clock. Everyone is astonished. He is terribly excited. Conversation about demoralization, drunkenness, and crime. He begins to talk about his theory about madness. The inspector says: You don't take into account the moral foundation at all then. What would be capable of restraining the criminal then? [Neophytes] Force and fear. Civil society. That is not enough. Be assured that up to now this alone has restrained society: Voices: that's the way it is, right? And blood? Did blood restrain Napoleon? That's not a crime. Why not (Pestriakov tells how they entered the room and saw the bodies). (By all the signs the murderer is an educated person.) Why lose 100,000 at Marengo—that's not the

---

* A well-known restaurant in St. Petersburg.

[1] In some kind of lodging house; doesn't say which one, but it's close by. Lebeziatnikov.

[2] But nothing can be compared with that madness, when he ran out on the street (before the *Palais de Cristal).*

This manuscript page corresponds to p. 176, beginning with the title "Current References" and ending with the phrase "Rule over them." Two marginal notes at the side are not precisely located, a rather frequent feature of these notes. The church cupolas are characteristic drawings.

same thing as killing an old woman. Pestriakov: actually the old woman was of no use to anyone. Aristov: she is needed there! There's no crime then for you? There is a sin and it is great. How can you say then that it's permitted? Theory of arithmetic. How a German acquires a moral obligation, which he takes on himself . . . etc. Aristov is in rapture (one can really live well, easily). According to this theory then one can do it to another (you are less needed) and therefore the only motive left: force and fear.

That's not true (. . .); one objects. We don't know Chatov. About the Rut. Would you do it? I don't know. Well, not at all: you couldn't commit the crime.

After you've lived a while, you'll see that there's something more than arithmetic in a crime. You're thinking about arithmetic, but it's a matter of life. God grant that you don't fall into ~~crime~~ misfortune. [Yes, I guessed that from your article. That's all theory. Believe me that no crime was actually done; nevertheless you've been having me under surveillance a long time.] You won't be able to bear it. You, that is you, won't bear it. I can judge by your face that others (he glanced at Aristov) will bear it. For them it is too early to get rid of corporal punishment. (He gets up.) [His face is pale and sickly. Razumikhin sees him home. Listen: he won't suspect you now after what you said.

"I knew that."

"How did you know it . . . Yes. Raskolnikov talks in riddles and rapturously; he falls into a faint on the street.]

What, are you sick?

Yes, I've heard, heard about your sickness. [Such illnesses] can be dangerous. It seems that you don't pay enough attention to what is wise.

He heard about my irritability and wanted to irritate me.

After Razumikhin [and the enigmatic words under the street lamp], a meeting with his mother in the apartment (Nastasya), a slight falling out. Razumikhin makes himself indispensable. The next day Sonia (by the way, she speaks of Luzhin, 10 rubles). Mother and sister. He seated Sonia. Razumikhin is there also. Silent insult (a sad explanation). Razumikhin had blabbed: letter from Ly[u]zhin, requesting that he not be there in the evening. (And the mother asked: you won't be there, better to lie at home.) He says to Razumikhin: I'll bet that Luzhin will be there. Razumikhin had let it slip. In the evening he enters. Razumikhin meets him on the stairs. [He was doing an errand.] *Qui pro quo* and malcontent.* The mother is troubled. Pyotr Petrovich says that you're being kept: True I didn't give back the money. He's not worth my little finger. Insult. He tells what happened briefly and clearly to Sonia. Look here's what I want to know: Is it true that there was a definite condition that I not come? I noticed, Mother, how you asked about it a little while ago. Here's what I have to say: I was so crazy that I made this kind of proposal, that is, either me or chase Luzhin away. I was a despot. I came to arrange and unravel everything. 1) I'm not in condition to help you. 2) If, as I have supposed, my sister is getting married for my sake alone, then I will never want that kind of career and work with Luzhin, or receive any help or whatsoever from Mr. Luzhin. My fate is unknown to me, but God (obscure words) and therefore, if it's only *for that,* then I'm obligated to declare this in order to release my sister. If other motives forced her to give her agreement, then I feel myself obligated to say then I will not insist that Luzhin be chased away and I will not dare to quarrel with my sister. Luzhin asks: Is it true that it's only for them? She says suddenly: only for that, and she went out. Luzhin gets up and says something rude. Without saying anything they throw him out. Razumikhin is delighted: a new life, good! General delight. He says: I can't. Leave me alone, I can't live with you, or perhaps even work. My fate is cast, tormenting (. . .).

Razumikhin supports everyone, his tears. The mother thanks Razumikhin. Then Marmeladov's funeral. The wife—more tragically.

---

* A Gallicism for *quid pro quo,* "one thing for or in return for another," "tit for tat."

Notebook Three

VIII

Luzhin's intrigues against Raskolnikov and Sonia—Portrait of Svidrigaylov—Comments on Raskolnikov's motives—Katerina's efforts to find justice—Characterization of Razumikhin

In addition to fragments on a variety of subjects, this section consists of an analysis of Luzhin's intrigues against Raskolnikov and Sonia, a detailed characterization of Razumikhin, and a rather full portrait of Svidrigaylov. The fragments include the following: random thoughts of Porfiry about Raskolnikov, fragments of dialogue concerning Raskolnikov's motives, a definition of Orthodoxy and suffering, and brief references to Katerina's efforts to strike out against injustice. It seems clear that Luzhin's intrigues against Raskolnikov were meant originally to be more elaborate and ferocious: he enters into a pact with Lebeziatnikov against Sonia, has her arrested, and even makes friends with Porfiry in order to gain some advantage over Raskolnikov. The characterization of Razumikhin differs primarily in the way he thinks of Sonia. He first comes to hate her because Dunia hates her; then he comes to respect her and because of this has a terrible row with Dunia.

Most of this section is taken up with a characterization of Svidrigaylov. The portrait that emerges from descriptive detail about him, reflections on his part, and fragments of dialogue with Raskolnikov is not very different from the Svidrigaylov we meet in the novel itself. As in the novel, he is cynical, bored, amoral. Dostoevsky's intention to make him the embodiment of terrifying amorality is put forth perhaps more strongly. We are told that he has a "convulsive and bestial need to tear apart and to kill," and the crimes that are hinted at in the novel are frankly admitted here. He has a curious relationship with Sonia: they discuss ideals; Svidrigaylov falls in love with her; and he conceives of the possibility of being a better man with her. Love for anyone, though not the desire for love, would be inconsistent with the character Dostoevsky intended him to embody. Impulses to love as well as moments of despair wisely were not expressed in the final version.

In this section Svidrigaylov is somewhat astonished at his ability to entertain contradictory impulses: a respect for Dunia and a desire to ravish her: "What a strange, almost unbelievable doubling. And yet that's the way it was; he was capable of that." In the final version he is purged of emotions of astonishment, and indeed of any emotion that qualifies his amorality and disattachment to life. Also, Dostoevsky in these notes puts, unbelievably, an argument against socialism in Svidrigaylov's mouth. The Svidrigaylov of the finished version would hardly bother with the topic, except to annihilate it with cynicism. In the novel, too, we are not sure that Svidrigaylov loves Dunia. In the attempted rape scene, he seems to be hanging on to a kind of last hope that he can love and be loved. In these notes Dostoevsky seems undecided whether Svidrigaylov loves Dunia: "Love for Dunia: it turns out that he doesn't love her very much; he himself says so; he criticizes her to her face and laughs at her, which pleases her very much. But he insists on the marriage, but not very much."

Raskolnikov's humanitarian motives are most prominent in the first two notebooks, but in this and subsequent sections of the third notebook, references to his proud, wilful, and despotic nature become more frequent. We find, for example, the following: "In his image the thought of immeasurable pride, arrogance, and contempt for society is expressed in the novel. His idea: assume power over this society ~~so as to do good for it~~. Despotism is his characteristic trait. She opposes him." The stroke of the pen through the humanitarian motive is perhaps our clearest evidence that Dostoevsky had come to see that this is not the real motive. It is also of some significance that the following quotation is transferred from notes to novel without change: "N.B. Whatever I have been, whatever I might do later—whether I would be a benefactor of mankind or someone who would like a spider suck out its vital fluids—that's my affair. I know that I want to wield power over others and that's enough."

I don't think that this is the motive for the crime, but it is the "conscious" motive that comes closest to that psychic core from which radiates a range of motives. The conscious motives—whether the humanitarian motive (for mother or sister or for mankind) and whether the superman motive (which also has its humanitarian side), all have their "beautiful" side. We know enough psychology today —and Dostoevsky knew it before us—to know that we permit our conscious minds to confront usually only our most flattering motives. When Raskolnikov acknowledges the motive of raw power, he, and Dostoevsky, have finally stripped away what is flattering to the ego—but not entirely. Power and daring have their attractive side too. We have no explicit mention of unconscious motives in the notes or in the novel, but the many references to aggression against his mother and sister—more bald in the notes than in the novel—hint at something less flattering and more painful. I am not suggesting some kind of incestuous feeling as the painfully repressed motive, but I am suggesting that the conscious motives are flattering analogues to unconscious motives.

What links the conscious and unconscious motives? The conscious motives are the humanitarian impulses, the division of humanity into extraordinary and ordinary people, and the self-willed act accomplished for its own sake. The unconscious motives are the drama of aggression against his mother and himself. What strand links one to the other? On the unconscious level it is clear that Raskolnikov resents his mother for expecting him to live up to an ideal, and hates himself for resenting his mother. What is the source of the grudge? The answer for the orthodox Freudian is simple and dreary: the Oedipal complex. But, leaning on Kenneth Burke, I want to suggest something else. Kenneth Burke is right in claiming that everything in a work of art is symbolic, although the codex of symbolism must be derived from the work itself. Freudians have always treated everything in a work of art as symbolic, except for the sexual base, which has been taken in an entirely arbitrary way as the literal referent for all other symbols. Why? Sex itself can be symbolic of something else —it surely is in life—and I'm convinced that it is symbolic of something else in *Crime and Punishment*. The conscious motives are not simply "false"; they are false in a particular way: they are flattering distortions and as such imply what they are distortions of. Raskolnikov's conscious motives are all connected with "freedom"; and his unconscious motives are connected with freedom. The difference is perhaps only aesthetic. On the conscious level, this freedom is conceived of in dramatic and even awesome terms; on the unconscious level, freedom is painful and even shameful, because it involves uncomfortable feelings of hate and resentment against what society and tradition insist one must only love and revere. Raskolnikov's mother "preys" on Raskolnikov with love, as the pawnbroker "preys" on the youth of St. Petersburg. Is it any wonder that Raskolnikov reacts in fury and hate against what refuses to permit him to be what he must be? Is it any wonder that he symbolically chooses and kills an old woman who refuses to permit the youth of St. Petersburg to be what they can be? In the dream of the beaten mare, Raskolnikov is identified with all the characters in the dream, and the dream expresses at once the wrong and the right ways of achieving freedom. The wrong way is by hate and force; the right way by love and forgiveness. The wrong way is to whip the eyes of the horse; the right way is to kiss the eyes of the horse and take the whiplash meant for the horse. Mikolka, the slayer of the mare and a surrogate for Raskolnikov, is the wrong way, and the little boy—the ineradicable Raskolnikov that still exists in the grown man—is the right way. Freedom comes paradoxically not from destroying what oppresses you and limits your freedom, but from accepting, bearing, and forgiving what oppresses you and limits your freedom.

Characters and places in the novel.

Andrey Semenych Lebeziatnikov, Bakaleev's building.

V

Fifth chapter. Conversation, Porfiry. His confusion. Is he brilliant or not? It's clear that Porfiry has prepared everything; he's only having some fun. It's clear that he is embittered against me because there aren't any clues. But he's made up his mind; he was too rude (about the article). That's not natural; he has some kind of design. What kind? To irritate or let one know. But perhaps he himself became irritated. He is a man [too].

Svidrigaylov. To Dunia. "Do you remember once there was almost a moment when you were really falling for me and were thrilled by me?"

N.B. After the evening with Luzhin and the goodbye with her brother, near the lamp, Dunechka became more and more deeply reflective.

If there were people who would always submit—then nothing would happen in the world.

Raskolnikov, Dream. I'm young, I don't know. I can't even understand who can foresee it. But I had to take the first step. I want power. I don't want . . . I want everything I see to be different. For the time being I needed only that and I murdered! later I'll need more. I don't want individuality; I want to act. I want to act myself. (Holland, Pyotr) I don't know where I'll end up. [I don't want to submit.]

You didn't do it to help your mother; no, not at all; you did it for yourself, for yourself alone; I didn't want injustice,—or: I didn't do it for others but for myself, did it for myself alone.

"Oh, why did you tell me," Sonia said, running all over the room and wringing her hands. He wanted to go away. "Stay," she fell on her knees . . . "Tell me why (. . .) rob? You didn't have anything to eat? You were hungry?"

"I didn't want (. . .) I don't want to act meanly."

July 22.

Luzhin brings about Sonia's arrest with the help of Reisler. Mrs. Marmeladov is in despair, 5 sous; but Razumikhin has Luzhin arrested. Helps Sonia and *by that becomes reconciled with him.*

(3rd part)

N.B. He sees that Sonia loves him; he leaves her, *knowing what will come of it.* (That is, he treats her heart not like a rag, but like a treasure, respects it.) Sonia looks on this as contempt from his point of view. The incident with Luzhin and Lebeziatnikov (stole) and then the explanation at her place: I'm worse than you (I killed). Sonia can't bear it, becomes sick—Cinq sous.

Oh you mothers why did you bring them into the world!

N.B. Sonia told me it because it was necessary to live with someone.

"I love you and that's why I told you."*

"You need me that's why you love me."

The Idea of the Novel

1

The Orthodox point of view; what Orthodoxy consists of.

There is no happiness in comfort; happiness is bought with suffering.

Man is not born for happiness. Man earns his happiness, and always by suffering. There's no injustice here, because the knowledge of life and consciousness (that is, that which is felt immediately with your body and spirit, that is, through the whole vital process of life) is acquired by experience *pro and contra,* which one must take upon one's self. (By suffering, such is the law of our planet, but this immediate awareness, felt with the life process, is such a great joy that one gladly pays with years of suffering for it.)

2

In his portrait the thought of immeasurable pride, arrogance, and contempt for society is expressed in the novel. His idea: assume power over this society. ~~so as to do good for it~~ Despotism is his characteristic trait. She opposes him.

N.B. In giving it artistic form, don't forget that he is 23 years old.

He wants power, but he doesn't know how to get it.

Get power as quickly as possible and get rich. The idea of murdering comes to him ready-made.

N.B. Express all this at Razumikhin's evening gathering.

---

* Apparently Raskolnikov is speaking and is answered by Sonia in the next line.

N.B. *For the novel:* find and set in action (in the novel) a Russian merchant (Babushkin) factory owner, so that later he will give Razumikhin a position paying 3,000 r.

Katerina Ivanovna goes to the gentleman who had crushed. Scene. Throws 10 rubles into his mug and goes out on the street.

N.B. Whatever I've been, whatever I might do later—whether I would be a benefactor of mankind or someone who would like a spider suck out its vital fluids—that's my affair. I know that I want to wield power over others and that's enough.

January 2, 1866*
Notes for the Novel
Characteristics

1.

Razumikhin

Razumikhin has a very strong nature, and as often happens with such strong natures he submits completely to Dunia. (N.B. This trait, too, is often met among people, who though most noble and generous, are rough carousers and have seen much dirt: he for example sort of humbles himself before a woman, especially if that woman is refined, proud, and beautiful.) At first Razumikhin became the slave of Dunia, (an efficient young man as the mother called him); he humbled himself before her. The thought alone that she might be his wife seemed to him at first appalling, and yet he was hopelessly in love with her from the first night that he saw her. When she let him know that she might possibly be his wife, he almost went out of his mind (scene). Although he loves her terribly, even though he is wilful and audacious to the point of doing crazy things; and despite the fact that he is her fiancé, he always trembled before her and was afraid of her. Even though she loved him, she was spoiled, conceited, and dreamy, and at times sort of disdained him. He didn't dare talk with her. And therefore from the very first he conceived a hatred for Sonia, because Dunia also had conceived a hatred for her and had insulted her. (He went far) and because of

* This entry was being written at the time the first instalment of *Crime and Punishment* had begun to appear in *The Russian Messenger.* The novel was serialized from January, 1866, to December, 1866.

2-го Января 1866 год.

Замѣтки къ роману.

Характеристики.

1

Разумихинъ

Разумихинъ, очень сильная натура и, какъ часто случается съ сильными натурами, весь подчиняется Авд. Ром. (А. Ещё и та черта, которая часто встрѣчается у людей, хоть и благороднѣйшихъ и великодушныхъ, но грубыхъ буяновъ, много грѣшившихъ, бабниковъ — что н. прим. онъ самъ себя какъ-то принижаетъ передъ чистой женщиной, особенно если эта женщина изящна, горда и красавица). — Разумихинъ сначала сталъ рабомъ Дуни, (расторопность молодого человѣка, какъ нянька по матери); унижался передъ нею. Одно лишь, что онъ [illegible] [illegible]

This manuscript page corresponds to pp. 189–91, beginning with the date "January 2, 1866" and ending with the words "But when he learned that Dunia had visited Sonia . . ." This is a thoroughly clean and regular page, corresponding to the neatness and unity of the sketch Dostoevsky draws of Razumikhin.

this quarreled with him.* But later (beginning with the second half of the novel) having understood who Sonia really was, he suddenly went over to her side, and kicked up a terrible row in front of Dunia, quarreled with her, and went on a spree. But when he learned that Dunia had visited Sonia, etc. (and when he himself could not bear his own despair) Dunia found him and saved him. She's begun to respect him more now for his character. In brief, Razumikhin's character.

N.B. Razumikhin took to drink; she herself came to him, to the drunkard. No, young lady, I don't want to. And later, when she fell at his feet. She laughs in delight:

"What a fine guy you are. And you're not going to drink."

"I will."

"What a little devil you are, you are worth 15,000 to me now, you know."

"I'm going to bite your little finger." He bites it very hard.

3rd character

Pyotr Petrovich—Luzhin.

~~Vain and in love with himself to the point of coquettishness, petty, and possessed of a passion for gossip. With heart and soul he became Sonia's enemy to spite Raskolnikov, solely because Raskolnikov had said that he's not worth her little finger, and talked with fervor about her *heroism*. Luzhin laughed then at this heroism and therefore conceived a hatred for Sonia, a bitter personal hatred and even entered into a pact with Lebeziatnikov to humble Sonia.~~

He constantly considers Raskolnikov his worst enemy. He is so taken up with this enmity that he even neglects his affairs.

He gets close to Reisler and menaces Sonia. N.B. But Luzhin is a man who had come from the seminarists, from a low class, and from routine life. Nevertheless, he's not an ordinary person. Despite himself he is forced all the same to notice the fine qualities of Sonia; and suddenly he falls in love with her and becomes hopelessly attracted to her. (Tragedy)

~~He makes friends with the inspector in order to do harm to Raskolnikov. Slander, Reisler~~.

~~N.B. He fell in love with Dunia because she was beautiful and proud, and his vanity was flattered that he could say, look what a~~

* The reference is apparently to Raskolnikov.

~~wife I have. 2) It was flattering to him, to the point of exquisite pleasure, that he could say, look, I hold power and tyrannize over such a beautiful, proud, virtuous, and strong character.~~

~~N.B. *He's stingy*. There's something of Pushkin's avaricious baron* in him. He has dedicated himself to money because everything else perishes but money endures; I am from a low class and I want absolutely to be at the top of the ladder and hold power. If I don't have the talent, know the right people, etc., I will still have money, and therefore I will dedicate myself to money.~~

Svidrigaylov and Dunia

The sound of a key.

Svidrigaylov: Listen Avdotia Romanovna, even if something were to happen (that is, this is only a supposition: It won't, let's assume, happen for anything in the world), the door is locked and I've taken care of everything. [The cries will not be heard and I'm three times as strong as you.] And then: Yes, most assuredly it will happen: can it be you haven't understood?

N.B. The pistol is aimed.

Svidrigaylov. "You are destroying your brother, Avdotia Romanovna."

"On the contrary, if I shoot you."

In order to hold power:

When they show Raskolnikov that in order to get power he must do so many base things that later he will not be able to make up for them, he answers [with sarcasm],

"Well, one need afterward only to do more good and then add it all up, and perhaps it'll turn out that there is more good." And then getting angry: "I don't have to do any good. I'll do it for myself, for myself alone."

(Important point, no issue)

Svidrigaylov. "Everything on earth is a lie [and besides] that's the way it ought to be."

Raskolnikov to Svidrigaylov. "What kind of impression does Sonia, etc., make on you."

Svidrigaylov. "The impression of the beautiful and deceived, and because of that rather sad (boring)."

---

* A reference to Pushkin's play *The Covetous Knight*.

Svidrigaylov.

Our democrats are insufficiently democratic.

(Freedom with a crown in one's hand. The democrats are not standing up for the people.

Seminarism in Russia, an important thing, seminarism.

Svidrigaylov to Raskolnikov. "What do moral questions have to do with the matter? (decided and did it, that is, he killed)."

"And if it's impossible otherwise?"

"Well then, don't do it."

"The peasant butchers and has no remorse."

"But the peasant is a different matter; that's true."

Raskolnikov understood with some difficulty.

"How is it that you could come to me?" asked Raskolnikov.

Before his death after the incident of the money she gave, here is Ark. Iv. in order to cheer up V.

"But didn't you kill her?"

"You think that I killed her?"

"What's the matter with you?"

"No you know it's natural, but apoplexy and anatomy were all."

N.B. Svidrigaylov in the hotel at night looks through the door and sees an officer with a whore. [N.B. Among other things the thought came to him: how could he a little while ago, talking to Raskolnikov, speak of Dunechka with veritable fervor, compare her with the martyrs of the first centuries, advise her brother to guard her in Petersburg, and at the same time know for sure that in no more than *an hour* he was preparing [to rape Dunia], trample on all that heavenly purity with his feet, and catch fire with lust from that holy indignant look of the martyr: What a strange, almost unbelievable doubling. And yet that's the way it was; he was capable of that.]

He happened to remember that an hour before the rape he had intrusted Dunia to Razumikhin. Yes, actually I did that perhaps from lust. What a scoundrel Raskolnikov is! He had seen through it and had not believed. He'll be like that all his life: seeing through it and not believing.

Ugh, what have I said! Every man penetrates into his life like cracking a nut, and won't believe what he has in his mouth. How empty words at times become significant.

N.B. Svidrigaylov in a tavern talked a lot with Raskolnikov (about his corrupt adventures), but it is impossible to recount this. He wasn't embarrassed by anything and even revealed things with *delight.* You pleased me because your situation was so fantastic, and he hints directly that he committed the murder.

Svidrigaylov (continuation)

Very often (in passing) he gives forth with extremely significant reflections about certain subjects (literature, etc.), but without interest, surprise, or emphasis; he is not even interested in his own opinions.

N.B. *His thought about the appearance of spirits.* He says that ghosts appear only when a person is ill, consequently an absurdity. An incorrect logical opinion: why not say that they *can only* appear in (. . .) an inorganic state and we come in contact with them only when our organism begins to be destroyed. And the fact that ghosts do not appear to healthy people is understandable: nature herself stands in opposition to ghosts, because for order and fulness [of life], and most [of all] for order, it's necessary that we live one life and not two (after two rabbits), so that nature itself defends and guards itself [against the other world, that is, against ghosts]. As soon as our organism breaks down a bit, we become capable of coming in contact with ghosts [and with other worlds]. So that it is true that the appearance of ghosts is a sign of a sick organism, from which, however, it is completely impossible to conclude that ghosts do not exist.

[He had therefore thought about this before.]

Svidrigaylov. If I were a socialist, I would certainly continue to live, because I would have something to do. No people have more conviction [than the socialists. And the chief thing in life is after all conviction]. Try to shake his convictions. He'll feel that he's losing the very stuff of life. For him the important thing is conviction. What does the conviction consist of? The chief thought of socialism is *mechanism.* Man in socialism becomes a man mechanically. There are rules for everything. Man becomes a stranger to himself. The living soul is cut away. It's clear that one can be peaceful—a veritable Chinese spirit, and these gentlemen call themselves progressive! Lord, if that's progress what is the Chinese spirit then?

N.B. Do you believe in the future?

Much skepticism.

Socialism—that's the despair of ever creating a real man; hence they create despotism and say that it is freedom!

And so that he not think too much of himself, they like terribly the opinion that man is only a mechanism.

"What is time? Time doesn't exist; time is numbers; time is the relationship of existence to non-existence."

Dunia shoots at him; how beautiful she is, however, thought Svidrigaylov.

The symbol of faith, "He lied even about the sense."

N.B. *Svidrigaylov.*

The ghost of Marfa Petrovna.

N.B. An *unoccupied* man (all his life he was lazy, did nothing).

There was an age; good eating.

N.B.—Like a crawling reptile. (He even frightens one by unexpectedly showing such a strong imagination and expressing so many questions nesting in him.)

What, you don't believe in anything better, more just?

But that will be perhaps just, (like a crawling reptile). [You have a vivid imagination; only science has been invented; but it's not only a question of that.]

Her breath smelled bad (she was holding a piece of cinnamon). An observation made in passing, only *once.*

Svidrigaylov, knowing the secret, never revealed it, and strange: he sort of respected Raskolnikov for that.

As a thought the rape appeared suddenly, but it became tied to Avdotia Romanovna completely by association with another idea.

He arrived in Petersburg in love with Dunia, and it turns out that he is not so completely in love (sees this himself).

Nevertheless, he ends up being in love.

[very frank]

But why act differently then?

Why not be frank? I'm not trying to gain anything. And besides if need be I can make a fool of people.

You seem to be bragging about that.

And you, wouldn't you brag about it?

Raskolnikov. Murder—hung on the gate. Svidrigaylov. No, that's not true, but something is crying out. Blood is calling. Raskolnikov.

I myself also thought. *Svidrigaylov.* What were you saying a little while ago about the gate: Raskolnikov. I spoke about it thus.

Svidrigaylov. I know that you spoke about it that way.

Svidrigaylov says: (I know a German woman who drowned her daughter), but he doesn't say that it is his landlady. He tells about it as an example of insensitivity and of a gratuitous ability to control one's self. (N.B. Many [similar] anecdotes and episodes from the past and present life of Svidrigaylov.)

[He says about the landlady that the daughter was raped and drowned, but he doesn't say who did it. Later it becomes clear that it was he.]

N.B. He flogged her to death; the spirit appeared.

Svidrigaylov says half-laughing: You'll be Providence itself, for example, for poor orphans. Doesn't that tempt you? In the presence of children, the aunt, Marfa Petrovna, left a will.

"Well, what Razumikhin? I don't find anything in it."

Svidrigaylov does not show further that he knows that he was the murderer and suddenly he says, "[Don't worry I've known many affairs of that kind. I myself have a part in some.]"

Marfa Petrovna died a week before their departure (immediately after the letter from his mother). She died in this way: Svidrigaylov lost control of himself and beat her (the first time in his life. He became frightfully angry that she was marrying Luzhin; he announced to Marfa Petrovna that he would go to Petersburg). Marfa Petrovna was upset, went off to sleep, didn't succeed in going off to town and gossip about her misery; toward evening she took a bath and died of a stroke. That's all.

[N.B. He relates comically with a cynical laughter how he beat her. Physical details—took hold of her nose and pinched it.]

Power. But power would not have tempted you. And justice. But that's an impossible thing. That's the way the whole world is constructed, matter and spirit.

There ought to be equality. Life comes from that.

On a canal near the Moyka* (. . .)

---

* A tributary of the Neva River.

Svidrigaylov tells how [he himself] naïvely. He is living at Reisler's. Why is he a rich man at her place? The answers he gives, though not evasive, are not complete; I don't want to meet people, don't want any of that society, etc. But the important thing is that he has a desire to keep in the background, to obliterate himself, to disappear in Hay Market Square, etc. Characteristic traits: 1) He relates how he was a cardsharp. Now he doesn't want to be one. 2) He relates that he was a good agronomist. 3) Relates without any twinge of conscience that at the time of serfdom he had whipped two men to death and took advantage of innocence. 4) That he doesn't drink wine [drinks rarely]. 5) Marfa Petrovna's ghostly appearances. 6) Wants to marry a 16-year-old. 7) Wants to give a lot of money to Dunia. (Refusal) 8) Gives money and takes care of the family of the deceased Mrs. Marmeladov. Unlimited gratitude of Sonia. 9) Hate of Luzhin, not much. 10) Love for Dunia: it turns out that he doesn't love her very much; he himself says so; he criticizes her to her face and laughs at her, which pleases her very much. But he insists on the marriage, but not very much. 11) He knows the secret of Raskolnikov, but doesn't speak of it to him.

[N.B. About the children and little beggar girls.]

[Raskolnikov meets him hunting. Description.] And he respects him for that, and admits it. 12) The rape is done accidentally. 13) Relates it suddenly as if by chance, and as if they were simple anecdotes like the one about Reisler. 14) About the rape of children, but dispassionately. N.B. (His anecdotes are terrible. He doesn't let things slip. Talks as if by accident. Extraordinarily agreeable and easy of disposition. Very indulgent. Appears to be cold, but is horrible. *Doesn't know what to do.* [wanted some kind of excess] Starts a conversation about one thing and then suddenly is ready to change the conversation. [But do you know that Petersburg is terrible? In Russia you still believe in something, you still hope for something, but in Petersburg. It's a city of seminarists and clerks.]

He offers money to Raskolnikov. He reasons cold-bloodedly about any project, for example, Raskolnikov's power. He believes in future life, in *spiders,* etc. He's not derisive, excuses everything and everybody. [Because he is cynical he rejects everything and allows everything]; he is strong, *moments of deep despair,* wanted to marry a 16-year-old. *He fell in love a bit with Sonia* and profited from her advice. He came to say goodbye to her before shooting himself, rather happy. N.B. (Came to him previously to say goodbye). N.B. Neither enthusiasm nor ideals. Not given to him to have a direction.

Without intending anything, he has Dunia come, and then suddenly by chance.

N.B. At times conversations with Sonia about beautiful ideals. He admits that he would be better with her. He speaks of this to Dunia and he praises Sonia; but afterward (judging himself by his bestial and animal tendencies) (16-year-old and the rape) he says that he is not capable.

N.B. *Most Important.* Svidrigaylov knows mysterious terrors about himself which he doesn't relate to anyone, but which are revealed by the facts: This is a convulsive and bestial need to tear apart and to kill, coldly passionate. Animal. Tiger.

He regrets the loss of poisons; he puts forth a theory about this in passing. N.B. If they refute him very strongly, he never defends himself very heatedly. He speaks of gambling, of roulette. In that way he puts forth his opinions by chance, extremely remarkable opinions. It's clear that he thinks. N.B. He said once very coldly (completely in passing) *that he had murdered* a man. That he happened once to murder. That happened to me once also; if you're going to be strict about it, *twice* (that's when he's revealing to Raskolnikov that he knows about it).

[Svidrigaylov says to Raskolnikov: "You didn't want to, so to speak, splinter it by analysis, but wanted a Synthesis."

"Yes, from such material Napoleons are made" (derisively).

Raskolnikov says to him: "Go on, go on."]

"And you know, I believe in the resurrecton of Lazarus" [*Svidrigaylov*].

Fear of the beautiful is the first sign of weakness.

It is impossible to live [only] the general life of humanity; nothing to do, civil feeling is not developed; the feeling of nationality is not developed.

"Well, does that man have a sense of nationalism?"

"What! He spent his whole life hunched over books. I'll tell you an interesting anecdote about that. *Symbol of faith.*

IX

Raskolnikov and Porfiry—Sonia and Raskolnikov's family—Raskolnikov's love for his mother and sister —His love for Sonia

Most of the fragments of this section, diversified as they are, have to do with Raskolnikov's relations with his family and with Porfiry. We have here Porfiry's interrogations of Raskolnikov, Raskolnikov's concern over the possible evidence that Porfiry has accumulated, the importance of Raskolnikov's discussion with Zametov in the restaurant in arousing Porfiry's suspicions, the various traps that Porfiry has set for Raskolnikov, and the surprise confession of the painter, here referred to simply as a worker. For the most part, the fragments—schematically put forth—correspond to the finished version. There are some interesting variations, such as reference to a dream that Raskolnikov has of killing the petit bourgeois (the artisan in the final version) who mysteriously accuses him of murder.

Dostoevsky's dramatic action is usually an analogue of the meaning he wishes to express. Often, at his very best, the organic unity of idea and action takes the form of a summary gesture which externalizes and unifies complex moral and psychological relationships. I am thinking of such gestures as Nastasya Fillipovna's throwing a hundred thousand rubles into the fire, Stavrogin's bearing of Shatov's slap, and the Elder Zosima's deep bow before the would-be murderer Dmitry. The notes for *Crime and Punishment* show us that he had a great deal of trouble in finding the correct analogue in action to the relationship he wanted to express between Raskolnikov and his mother.

In these notes Dostoevsky seemed to entertain the possibility of more extensive relations between Sonia and his family. The contacts are few in the novel: Sonia comes to Raskolnikov's room to invite him to Marmeladov's funeral when his mother and sister are there, and Raskolnikov takes a certain bold and possibly cruel pleasure in humiliating his mother's sense of propriety in inviting Sonia to sit down. In the notes, however, Raskolnikov's love for Sonia was meant to be a bone of contention between the family and Raskolnikov. The mother, Dunia, and Razumikhin (because of Dunia) are all at one point or another vigorously opposed to Raskolnikov's love for Sonia. In the novel itself Raskolnikov's mother worries a few times about his association with a prostitute, Dunia seems to have some sympathy, and Razumikhin does not seem to have any opinion at all. In the notes we get the following: "Mother, sister, and Razumikhin. Decisive quarrel about Sonia."

What Dostoevsky seemed to have planned at one point was some analogue on the level of action to the psychological drama underneath. It would make very good sense to have his mother oppose his love for Sonia on the dramatic level, because she is unalterably opposed to the love on the unconscious level—and perhaps to any love her son might have for someone else. Such interference would give us signs of her overt hostility to the relationship and to the love Raskolnikov needs most. The notes should dispel any doubt that Dostoevsky meant his love for Sonia to be the counterpoise to his love for his mother. Raskolnikov himself comes to the reluctant admission that he does not love his family: "I can't reach my family. How could I have loved them? It's as if now I didn't love my mother and sister. I know that I don't love them. It will be painful for me to embrace the woman that I'll love. Is that possible? If only she knew that she was embracing a murderer. She will know that. She ought to know that. She ought to be *like* me." Sonia, who is the woman he loves and who is like him, is contrasted sharply to the family: "Why have I attached myself to you? because you alone are mine; you are the only person who is left for me. The others, mother, sister; they are all strangers. We will never again be at one. If I don't tell them, then I will not go to them; and if I reveal everything to them, they will not come to me."

The struggle to liberate himself from the punishing, painful, unfree love imposed upon him by his mother and the struggle to accept the new love offered by Sonia are much more intense in the notes than in the novel. The notes are full of alternating feelings of hate, anger, shame, and repentance toward his mother, and feelings of anger and hatred and reconciliation toward Sonia. The following notes bear out this parallel struggle: "Coldness toward his mother." "When Dunia wasn't home, he came once to his mother in anguish, kissed her feet, cried, sobbed, and begged her without explaining anything." And about his relationship with Sonia: "At first, hatred for Sonia, and then reconciliation with her." The conflicting feelings toward both women are, of course, understandable, for it is difficult for Raskolnikov to give up one kind of love and to accept another. In a strange way Raskolnikov may have committed the murder, in part at least, to liberate himself from one love and to find the kind of unconditional love of the other. Even he, in the notes but not in the novel, recognizes that he did not do it to help his mother: "He is struck later during the whole novel by this thought: I wanted to make myself and my mother secure. There was no time to do it by German grubbing. I took the sin and the suffering on myself. Nevertheless, from the very first I couldn't do anything right; I didn't even know how to rob well, proof that this act was not meant for me, and that the whole affair was a false path. It was not a path to be followed." Raskolnikov recognizes that it was a "false path"; but he does not seem to recognize that the false path was also a distorted way back to the true path.

Nota Bene

For the Novel

1) He is struck later during the whole novel by this thought: I wanted to make myself and my mother secure. There was no time to do it by German grubbing. I took the sin and the suffering on myself. Nevertheless, from the very first I couldn't do anything right; I didn't even know how to rob well, proof that this act was not meant for me, and that the whole affair was a false path. It was not a path to be followed.

2) The chapter, Christ, (like Oblomov's Dream)* ends with a fire. After the fire he came to say goodbye to her. No, I'm not ready yet; I'm full of pride and falseness. I'm only beginning the whole process of transformation—in prison (7 years in prison, reduced by the highest of orders).

N.B. Svidrigaylov, having run away from Marfa Petrovna, arrives in Petersburg.

N.B. Zosimov and Porfiry Semenych cook up something.

(N.B. He testified for Raskolnikov against [Porf. Semen] suspicions.)

N.B. Sonia the next morning at his place. He doesn't ask why she came. At first a *dogmatic* conversation. He expresses himself in half phrases. Perhaps God doesn't exist. I'm sad, let's stop this conversation. About Katerina Ivanovna, that she went off. Dreams. *Sudden movement of Sonia;* she went up to him. Why did you do that? Tears. I love you—fervent conversation.

"Sonia, you ought not be in this situation."

Arrogant attitude *toward her about* this point.

N.B. DON'T: I LOVE YOU

[I'm sure that you spent all night praying to God. Silence.]

[N.B. For a long time he does not believe.]

N.B. *Sonia says:* how you talked yesterday, as if you had the power. Sonia goes to Katerina Ivanovna and says: don't take anything from him.

She came home and fell ill. Svidrigaylov is a neighbor. Becomes acquainted. Long conversations with Raskolnikov at the side of the sick girl. The death of Katerina Ivanovna.

N.B. He separates himself from his sister and mother so completely that he doesn't even interest himself in how they manage to live. (And not that he didn't suffer from that.)

N.B. His pride and arrogance and his self-assurance in his innocence continue to mount in crescendo and suddenly at the time of the most intense phase, after the fire, he goes to give himself up.

---

* From the novel *Oblomov* (1859) by I. A. Goncharov.

About his love for Sonia—say little; only give the facts.

Confession to Sonia that "I am myself a criminal." Done without any particular sensitivity.

N.B. Razumikhin in accompanying the mother says that he had just talked a terrible amount of foolishness (about the murder. It wasn't necessary to talk about that). N.B. The next morning Razumikhin, an ambassador from the mother, tells him, among other things, that he had lied a lot to him yesterday.

Razumikhin's thoughts finally come to ripen into the conviction that the idea has made him mad.

Porfiry heard about that; interrogation; he didn't find anything out, but the fact is that Raskolnikov denies that he is the murderer. ~~He's not the murderer then, he thinks.~~ Porfiry remains convinced that he is the murderer. Meeting during the storm; he sees Porfiry in a dream. N.B. Disgusting, humiliating, childish dream about how Porfiry is tracking him.

Razumikhin accompanies Zametov and *Porfiry*. Porfiry comes to get acquainted. Or this way: he comes to know Porfiry somewhere, without knowing that it is Porfiry.

(All the facts without reflections.)

N.B. Coldness toward his mother, which particularly astonishes them. The whole third part. Their uneasiness grows. Reconcile yourself with us. It's painful for him to be with them, doesn't go. At first, hatred for Sonia, and then reconciliation with her. At the moment of reconciliation, when his mother and sister are at Sonia's (a new apartment—Svidrigaylov gave up his), he appears to say goodbye to her. Lieutenant Gunpowder.

The characteristic trait of the third part.

Coldness toward his mother, which particularly surprises them. N.B. Don't forget the landlady. All the facts without reflection.

Third Part

Program

[1st Chapter] Several puzzling words, said by him immediately after the fainting. Come closer, let's have a look at you. Since I'm weak. (N.B. in a weak voice), and I must lie down and don't have time.

N.B. He says, straight to the point: Did you receive a letter from Luzhin? No, we only notified him of our arrival and [all] simply sat here. Good, I kicked him out. What? Without answering the exclamations: I don't accept the sacrifice, and the proposed marriage ought to be broken off. It's stupid. She's doing it for herself. It can't be and therefore sit down immediately and write out a refusal. But what right do you have? Listen, it's him or me! You have a night to think it over. Goodbye. Quarrel.

Razumikhin takes them aside and consoles them (show that Razumikhin is already in love with Dunia). Beat up.

[For God's sake, hurry to him. What's the matter with him now? You know I'll run off and see and return to tell you. (. . .) them for himself.]

[At his mother's] The mother is in despair. He relates how he hurt her formerly. Dunia, a bit haughtily, comes around. [Letter from Luzhin] Razumikhin promises that he will spend the night at his place, in that house. He spent the night at Nastasya's.

[2d Chapter] The morning at his place [don't come in the evening]. ~~Letter from Ly. Letter from Luzhin.~~ A talk with Razumikhin. At his mother's—advice. ~~Letter from Luzhin.~~ [Introduce me to Porfiry. I went there to pawn.][1, 2, 3]

Go to him. Sonia[4] comes to Raskolnikov, has her sit down. [Today is the funeral.] In the evening does not come.

[I'll come. I'll come for sure and on purpose.]

(Arrange the meeting with Porfiry and Svidrigaylov.) ~~He stops in on Mrs. Marmeladov~~ On leaving Mrs. Marmeladov, he parts with Sonia. Svidrigaylov eavesdropped[5] and heard the address. He goes after Sonia. And this is in my house. ~~In the evening at M.~~

[With Mrs. Marmeladov a boarding school for well-bred girls. Advice to go to the oppressor and to the general. The funeral meal.]

In the evening at his mother's, finished with Luzhin. I can't work; ~~I need capital, says Raskolnikov.~~[6] Plan to live; Uncle. ~~I can't do anything, I can't work~~.[7]

---

[1] I pawned things at the old lady's.

[2] He doesn't want to lose his father's watch.

[3] He's summoned to see Porfiry.

[4] N.B. A skeptical conversation with Sonia.

[5] Svidrigaylov with Raskolnikov. (. . .) reward with money.

[6] One thousand rubles for Razumikhin, and if it turns out well, I will get it. Why are you so gloomy!

[7] Death of Marfa Petrovna. I suspect that Svidrigaylov is here.

At Mrs. Marmeladov's. Funeral. Dinner. Landlady. [Porfiry and Zametov. Pawner. And why were you in the apartment? *Svidrigaylov*] Conversations.[8] Advice. They summon Sonia to Luzhin's. She stole. Lebeziatnikov flatters and then repudiates. Mrs. Marmeladov is in a rage; he goes to Sonia and tells her that he is the murderer. Svidrigaylov listens in. 2) Mother, sister, and Razumikhin. Decisive quarrel about Sonia. Visit of Svidrigaylov to Raskolnikov. An unusual conversation. Sonia at his place. Puts Katerina Ivanovna on her guard. [Perhaps there's no God; bows to him.] They didn't give anything to Katerina Ivanovna. Sonia's sickness. The sick girl at night in order to get money for Katerina Ivanovna. Katerina Ivanovna learns that Sonia is sick. The madness of Katerina Ivanovna. Sonia runs into the apartment; they go out onto the street. Madness and death. Svidrigaylov appears in passing and promises Sonia help. Sonia's sickness.

He goes to Zametov and announces that he too has things pawned there. Goes to the police station. A worker gives himself up. Scene of interrogation. And why were you in the apartment?

[Svidrigaylov at Sonia's place.]

[Sonia at Raskolnikov's; why did you do it; Svidrigaylov comes in to see Sonia.]

[Isn't it after the scene with Sonia that suddenly Svidrigaylov, and then Porfiry. He (with Zametov and Raskolnikov) lies in the presence of Sonia and Svidrigaylov.]

N.B. 4th Part. Svidrigaylov. Conversations with Sonia. His despair. Porfiry tracks him, rejects his mother.

In the Fifth: the storm.

They became acquainted at Porfiry's. A conversation about the quarrel they had at the evening gathering. Tries to get at his thoughts; Raskolnikov guesses. He was in good form. About the workman. About various topics. About the murder, about the *power* of being in a rut and *exceptions,* etc. He goes out and laughs. (To Razumikhin: You know he was interrogating me) [and suddenly]. The petit bourgeois testified that someone had come. But it was me.

N.B. In a conversation with Sonia: I don't want good for them; I didn't do it for good but for power.

But you are doing good.

I want power; in order to do good, you need power first of all. Is it

[8] He talks also of the murder of the old woman.

good that you walk around the streets like that? Polechka also will do the same thing. I don't want to pass by and remain silent . . . A law is necessary for everyone, but not for the chosen few. Suffering for sin. [A bitter, bilious conversation without expressing everything, that is, sort of *reluctantly*.]

Nota bene (important). The petit bourgeois had testified to Porfiry (two days after) that he had been in the apartment of the murdered woman the day before. Nevertheless, Zametov told him about the conversation and the scene in the Crystal Palace and showed enthusiasm for Raskolnikov. He also told of the irritable state of Raskolnikov, etc. That weakened the denouncement. Then they learned of the death of Marmeladov and of Raskolnikov's role there. That weakened the denouncement even more. But doubts remain and Porfiry doesn't know what to do when suddenly Raskolnikov himself comes in. Testimony of the workman. Porfiry talks to Raskolnikov about the quarrel at Razumikhin's. Raskolnikov's decision. Why did you go to see the petit bourgeois? I swear I don't know. But admit that you wanted to examine me. An ambiguous and cold parting.

(N.B. More skilfully)

N.B. On awakening the next morning [after the meeting with his mother] Raskolnikov realizes that he had said a lot of stupid things and had let things slip the night before; the conversation with Zametov turned to his favor, but the fact that he had been in the old woman's apartment might become known because he had given his name. All that had to be made right then.

The worker's testimony confuses and stops Porfiry for a time. I killed with their own ax [and the pawned object?]. There really was an ax in the kitchen. Only the ax was found lying in its usual place. I wiped it and put it back.

N.B. Why were you in that apartment? Porfiry's question was put forth in the presence of Sonia, of Svidrigaylov (who on coming in quickly made the acquaintance of Sonia and kept her from going). Just as she wanted to leave, Porfiry and Zametov came in; Zametov knew her and stopped with Razumikhin.

Zametov began to ask questions about Mrs. Marmeladov. She remained. (The whole conversation with Porfiry, etc.) The others left. Porfiry's suspicions melt away. (Raskolnikov, in answer to the question: why were you in the apartment, answered that he could hardly remember; Zosimov was there also. After the conversation with Zametov in the Crystal Palace, in the Crystal Palace, it seemed to him suddenly that he had lost his watch. Then he turned suddenly to

Zosimov and began to describe the psychology of this situation, and left in good shape.) When everyone had gone off, Sonia got up.

(N.B. Even though Raskolnikov had not explained the theme of the conversation with Zametov, he was sure that Porfiry knew it.) (N.B. Razumikhin announced to Raskolnikov in the morning that Porfiry knew that he was in the old woman's apartment. Razumikhin came earlier than they and was quite astonished by their arrival, and they in meeting him. How is it that you said that you would not go there, that you had things to do at home? Raskolnikov saw immediately the *qui pro quo** and assumed a very ironical air.)

N.B.??? How to do it more properly [and fittingly] that Porfiry himself comes to Raskolnikov. There has to be an incident, a pretext, so that Porfiry would take hold of the pretext readily to visit Raskolnikov.

Raskolnikov went to see Porfiry on the eve but didn't find him at home.

Suddenly, turning pale she said [whispered to him]: "That's terrible, it's unfair, no that's horrible," and she went off to Katerina Ivanovna. Then he turned to Svidrigaylov: "Well, what do you want?" Conversation with Svidrigaylov. Enigmatic allusions of his. (He went to Sonia; she wasn't at home; roams about at night, finds her on the street. She, to earn something.)

Nevertheless, Sonia came to Katerina Ivanovna: "Don't take anything!" And she tells how she went here and there and wants to go to Raskolnikov: Sonia says to her: "Don't go to him."

Mrs. Marmeladov starts to go out of her mind. Sonia runs out on the street to earn something. Her night. (meeting: *Ich mache ein Kreutz.*)** Meeting with Raskolnikov; runs away from him; he catches up with her. A few words; she is in despair. Meeting with Katerina Ivanovna; scene on the street. Death.

[Went to see his mother, [wanted to be good and was very bad], sad. I can't, don't want to; leave me.

"One has to be on top!" despotic and sharp words; goes away from them.]

---

* See note on p. 179.

** German: "I make the sign of the cross."

[Young girl who gave herself for 10 rubles; Svidrigaylov's story (and drowned herself).]

Katerina Ivanovna at Sonia's. (Katerina Ivanovna tells them everything about the boarding school [madness] and *ne parlez pas russe.** [Coughs.] And dances and everything.)

Svidrigaylov gives money. He goes to Sonia's.

"Well, then, I'll start a boarding school for well-bred young ladies."

She seized a stone and *threw it* into the window and ran away.

They bought shoes for the funeral. They can't walk with bare feet?

I'll mend the boots with thread and blacken them with ink.

N.B. His mother to him: "Make .peace with us; you look so strange."

"What do you mean I look strange! I look as I ought to look. Don't talk to me about the way I look. Don't ask me about my health. Nothing is more unpleasant than questions about the way one looks and about one's health."

N.B. Razumikhin says that Zametov whispered to him that there had been an official testimony that Raskolnikov was in the apartment. But Porfiry hasn't said a word about that to me. A very cunning fellow.

N.B. Razumikhin to him: "Rod'ka. Do you believe in presentiments? Well, I believe in them. Why was I drawn to make friends with you?"

I am doubtlessly [in love].[9]

N.B. Dunia comes to him alone with an explanation. You are frightening your mother; you have tormented her. His answer is frightfully fantastic, mad. I can't do anything with you. Marry him.

N.B. Since he was making his mother and Dunia uneasy, had

---

* French: "Don't speak Russian."

[9] [The children on seeing Sonia rushed to her yelling.]

chased Razumikhin away, and had given them up altogether, they started to urge him to go to Sonia's and the mother went to Sonia. Dunia got angry because of this, (but then ~~Mother~~ she also went). Then Svidrigaylov made up to her. Scene. Brute force. Saving from the rape. And then the fire. He saves. He says goodbye to everyone and then gives himself up.

N.B. Don't forget the landlady.

N.B. Very Important:

N.B. Must not forget that on the next day Razumikhin is completely serious and sparse with words for many reasons. 1) Dunia and yesterday's memories 2) Luzhin, and instead of "I'll crush Luzhin" decent relations both with Dunia and with Luzhin.

3) He is extremely worried by the fact that yesterday, while drunk, he let out to Raskolnikov that he was suspected of the murder.

4) Whispered (and enigmatic) words of Razumikhin to Raskolnikov about his presentiments.

and finally:

N.B. Raskolnikov remembers in the morning that he had said many foolish things and had given them an important clue [(had visited the apartment)]. He speaks to Razumikhin about the watch and the small ring. Razumikhin goes to see Porfiry. The interrogation is extremely polite; (like two good friends) (they speak of various questions taken up at Razumikhin's and about routine and the chosen few). Raskolnikov guesses that Porfiry knows about the conversation he had with Zametov in the inn and considers the conversation important. He jokes back and forth; but, nevertheless, he takes down his testimony [seriously] on paper. But even though he knows about the conversation with Zametov, and lets him know that he knows, he doesn't speak about it. In the third part the worker has not yet confessed, but only at the very end of the third part.

The petit bourgeois gives testimony of Raskolnikov's visit to the building at the end of the third part, so that the reader will sense that this will be important in the fourth part.

N.B.

(In the fourth part)

In the fourth part Raskolnikov is searched; they subject him to a serious interrogation (they decide not to arrest him).

N.B.

She stole

Luzhin asks Lebeziatnikov to call Sonia, gives her 10 rubles and quietly shoves a *serie** in her pocket. Lebeziatnikov sees [that he had sort of slipped something in] [stole the *serie*]. As an honest man Lebeziatnikov repudiates him.

N.B. Razumikhin in the second chapter yells to him [to Raskolnikov].

If you yourself say that she is marrying simply because of you, then how can you talk to her in that way? You are a despot and tormentor. It's not my affair, of course. Yesterday, I was drunk and I lied, and today I decided to remain quiet because I'm ashamed, but I can't be quiet.

N.B. Razumikhin talks to the ladies about Luzhin with extraordinary respect the next day and treats Luzhin well. He understood that it was impolite of him to dress down Luzhin yesterday, because he himself was in love, and consequently Luzhin was a rival to him. N.B. Dunia begs Razumikhin especially to come to tea in the evening in order to make clear to Luzhin that Razumikhin (Dm. Fyodor) had helped them greatly when they first came and without him they would have been completely lost . . .

"I couldn't meet you," remarked Luzhin.

Arrogant words of Raskolnikov when they kicked out Luzhin. People are pigmies; one has to dominate them. In your place, Dunia, I would not, of course, to reach my goal, stop myself from marrying a wealthy man, but you must not, and Luzhin isn't worth it. The sister is astonished by these thoughts. [Dunia contradicted him; how you've changed Rodia!] He doesn't deign to give any explanation.[10] Yes, the translations are fine. That's the first step. They will provide the first piece of bread, miserable, but still bread.

N.B. (A precious question)

N.B. During the questioning by Porfiry he asks in passing: "When you were going up the stairs, didn't you notice the painters in the apartment?"

---

* A redeemable note.

[10] N.B. I judged completely incorrectly, Dunia. Marry, take the wealth and hold power.

"Yes, I" (something transfixed Raskolnikov) "None, all the apartments were closed. Furniture was being carried out of one upstairs."[11]

"But that wasn't then," yelled Razumikhin. "The painters were there on the day of the murder."

"Oh, yes! Excuse me. No, I asked because no one had seen them, and that poor painter."

Raskolnikov understood that he wanted to confuse him.

Razumikhin became surprised and then furious.

FUNDAMENTAL N.B.

Such an order:

1) First Porfiry interrogates about trifles.
2) Then the accusation of the petit bourgeois. Porfiry makes an arrest.
3) He is under arrest. Love of Dunia and Razumikhin. Svidrigaylov's attempted rape. Dunia learns about it, visit to Sonia.
4) The petit bourgeois gives testimony against himself. He studied the circumstances. At first he gets confused and then he corrects himself.
5) Nevertheless they busy themselves in helping Raskolnikov. They release him from the inquest.
   (N.B. Can that be done?)

N.B.

N.B. Raskolnikov about the dead landlady's daughter: She was such a sick girl, and liked to give to beggars (she was so humble, so meek; she used to dream of a convent, and once she broke out in tears when she was telling me about it). To tell the truth, I don't know why I loved her, because she was sick, it seems. Truly, if she were a cripple or hunchbacked, I would have loved her even more, it seems. It was such a spring madness [no, it was not spring madness].

"She wasn't bad looking?"

"No, you know, is anyone in their youth bad looking? But the devil with this."

---

[11] "Well, I remember only that they had blocked."

"Blocked what?"

"The soldiers. . ."

"And so you knew then already that the apartment across the way would be empty. . ."

"Yes, I learned about it then."

"Ah, I mentioned this to no purpose. I put my foot in it."

N.B. N.B. Mention this only once again.

N.B. He has a small portrait in an ivory setting of his fiancé (Zarnitsina).[12] He kissed it before going to prison.

N.B.

Don't forget:

N.B. *His mother to him:* we haven't even had time to talk to you. I have to. I have to get to know you after all these years. You are my . . . Why do you withdraw? . . .[13, 14, 15]

N.B.

February 23. [When did I go there?] Two days before the death, it seems that I was . . . That's why it so struck you.

"Yes, but worry about that is purely egoistical. The point is that even though the watch is not worth anything, it belonged to my father and I wouldn't want to lose it. Besides that, Dunia's little ring . . . I admit that I was so busy, and"

"You raved in your fever about little chains, rings, and bracelets."

Raskolnikov smiled; "I'll say it then more simply."

Razumikhin left.

Raskolnikov is alone: he would perhaps let himself be crucified for me, he thought; but he is awfully glad that the reason I raved about chains and rings in my sleep has been cleared up. Hasn't that thought crept into him despite the fact that he pulled Zametov by his hair [for me]? For all I know! (And he turned to Sonia. They left.)

N.B. About the watch—they went to see Porfiry and Porfiry, Zametov. Razumikhin: Aren't you acquainted? Zametov became embarrassed. Porfiry says that this is surely high society. Raskolnikov gets irritated. You'll do it then tomorrow officially. I'll send you a

---

[12] He gives it to Sonia; she predicted your arrival to me.

[13] "I understand that," said Dunia. "You you are different and unusual, brother. You're not like us."

"Do you think so?" Raskolnikov asked.

"The devil take it, Dunia, I ought to beg your forgiveness, yesterday. . ."

"But I remain with the same intentions."

"But I know that," she said.

[14] Dunia: "The matter ought to be decided with one stroke."

[15] "Leave it, I'm finished with all that, it's as if it happened in another world."

summons. These are trifles. No, you can be a witness. Take this worker; incidentally, you haven't seen . . . Mamonov? etc.[16]

N.B. When Raskolnikov started to talk about the watch, Razumikhin began quickly to explain himself. Ugh, what nonsense!

But at Porfiry's Raskolnikov tells frankly about Il'ya Petrovich's* question.

N.B. Fine, it seems! he says when he came out. Overcome!

N.B. Psychological trait.

N.B. He's with his mother, or somewhere, or walking along the street, and suddenly he throws up everything, runs home to the corner, the wallpaper, the hole: had he left something there, hadn't he forgot some object when he took them out of the hole to throw them away?

About the petit bourgeois

He's afraid of the petit bourgeois. The bourgeois met him and yelled at him: "Murderer."

Dreams (wants to kill the petit bourgeois)

The petit bourgeois gives evidence almost on the eve of the arrest. Raskolnikov handles this masterfully.

[Porfiry judges the scene between Zametov and Raskolnikov in the inn:

"Why joke in that way. *Ne touchez pas à la hache.*]"**

Meeting with Kokh. (rather fantastic)

That was you then? But suppose he recognizes me by my voice? No, I didn't say anything, after all.

N.B.?

The next day after the conversation in the inn (*Palais de Cristal*) Zametov's thoughts change suddenly for the most trifling reasons, precisely when Raskolnikov spoke to him about the murder of the old woman, he became very serious, pale; his lips fluttered, and he trembled. But he doesn't say anything about this thought for a while yet.

---

* Lt. Gunpowder.

** French: "Don't touch the ax."

[16] Raskolnikov listened carefully to Razumikhin's question as to why Zametov was here. That irritated him.

N.B.

When he revealed everything to Sonia, he did not say to her at all: "Don't speak to anyone." She is struck by this thought: he thinks highly of her then. She feels somewhat better because of this.

He says to Sonia: "They're looking for me." She becomes frightened. "Why, you've just been begging me to give myself up?"

Answer. It's better to give one's self up. There's a difference. What kind? An important one? Sonia has the habit of saying something.

N.B.!!!

When Dunia wasn't home, *he came once to his mother* in anguish, kissed her feet, cried, sobbed, and begged her without explaining anything.

Luzhin at the evening gathering.

Explanation of these words: "You have transmitted."

I transmitted them as I understood them. I don't know how Rodia transmitted them. Perhaps he exaggerated something. He couldn't have exaggerated without your words.

"Pyotr Petrovich," said Pulkheriia Aleksandrovna with dignity. "The proof that we did not look at your words (only) from a very bad point of view and that we trusted you is that we are *here*."

"You said it very well, mother," Dunia remarked.

"I'm to blame for everything then," Luzhin said feeling insulted.[17]

1,000 rubles from Marfa Petrovna.

Marfa Petrovna's will. She didn't have time, but she declared it to Svidrigaylov, and he insists that they take it. Find out for yourselves; the whole town knows that she wanted to leave it to you.

N.B.

"Can't you see that I have to marry him, Rodia?"

Or in the evening she says to Luzhin: "You understand [know] that I must marry you now."

---

[17] ["And you gossiped about me in your letter?"

"Excuse me, sir, I fulfilled the request of your sister and mother, who, when I was leaving, not hoping to get away soon, asked me to send a letter quickly with an *account* of how I found you and what kind of *impression* you made on me. As for what I wrote in the letter, I challenge you to find even one unjust line—that is, that you did not spend the money, and that in this family, unfortunate to be sure, there weren't any unworthy persons."

"Who then?"

Unworthy persons. My little finger, etc.]

When Luzhin went away: "Mother, dear, I've decided to marry him. I decided a little while ago." But that was impossible; you saw it.

"How is that you didn't see it earlier?" the brother said.[18]

At his place

Zosimov.

"We haven't spoken of anything, Rodia. I've got so much to tell you."

"We'll have time, mother dear."[19]

Dunia looks: "Don't you really have any tender words for him as he leaves?"

N.B. "I'll come for sure," said Rodia.

"You must," said Dunia.

"Well, then, as you've decided that that's the way it'll be: I prefer it that way; I don't like to pretend and to lie, but he will tell the truth. Only, Dunia I'm still afraid . . . You know that?"

"And I, mother dear, am not afraid," said Dunia.

N.B. (Nastasya has reported) on your angel.

N.B. "I know the German [language] perfectly." N.B. With a reflective air.

["How is it that once you said that you don't know it?"]

"Ah, yes, [that's the truth, damn it] I did say that [then]. I lied. I know."

"And why did you [lie]?" (Dunechka)

"Well, you know."

"No, why?"

"Well, it's not worth talking about."

"No, no, no. Why?"

"Oh, my God, there's feminine curiosity for you; why do you have to know; we're talking business and you."

"Yes, I want to know under what circumstances you lie and under which you tell the truth."

---

18 Reason. Dunia aren't you ashamed? I saw Pyotr Petrovich [truly] only one time, but you're right. I'm ashamed."

19 ["Tell me how did you live all this time?"
"We'll manage to all have a chance to talk, mother dear, but it's impossible to do it all at once. . . Let's finish this first."]

"And you're interested."

"Yes."

"He did it," said Raskolnikov, "to convince me to take the translation and the money for it in advance, so that I would think on top of everything that I was doing him a favor and helping him by it."

"And you know, the worker confessed—in that station."

N.B. At the evening gathering at Luzhin's he suddenly stopped talking as if transfixed. He remembered that the petit bourgeois was from that building. (everything in the third part and the worker)

N.B. Nothing can happen to the worker, thought Raskolnikov. Sonia reminds him about the worker.

N.B. Raskolnikov follows the petit bourgeois more than once.

Fundamental and Most Important

Never was there a single word of love expressed between them. Sonia fell in love with him on the evening her father died; and what struck her from the very first was that in order to calm her, he said to her that he had committed a murder. Consequently, he respected her since he was not afraid of telling her everything. Although he did not say anything to her about love, he saw that he needed her as he needed air, as he needed everything—and that he loved her immeasurably.

(On the next day) he even said to her in conversation:

"I respect you."

"I know that. You wouldn't have come to me otherwise. That's why it seemed to me that I definitely had to come to you and be at your side."[20]

N.B. (The father, Marmeladov, had talked to her about meeting a learned student and told her much about him. Also Katerina Ivanovna).

N.B. Sonia read books. Lebeziatnikov gave them to her.

Nice touching stories of Sonia about how her father came to her and told her about how he had talked with a learned student.

---

[20] [Perhaps you and they (. . .)
No. Don't you understand that?
"How young that is, Rodia. . ."]

N.B. Fundamental

"What difference does it make to me what will happen?" (Raskolnikov let slip to Sonia) "Is it possible to live now (I can't pass by all those terrors, sufferings, and misfortunes cold-bloodedly. I want power)."

In the 3rd part.

"What did you gain in killing the old woman?"

"That was stupid," Raskolnikov said. "I didn't even have time to take the money. It wasn't even stupid, but an *urge*. What's important is that an idea came to maturity in all that."

"What idea?"

"Let's go together, etc."

Dunia in the fourth part.

"Brother, you need me!"

"Leave me alone."

"Will you come?"

"Yes."

Sonia in the 5th part.

"Do you have a cross?"

"Here's a cypress cross."

N.B. You've got to write officially to the police about your things; they'll take care of the form there. Nevertheless, he did not make out a request to the police.

N.B. Mother to Dunia: "He's affectionate with us, but it's as if: 'Leave me alone, please!' "

N.B.

N.B. Luzhin had promised Katerina Ivanovna to dig up a boarding school, but she got excited, and then: I'll go myself. She went there—they chase them away. [At Sonia's]

N.B. See Page N.B. 3

I kissed my mother a little while ago.

I can't reach my family. How could I have loved them? It's as if now I didn't love my mother and sister. I know that I don't love them. It will be painful for me to embrace the woman that I'll love. Is that possible? If only she knew that she was embracing a murderer. She will know that. She ought to know that. She ought to be *like* me.

The sum of evidence? What does it amount to? I'll get rid of all the evidence.

N.B.

This also, that Zametov did not mention anything (at Porfiry's) about yesterday's conversation at the Crystal Palace.

(The old woman is a bit of stupidity! I did something stupid.)

[How will I be able to talk about it; whom will I talk with? No, I didn't think of that.]

[N.B. Lizaveta? [Poor thing] Lizaveta! And why is it that I haven't thought of her a single time since then. It's as if I had not killed her. Killed her? How horrible that really is!]

18 N.B. A woman is always only what we ourselves want to make of her.

N.B. He had to think over his situation. They didn't give in the morning [and how could I kiss her [mother] a little while ago, he thought].

N.B. And I had the misfortune to quarrel with a thoroughly worthy man, a quarrel that broke up the marriage of my sister.

[A little while ago Dunechka bowed down to her. He was in ecstasy. And then, he forgot it. What? What?]

N.B. (Never, I must never *speak* with people.)

[Never talk to anyone, and don't communicate one's thoughts to anyone. Because that's not a conversation now. Can I really talk about anything sincerely?]

Alone at night.

How painful it is, however, for me to talk with people. Stupidities! Strange, I so loved them from afar, and yet close to them it's as if I don't love them.

Is it that all the love for them was over when they arrived [almost, almost]?

[It's good that they take me for a madman. God knows in what way the crime will be discovered. No, only a fool or a madman takes the risk of committing a crime. It's better really to commit legal crimes, that is, be an out-and-out scoundrel.]

[Yesterday's errors must be corrected. Today at Porfiry's I played the part of a prattler.

Accidentally and quite by chance.] [How *frank* Porfiry is.]

[N.B. They came into Porfiry's apartment with *such laughter.* But isn't such a point improbable?]

[Dunia is haughty; she didn't want to admit today that she's getting married for my sake, and yet she herself had already decided on breaking it up. But I found it pleasant a little while ago to make peace with her.]

[I don't like anything here; there's nothing especially noble; I'm a despot; I hate everyone.]

[How I detest the old woman, especially now, now after *that.* [I'll never forgive her.] *I can't forgive.* I would perhaps kill her again if she were to come back to life.]

[Porfiry to him: "Do you know Luzhin?"

N.B. (Absolutely—Luzhin's intrigue)]

N.B. I am surprised, Dunia, how you could really take this man to be honest after he basely slandered me in saying that I did not give it to Katerina Ivanovna.

N.B.

Porfiry. "And you know that would even be a clever trick on the part of the criminal," Raskolnikov said: "Admit the crime and then lie and get confused . . ."

"You really have some ideas!" Porfiry said. Zametov smiled [Porfiry] and suddenly when saying goodbye: "Do you know what I think, sort of looking at him in a special way, your ideas are extraordinarily witty, but here's what's wrong: all that would be fine if man were something like a machine or if, for example, he directed himself only by reason. Reason is a fine thing. Reason can think up such tricks that a poor inspector would never see through them. But, you know: nature will not hold out, and that consequently helps out. A man will lie magnificently [here an example is needed, but he suddenly] but suddenly he falls into a faint. He'll arrange everything beautifully and then will turn pale, or won't count the money.[21] You're a young man, and as usual with young people, you don't take nature seriously; you respect the mind alone . . . What's matter with

---

[21] [About the scene with Zametov in the inn. And he turns pale very naturally] [After seven o'clock he tripped me up very well, by chance; if not after seven o'clock, then at what time] [He's convinced; how sick I am of it all.]

you, are you sick, you're sort of pale a bit? No, don't worry, no don't worry," and he burst out laughing. Porfiry Petrovich himself began to laugh.

Zametov exchanged a glance, goodbye.

"Better to arrest me."

Porfiry looked at him without saying anything. "Well, then, I will and I'll do it even today."

Porfiry N.B. "Say, is the article in *The News* yours? Either learn or write?"

Most Important

Porfiry [Porfiry's] idea that there were a lot of criminals (among others, the worker) and Kokh and Pestriakov might have been in on it, and Raskolnikov even, and that the whole thing was a very cleverly played comedy.

N.B. Porfiry doesn't tell the visitors that the worker had confessed. [Porfiry interrogates.] N.B. About Marmeladov's money.

You'll never get a horse from a hundred rabbits; you'll never get evidence from a hundred suspicions.

(A judicial English proverb)

Porfiry. I studied law. Look at them. (Theory of the sick state of criminals.)

"Whoever is sick, is not called."

"What? called to commit a crime?"

(So I'm a prattler went through his thoughts, so I'm a mischief-maker, [all the same] in that way the suspicions will be dissipated.)

"Tell me, is that your article in *The News?*"

"It's mine. I've read it."

At Sonia's. Books. Not necessary.

At Luzhin's. They give him money, from Marfa Petrovna; he doesn't accept it.

[(Porfiry) lets slip that he knows that he gave some money to the Marmeladovs.]

Fundamental.

He to Sonia.

"Why have I attached myself to you? because you alone are mine; you are the only person who is left for me. The others, mother, sister; they are all strangers. We will never again be at one. If I don't tell them, then I will not go to them; and if I reveal everything to them, they will not come to me. But you and I are damned; therefore our road is the same, even though we look in different directions. [You are now my sovereign], my fate, life—everything. We are both *damned,* society's pariahs."

After Luzhin. Move in with us.

At Sonia's. "I was the murderer."
"Why did you tell me that?"
"Yes, I came on purpose to tell you that."

To himself N.B. And besides, am I not indifferent to everything? Let her marry whomever she wants. I've got to talk to someone . . .

At Sonia's. *Sonia.* "What should I do?"

"What must be done? Take and break something, but get out of this situation."

At Sonia's. "You yourself have given us everything," said Sonia.

Fundamental

At Porfiry's for the interrogation. When he came out of the special room where the petit bourgeois sat and walked past the worker, perhaps the first question Porfiry put to Nikolay was: "Do you know this gentleman?" He had brought me here for a silent confrontation.

N.B. No one to talk with.

Sunk in thought Porfiry stands at Lebeziatnikov's.

At the evening gathering. Luzhin. Marmeladov is such a sugary surname.

"Why is the name Raskolnikov any better?"

Mother: "Raskolnikov is a good name, even though your father was a teacher; the Raskolnikovs have been known for two hundred years."

After Luzhin leaves, he says: "I can't do anything for you."
"Let me go."
"Rodia, why are you acting this way?"

When the latter (Luzhin) has gone away, the mother says:

"Now, we ourselves are to blame because we have gone along with an unjust affair, and I myself am to blame."

And to Luzhin: "Do you think I'll let someone like Dunia marry you? You've got another thought coming."

"We are more to blame than you. We went along with something unjust, and most of all, I did."

"Good for you, mother dear."

Generally speaking, she distinguishes herself.

N.B. Lazarus. Arise and the dead man arose (a little before).

At his mother's for the evening N.B. Mother about Sonia: "How I did not know that she was simply that kind of woman? And how could you acquaint her with your sister, Rodia?"

X

Reflections on how the novel should end—Raskolnikov talks with Sonia about his motives—Raskolnikov gives himself up—Characterization of Svidrigaylov—Svidrigaylov tells Raskolnikov about his life and beliefs—Porfiry tracks down and interrogates Raskolnikov—Raskolnikov prepares to shoot himself

Most of the fragments in this section are concerned with the ending of the novel: Raskolnikov talks with Sonia about confessing and about his motives for the crime; he is convinced that he is right because he murdered only a louse. Porfiry interrogates Raskolnikov, reflects on the evidence he has, and on the psychological considerations that he is counting on. Raskolnikov goes to give himself up to Lt. Gunpowder. Svidrigaylov believes Raskolnikov will probably shoot himself and that he too will probably shoot himself. Indeed, the notes come to an end soon after the statement that Raskolnikov has gone off to shoot himself. The function of Sonia and Svidrigaylov as embodiments of the antithetical principles that Raskolnikov carries within him is made explicit in the last words of the notes:

Svidrigaylov is despair, the most cynical.

Sonia is hope, the most unrealizable.

[Raskolnikov himself should express this.]

He became passionately attached to both.

There are interesting variations of the final version, and some interesting first statements in the notes that follow. It is here, late in the notes, after the many discussions we have had of motives, that Raskolnikov first introduces explicitly—in a word or two—his theory of superior and inferior people. Dunia dresses down Luzhin for his despicable plans to arrange matters to have her and her mother entirely dependent on him. And there are fragments of dialogue that vary from what we find in the novel itself, such as the following between Sonia and Raskolnikov:

"What does happiness consist of?" asked Sonia.

"Happiness is Power," he said.

Much of the matter in this section concerns Svidrigaylov. We meet very little that is different from the final version. Svidrigaylov's theory of debauchery as a support in life, his smirking satisfaction with "charming escapades," and his general cynicism about ideals and love are the same. This in itself is significant, indicating, I suppose, that the character of Svidrigaylov gave Dostoevsky very little trouble and that the portrait of Svidrigaylov was conceived in one coherent piece. I think there is evidence to support such a supposition. We are given phrases or single sentences that express in compressed form what is developed into little scenes or stories in the final version. We get hints that become fully developed scenes in the final version, such as "Theory of how to possess a woman. Flatter; how base a woman is," which in the final version becomes a long story told by Svidrigaylov about how he once seduced a virtuous woman by convincing her of her virtue. Or "Story of the dancing class, about the young girl," which in the final version becomes a story about how he chanced upon a mother and a thirteen-year-old girl in a tavern they had mistaken for a dancing class. The dream of Svidrigaylov about the young girl who had apparently drowned because of the outrage he had perpetrated on her probably has its germ in the little remark "There was a coffin . . ." The complicated situation between Dunia and Svidrigaylov and Svidrigaylov's eccentric relations with his wife are first expressed in this sketchy form: "Marfa Petrovna permitted him to have servant girls, as long as he told her about them. But she became outraged about Dunechka."

One item is different, though. Although we have several mentions of Svidrigaylov's attempted rape of Dunia, we have no reference to his "good" moment, when with clenched teeth he permits Dunia to leave. As a matter of fact, we have virtually no reference at all to the good deeds that have baffled some of Svidrigaylov's interpreters: the release of Dunia, the five-year-old girl whom he takes care of in a dream, the money he leaves for his young fiancé. The decision to give Svidrigaylov some seeming good qualities apparently came late and was motivated by the perception that an amoral individual will do indifferently both good and evil acts. There is no reference either to the last night of Svidrigaylov, which he spends in an obscure hotel, infested with vermin, troubled by his dreams. In the notes after the attempted rape of Dunia fails, Svidrigaylov apparently spends a night in debauchery before killing himself. On the whole Dostoevsky seems satisfied with his plans for Svidrigaylov; after a sketchy outline of his last days and his death, Dostoevsky remarks in parentheses: "This will be magnificent!"

Dostoevsky has a hard time deciding how to bring the novel to an end. We know that he thought of having Raskolnikov shoot himself, and he thought of having him commit new crimes. Confession looms larger—to judge by the number of notes—than these, but he is uncertain how to bring about the confession. He has Raskolnikov confess to Razumikhin, to Sonia, and to his family. After he confesses to his family, Raskolnikov goes off on a binge: "Since everything is already known to the family [he tells everything for the first time]; he can't stand up to it. Delirium. In the delirium all kinds of sufferings and then *in the evening, prostitutes.*" On more than one occasion after confessing to Sonia, he runs away from her. Such reactions find expression in the novel in Raskolnikov's impulses of recoil after he confesses to Sonia. The death of Svidrigaylov was planned, in both notes and novel, to move Raskolnikov to give himself up. In the novel Svidrigaylov's death coincides with the moment that Raskolnikov decides to give himself up. In the notes we have the following: "After Dunia, Sonia and other judge him; when it is decided that he must give himself up, he runs away; vision; in the vision the death of Svidrigaylov." In both novel and notes, Raskolnikov does not understand why he must confess, for he insists in both versions on his right to kill a useless louse.

Despite the fact that Dostoevsky wants the sleuthing of Porfiry to turn up only blind alleys, he pursues to the very end a parallelism between Raskolnikov's decision to confess and Porfiry's tracking of him. Notes about Raskolnikov's giving himself up and notes on his resistance to the tracking by Porfiry alternate in this section. Indeed, while Raskolnikov is making his way up the steps—with Sonia and Dunia trailing him—to confess to Lt. Gunpowder, Dostoevsky pursues him with fragments of dialogue about Porfiry's interrogation of him:

Makes his way up the stairs. Confess to Gunpowder; look at the dog barking. Everything's the same as always, but soon everything will be different.

(N.B. Golgotha. He didn't see Sonia.)

[*Porfiry*. "I'm sure, I'm sure that you didn't take a single ruble of her money. Isn't it so! Isn't it so! It's in the garden, right?"]

Raskolnikov gives himself up when there is no longer any possibility of Porfiry's catching him. Svidrigaylov, who knows about the murder, dies, and Porfiry has confessed to him that he has no evidence. Perhaps Porfiry plays his trump card when he assures Raskolnikov that he is safe and will no longer be pursued, for Raskolnikov needs to be pursued and punished, although he never understands why he needs to be punished. Dostoevsky provides us with an explanation by manipulating his conversion in the epilogue, but the novel—and these notes—provide us with many other explanations. Significantly, there is no mention of a conversion in the notes.

Fundamental

N.B. Present Razumikhin as a ceaseless bustler. N.B. The Requiem Mass in the third part [in the whole] and the chatter about the appearance of Marfa Petrovna also.

N.B. He most definitely talks to his sister [when she found out] or generally speaks about two kinds of people: about those chosen for greatness and those who are not, and she is fired up by his teaching.

At the evening gathering: Luzhin about Svidrigaylov. Raskolnikov relates that he saw him.[1]

Most Fundamental

At the end of the evening. Let's part for a couple of days. Forgive me. Complete collapse of the will.

---

[1] [Luzhin, meanwhile, reproaches himself for having really sacrificed very little money for Dunechka.]

With Sonia. Sonia once said to him: "I don't understand how you will live, how you will be able to marry, and have children?"

"I'll get used to it," he answered.

About the others, that is, about the mother and Dunia in the beginning of the third part, and about their relations with Raskolnikov. Raskolnikov in this chapter. *Dunia has a serious conversation with him.* Svidrigaylov makes a declaration to her. She is with Sonia and Razumikhin at his place, conclave. The news of Svidrigaylov's death. He triumphs proudly over all at the gathering. Then since everything is already known to the family, [he tells everything *for the first time*]; he can't stand up to it. Delirium. In the delirium all kinds of sufferings and then *in the evening, prostitutes.*

At the gathering, the news that the man [worker] was religiously minded.

Lebeziatnikov.

"Yes, but she is a free woman."[2]

"You know you can call her (Sonia) to read books. That's the way she is."

"(I'm very sorry not to have a father. Self-supporting person. I imagine how I would do there.) I am developing her."

"Well, take advantage of her."

"No, you know she's refusing me. I see that. What's more, I look upon that as woman's most natural state."

Lazarus, arise.

"And be meek, be more humble and you will conquer the whole world. There is no more powerful sword than that."

"And I know that God will find you."

"I am a sinner. That was a great sin."

I am hard of heart, the collars.

Picture

Convicts pass by

Fundamental

He says to Sonia. "I don't want to wait. I want my human rights right now. I can't pass by without giving back all the money. I'm not

---

[2] "And yet you beat up Katerina Ivanovna."

"That was another matter. You have a right to defend yourself. And what's more, I won't permit anyone to treat me."

like the socialists. And besides I don't need anything; I want to have power over others. Look at me as a student in 10 years: mother, sister. You Sonia," (picture of her life and future) Well then live and wait.

Sonia: "Yes, but how is it possible to kill another for that."

"She's a louse." *"No, not a louse.* And if she's a louse why are you suffering so?" ""Well, it's arithmetic: whoever will prevail." "Perhaps you're not so strong." "Don't torment me with that nonsense. Don't you think I haven't thought this and suffered over it? Others do it, Napoleon, etc., and I want to. Listen: there are two kinds of people. Those who are superior can cross over obstacles."

"You're sick."

"Yes, I'm sick. They are troubling me. The family. I can't be with them. I'm fighting against prejudices. *I'll get used to it."*

Napoleon, Napoleon, but perhaps it's not that.

Not that

During the age of barons it meant nothing to hang a vassal from the entry gate. To kill one's brother also. Consequently, nature is subject also to various epochs.

All great people were happy. [Their sorrow and suffering was happiness.] They must have been happy. A great man can't be unhappy. And the fact that they crucified them on crosses meant nothing.

At Sonia's. Sonia, sit with me a little. I went off to play (memories of Sonia). Katerina Ivanovna's shirt cuffs. Katerina Ivanovna burst out crying. He felt grieved. Oh I'm for Katerina Ivanovna now . . . What a woman she is! What a woman!

With Luzhin. Dunia. It's true that I am guilty in being attracted too rapidly, but that's the same as being guilty for believing you to be a decent gentleman; you are not therefore in a position to reproach me to my face. And besides you and not I were the first to refuse. What do you mean in your letter: you have only yourself to blame. That's a threat; at the beginning of our acquaintanceship you didn't dare to act that way, I'll tell you why you feel you can act that way now: You saw that we were now in Petersburg and consequently completely in your power, and so you've thrown off your mask. You didn't even bother to meet us at the station because of some business at the senate, and yet we were two women at sea in Petersburg.

Spent much. What did you spend? The trunk. There really are people like that: every one of the kopecks they spend seems to them dearer than 100 rubles of someone else.

[Here is his test]
[But he didn't find her.]
"You walk the streets at night then?"
"One woman told me, *Ich mache* [*ein*] *Kreuz und ich gehe.*"*
"Break something!"
As if he were laughing at it, but he was not laughing at it . . .
"You walk the streets but there wasn't enough for the funeral."
"It's necessary then to bow down to them."
"You also are not rich. And not in the university. Must suffer it."
"Why suffer it. The Hollander."
"About Lizaveta. She used to give me work. Trade. Yes, she was murdered."
"She began to cry. Cry."[3]
N.B. And when he declared: "I killed; well you'll go on the streets for a crust of bread for them."
"Yes, I'll go, go. Go away. I'll give them my body." (In the evening she walks the streets.)

N.B. *The Most Important.*

At the first meeting, he tells her about the Dutch method and prepares her to understand the confession he made the day before.
[The next day at the interrogation Porfiry reminds him:
"You spoke yesterday about some kind of treasure under a stone."]
In Porfiry's office.
"Well, then did you write it out? Now only one (detail) bothers me: why was their blood in your apartment (etc.)"
"And why does that detail bother you?" (he trembled inside)
"Well . . . because," (and he looked at him).
"Well, you see," a matter-of-fact tirade.
About Porfiry.
The matter was clear for Raskolnikov: Another would perhaps have arrested him, but Porfiry (that's clear) had been studying him

---

* German: "I make the sign of the cross and I leave."

[3] He at Sonia's. He tells her about *Ich mache ein Kreuz* and about the prostitute with the baby. The mother with the children (is it possible that she'll become a prostitute) and these wonderful and innocent creatures which the Savior. . . and they too will become prostitutes.

But what am I supposed to do. Daddy, children, I'm a sinner; cries. She rushed after him: wait, wait! Where are you going? He didn't hear and went out. Oh my God! was heard on the stairs.

for a long time and is studying him, and he understood, of course, that if he arrested him, he would not learn anything new; but if he was free, he would quickly compromise himself. And beside he has his eye on him, has him under surveillance, and as for a search, why search him when he has left his door open on purpose ever since that day? The stone impressed Porfiry.

But what reasons does Porfiry have to suspect him so persistently? After all, there are no facts. Is it possible that only psychological considerations turned his head? But psychological considerations are double-edged. Or perhaps he's a physiognomist. No, there are no facts whatsoever.

Isn't it clear that they are tracking him in order to get facts in order to make certain a psychological suspicion, especially since they know that the birdie will definitely not fly away in any case. If only an occasion would present itself; they're waiting for an occasion.[4]

Fundamental

Everything has become confused. What's happened to the promise that "the spirit of the ages" will be with you [and that consequently humanity will not lose its way in its development] to the end of the world. Christ? He must then be somewhere!

Beginning of the 3rd Part.

It wasn't necessary to go there, to learn and ask. And Porfiry says: *You yourself are giving everything away*. A moth and a candle. Therefore he won't learn about the worker. *He lost heart*.

But the worker, the worker. What is the worker? He's either a madman or an idiot, or they frightened him and he wants to get it over as quickly as possible. It makes no difference whether they hand him . . . and as a matter of fact he's already hanged himself . . . The worker will look around and see the truth. But, nevertheless, the important thing is, the most important thing is that he will start suspecting me again. And without that . . . what does it matter to me that you are psychologically convinced. He knows Luzhin then. Hmm . . . it's true that he has already sent after deputies.*

---

* These are official witnesses at a search.

[4] [Razumikhin was at Porfiry's and told him a lot.]

At Sonia's. About Lebeziatnikov. *He:* But he's crazy; there are many who are more intelligent; don't judge by one . . .

Pulkheriia Aleksandrovna is angry (mother chicken).

He is my son; he must obey me.

(Dies, blesses him.)

[Dies] Ah, what a painful field life is, my children.

[At Katerina Ivanovna's] A toy cockerel was found in Marmeladov's pocket.

He came to say goodbye to Sonia.

[That's when she convinces him, that is, before saying goodbye.] Now, kiss the Bible, kiss it, now read.

[Lazarus come forth.]

[And later when Svidrigaylov gives her money]

"I myself [was] a dead Lazarus, but Christ resurrected me."

N.B. Sonia follows him to Golgotha, forty steps behind.

Fundamental

~~Why don't they groan?~~ Why is this humble girl unhappy, and I want to live? I ought not live [if she is unhappy] . . . happier than she!

N.B. After Dunia, Sonia and others judge him. When it is decided that he must give himself up, he runs away, vision; in the vision the death of Svidrigaylov.

Fundamental

[First time at Sonia's] He intentionally starts a conversation himself about Lizaveta.

[Why did fate so decide it? Did it fix the cards. Oh man!]

Death of Katerina Ivanovna.

"Your Ex-ex-excellency [protect the orphans]. You see, Semen Zakharich, you were the benefactor . . ."[5] (in delirium).

"She has beaten up her children. The children have run away from her, don't run away!"

---

[5] One can even say aristocratically.

[About her husband]. The poor man would look at me at times and I could never say a good word to him, (she speaks with respect about him).

N.B. At the funeral dinner Amalia Ivanovna tells a story about how a gentleman was robbed. (The story pierced one's heart.)

(With Sonia) "Why do I use the familiar pronoun form in talking to you, Sonia?"

"And why don't I use the same form?"

And later when he went to give himself up and she hung a cross on him, then [for the first time] she began to use the familiar pronoun form.

N.B. Katerina Ivanovna died:[6]

"Why should a louse live and take interest, and people like that die? Is that more fitting?"

(That poor fool, Amalia Ivanovna; she won't be paid after all!)

Tell Avdotia Romanovna, that the 10,000 that she didn't want to accept I'll designate for these *orphans* and for Sonia.

Porfiry: "[No you] Walk, walk a bit more!"

About the stone. Yes, that's really the way it appears in dreams. (You dream then about it and then such dreams become possible.)

"Why are you compromising yourself in that way."

The worker confesses. But the petit bourgeois doesn't give any testimony.

It's because of that that I thought.

[The petit bourgeois talks.]

And then they began to say at our place, [the caretaker] that Mikolka admitted the affair, and I didn't go because I was gloomy, sick at heart.

Thus he put me face to face with Nikolashka.

Porfiry to the petit bourgeois at the end of the novel.

"Why didn't you appear. It was evidence after all. I would have arrested him then, but now I'll be frank. Now it's impossible to

---

[6] The letter of honor on the public square. She died with the honorable letter, dry feet [Oh, man]. And Sonia? Svidrigaylov in the third part. In another part, that Svidrigaylov took the orphans.

arrest him. I've studied him: he [was] sick [then]; his conduct strange, almost mad and later all his mannerisms and his actions do not bear it out; they even contradict it. There is no proof. We did well. But still, I don't know."

Svidrigaylov to Raskolnikov, meeting him after the conversation at Sonia's.

But what's the matter? *Don't be afraid.* I didn't hear your conversation, you know.

At Porfiry's. But they really turned pale too easily. That came to me at night while sleeping.

"True it was natural."

"And it may be really that he's a monomaniac. You know how far those monomaniacs will go; they'll obstinately stick at a thing [he gave 25 rubles; gave 20 and kept 5 for himself.]

The next day at the interrogation at Porfiry's.

"What civil servant are you talking about?" (about the 25 rubles given to Marmeladov)

"Yes, I went out yesterday to rent an apartment."

"True, I wanted to go to America; [and] I stopped in to see a most unusual apartment." [Eh, nonsense]

Hm. Tell me about it; it interests me very much.

(No, this can even be explained very well that way; that's really the way it was, thought Porfiry to himself.)

(And when he is sitting in the little attic room with the petit bourgeois: Raskolnikov: he is face to face with me now, denunciation, so that the other couldn't call a deputy as would be proper in the presence of such evidence.) ~~Razumikhin at Porfiry's.~~ Will a man do that (go to the apartment, if he were not delirious, go against himself).

"Well, then he betrayed himself while delirious," thought Porfiry.

(N.B. No, they're lying; they'll never think of that.)

(Mitka communicated all the circumstances of the matter to Nikolay. They arrested Nikolay.)

[But today he is lying sick in delirium.]

Fundamental

Raskolnikov and Razumikhin, after Luzhin, leave the mother's place: [Razumikhin] I've been to their place, nothing much; they were even surprised. I admit that I got hot under the collar. They look upon you as being a bit mad. [Your article . . . The hell with my article.] True I noticed that Porfiry is really a bit careful, but I'm going to beat up Zametov. He even had the nerve to laugh at me.

Raskolnikov: Good or not! that he talked with them. Good in part, and in part bad. Well, come what may! However it turns out . . .

Fundamental

[To Sonia] "Love! Don't you think that I love when I've decided to bear such a horror? Is it because it is someone else's blood and not mine? Don't you realize that I would give all my blood if it were necessary?"

He became reflective.

Before God who sees me and before my own conscience, speaking here to myself, I say: I would give it!

I didn't butcher an old woman; I butchered a principle.

So, live humbly. But I have the right. I realized that I have it and therefore I have it.

And it's curious that I do not think of the old woman but only of Lizaveta. Poor Lizaveta.

I've got to finish things with the family. But I can't do it now. I'm not up to it.

Later perhaps.

That's good: monomaniac. Necessary to uproot this idea.

Perhaps the article is *stimulating him* (and particularly at Porfiry's).

Most Important

Porfiry visits him. Private conversation.

[Luzhin, in the evening] Razumikhin's leaving Raskolnikov.

"Listen I was there. Nothing came of it. I sort of couldn't start a real conversation. Zametov was there also. Finally I took Porfiry to the window and began to talk, but [again] *not in that way*. He looked away and I looked to the side. Finally, I raised my fist to his mug and said that I'd give him a good smashing in a family way. He simply looked at me. I spit and went away. That's all! Very stupid! I'm not satisfied. I didn't speak a word to Zametov [said!]."

"Stop all of this," Raskolnikov said with disgust.

N.B.

N.B. Meeting with the petit bourgeois in Porfiry's small room. "But are you a fact?"

[*And later*]. "And that's what you call a fact? Aren't you ashamed, ashamed?"

Svidrigaylov and Dunia: Svidrigalov. "Well now, that's my revolver!"

"Yes, I took it when I was at your place."

After the fire.

Dunia came to, (pale).

2) The mother is sick; she talks deliriously about you. Talks about you.[7]

1) She lost her temper; looked at me and shook her head. Dunia fell into her arms, without saying anything. No explanations are needed.

"Goodbye, brother!"

"Goodbye."

Dunia went to see Sonia. Both follow after him.

Makes his way up the stairs. Confess to Gunpowder; look at the dog barking. Everything's the same as always, but soon everything will be different.

(N.B.: Golgotha. He didn't see Sonia.)

[*Porfiry*. "I'm sure, I'm sure that you didn't take a single ruble of her money. Isn't it so! Isn't it so! It's in the *garden,* right?"

"But I'll not let anything slip out; don't worry."

"But you said that a long time ago."

"Oh, you!" (but then suddenly he burst out laughing)]

[I have taken a liking to your face.]

Porfiry to him, at his place. "Do you know this word: *to suffer.*"

"I wanted to take advantage of your sickness; I tormented you then so as to make you lose your mind, so as to drive you mad."

"But now you are well."

Porfiry's admission to Raskolnikov.

"Do you know that I even supposed, having penetrated you to the core: I supposed, judging by your proud, dominating, and impatient character, by your tense nerves, and despite your intelligence and cunning, that suddenly you would not be able to hold out, that you

---

[7] (to his mother) I'm going to her. Be honorable, suffer!

would get up from your seat and blurt out all your cherished secrets. Right or not? Could that happen to you, think back on it? [I saw a case like that with my own eyes.] Haven't you been at times in just such a state, *so to speak, in just such a minute?* [But I didn't need a confession. I know, after all, that such a thing is rare, a full confession, rare that one would get up and blurt everything out, but I needed only a little sign (and I thought if only I had a little sign, a little everyday detail).] I'm not asking you to tell me aloud; it's enough if you admit it to yourself. I'll even remind you. Remember when you were at my place, at the station, and I suddenly laughed in your face. You got so angry suddenly that I thought you would . . . blurt it out. I had arranged things well then.[8] It was necessary to humble you morally with all that judicial procedure, sting your pride to the highest degree [and then I would let out my surprise from behind the door] and you would have confessed. And I swear that it would have happened if it had not been for that cursed Mikolka.[9] Of course, one could proceed in such a fashion only with you and not with someone else; am I guilty then that I saw through you completely [remember?] completely? Of course, now you have changed your tone and have begun something new, you have some kind of aim in mind . . . Perhaps."

Porfiry and Raskolnikov: "I didn't have your place searched; there was no point to it. [I knew, after all, without your telling me that that you didn't lock your door when you left. In the ~~first~~ second place, even without our acting, Zametov had done some searching of your place; remember that you mentioned the *stone*—two times in fact, on the day after you came to me, and you got angry at Zametov because he had changed yesterday's respectful and submissive behavior to you—well it was really too obvious that you had it actually lying under some stone in a garden of some kind."

The main thought of Porfiry in Chapter X, Part II.

"I wanted to convince myself definitely, and I did convince myself. And I took measures to be alone with you for about twenty minutes."

"I needed the petit bourgeois, just in case, in order to upset you completely; everything was prepared, and it was all set up for any eventuality."

---

[8] Taking advantage of all those things, of the sickness

[9] and perhaps it would have happened, if it had not been for that cursed.

[Or: "I had, of course, the obligation then to interrogate you according to official form. But I could do that the next day, and that time, since official form is confining, I wanted to look you over, as they look you over when you were, so to speak, *in a state of intoxication,* and get the feel of you alone, provoke you, etc."]

Svidrigaylov talks as if he were not bragging at all. He simply tells Raskolnikov straightforwardly (champagne) how he spent his time, dancing school, etc. As for detailed explanations and questionings he says very little and even frowns.

Svidrigaylov to Raskolnikov.

Raskolnikov. "It's only in ~~depravity?~~ debauchery that you see hope?"

Svidrigaylov. "A straightforward question. Debauchery?"

"In debauchery at least there is something constant, a small piece of coal in the blood continually burning, which will not be put out for a long time. Well, then, that's something to do isn't it? As long as there's variety. It's monstrous [so they say] admittedly, but . . ."[10]

"It is, admittedly, harder and harder to put out, but perhaps it'll last for a while yet. [What's the point of living if you're out of it. It's boring enough without having to pretend. I'm talking to you frankly.] I was [even] glad to meet you; I thought that you had something to say to me. But it was all an illusion. Everyone tries to distract himself with something, and it's all made up. Look if I were a drinker of wine, or if I were a glutton, or was good at cards, but my specialty is women. Yes, there is something in them . . ."

"But love . . ."

"Love takes time to develop, and ~~I'm not capable of deceiving myself.~~ I get bored, can't stand it, and what joy is there in fooling

---

10 [I've thought truly at times: if it weren't for that, I'd end up shooting myself.

"And you could shoot yourself?"

"Come now, on what grounds," with disgust.

"We're having a gay conversation, Rodion Romanovich."

Such a sickness, madness, so as (. . .) with the world (imagination) (the more imaginings the better).

"A girl 16 years of age, fiancée."

"And don't darkness, horror trouble you?"

"What was that business which Luzhin talked about, was it true?" Svidrigaylov (frowning) Well. . . (I don't like to) N.B.

one's self. But you know, I'm waiting for a piquant titbit. I've thought up a good trick."

"That's why I'm drinking champagne."

Svidrigaylov and Dunia

"There was a minute when you were giving in and getting carried away."

"You're lying!"

"Well, you were beginning to give in and to get carried away; I saw it by your eyes. But it's true one ought not to remind a woman of that."

Svidrigaylov and Raskolnikov.

Theory of seduction. Flatter, about everything; how he seduced a woman from her husband and convinced her that she was being virtuous (while indulging in horrible abominations).

That's the kinds of contrasts I like.

Tuberculosis the doctor says. (he is depressed because of the tuberculosis); for contrast he tells Raskolnikov. (You murdered and I'm talking to you about Christ.) Story of the dancing class, *about the young girl*. Charming escapades.[11]

Svidrigaylov. Svidrigaylov.

Contrast. [Sonia struck me by contrast and attracted me.]

There was a coffin . . .

About the fiancée. Marry or not?

Marfa Petrovna and I had an agreement, a girl was all right, but she lost her head about Sonia.[12]

N.B. *Important. After that.*

Svidrigaylov and Dunia (the scene of attempted rape) Didn't succeed. A night of debauchery. The next day he shot himself. Contrasts. Descriptions of dens (?) of St. Petersburg (?) (as artistically as possible).

---

[11] I'm a gloomy man, don't you know that? [I don't do any harm; but sit in my corner. It happens that no one can get a word out of me for three days.]

[12] (not seriously) Avdotia Romanovna did not speak to you about that; that was hidden from her, but I suspect that she knew.

(This will be magnificent!)

Svidrigaylov. *Sat for a long time and tried to catch a fly.*

N.B. This expression somewhere: "Just as each man answers to a ray of sunshine."

N.B. 13 November. Nihilism is base servility of thought. A Nihilist is a lackey of thought.

Svidrigaylov. [I will shoot.] I know that you'll shoot; a pretty little animal.

To Raskolnikov. You won't believe what courtesy means to these downtrodden people. (The fiancée. Compares his fiancée with Raphael's *Madonna.*) About Raphael's Madonna—a bit odd.

His opinion of Sonia.[13] What is important is that he came to say goodbye and according to his will he leaves his fiancée to her care.

About tuberculosis.

Theory of how to possess a woman. Flatter; how base a woman is!

Marfa Petrovna permitted him to have servant girls, as long as he told her about them.

But she became outraged about Dunechka.

N.B. If God created it (. . .); he's a great man!

N.B. Svidrigaylov and Dunia. You will denounce him. (That depends on you.)

D. "As you wish."

"Why?"

"(I'll simply rape) and with pleasure," and he began to relate with a dirty laugh. "I knew you were a scoundrel, a monster, a beast." "Beast? You'll love me perhaps (do you know) and you may make a new man of me."

One person from the crowd walked up and gave three rubles. I thank you. They are all well-brought-up children.[14] They don't give anything.[15, 16]

Polechka, fix your dress, the shoulder strap has dropped.[17] I was

---

[13] expressed his opinion of Sonia.

[14] You can even say that it is an aristocratic family.

[15] *du hast Diamanten und Perlen. Ed.*: ". . . you have diamonds and pearls." From a poem by Heinrich Heine, 1797–1856.

[16] In the heat of noon in the valley of Dagestan
(I love this romance to the point of worship)

[17] And all she could say: *M-me, Voulez-vous du pain.* (*Ed.*: French: "Madame, do you want any bread?")

saying then that the corset must be made longer; [the décolleté] has been completely ruined.

N.B. Katerina Ivanovna.

A priest is not needed. God ought to forgive without that; I've suffered too much. It's only an expense. [And if he doesn't forgive, then it's not needed.][18]

Sonia and Raskolnikov cry silently while embracing.

Svidrigaylov's conversation about the (16-year-old); how she deceived him and said that she would be a good wife.

N.B. "What does happiness consist of?" asked Sonia.

"Happiness is Power," he said.

At Katerina Ivanovna's funeral dinner.[19] Begin a chapter explaining Luzhin's fury and what it meant to him to lose Dunia.

DUNIA

She couldn't stand it and comes to him two days later and says to her brother: "you are killing your mother."

N.B. The last line

The inscrutable ways by which God finds man.

"What about it, Sonia, is Luzhin to live and commit his dirty acts or is Katerina Ivanovna to die?"

"Zametov? And why is Zametov at his place? He wouldn't have come by himself, *if he didn't know,* unless it were on business; otherwise he wouldn't have dared come. But if the other one had invited him to come, then (also) for no other reason except for business. What other reason would they have for becoming acquainted?"

I don't know whether it was good or not to pretend to be a *prattler.* It seems to be good. Now everyone is prattling about those subjects. And all the more so, our brother, "the socialist." It's natural then. Better than to keep quiet. Much more so. A prattler has an innocent air; whoever talks a lot is short on action. And if you prattle with too much enthusiasm, then you're not likely to do anything at all. And

---

[18] Ah, if you were to see a corpse with half-opened lips.

[19] at the funeral dinner; about the boarding school for well-bred young ladies. Amalia Ivanov: about linen and romances.
Katerina Ivanovna laughs at us. She even shows Raskolnikov (. . .)

most important I could talk about a murder with an innocent air. I was admitting to myself that I was prepared to kill. But a bit too cunning. He's a clever man, very clever.

And why was I the first to go? The fact that I went first was incriminating. A moth drawn to the fire. It's true that she might have written [on the watch that it was mine], but what did that matter. The objects were too insignificant, if I had not appeared. I should have sat at home. It's true that I found something out, much needed. You can tell by his look that he is in some ways suspicious.[20]

Porfiry didn't even deign to hide the traces of his plottings. Perhaps he was counting on my irritation and indignation.

But the fact itself that he [Porfiry] is so caustic is a sign that he's helpless. What does he have other than dim suspicions?

The next day a real battle. Zametov was there for that purpose.

There are no facts. That's perhaps why he's angry. And yet when he told me that I wouldn't be able to stand it he had much understandable suspicion.

Important, why didn't he even bother to hide things from me?

Was it good or not that I went?

Pass by and not help . . .

Oh, if I were sure of what I'm saying now! . . .

Appearance of Svidrigaylov.[21] He is lying with his eyes closed; and the other is sitting and looking at him.

That's another proof, a new proof! thought Raskolnikov? He saw or heard or knows something that I don't know . . . The end of a ball of yarn.

No the Old Woman was a bit of stupidity. I didn't even manage to rob her; I know only how to kill as they were saying yesterday. But then that's not the point . . .

Porfiry didn't have time to call a deputy.

Raskolnikov and Porfiry. I can't justify myself; I consider that humiliating.

---

[20] The next morning before the commissariat.

[21] What is science? Is it perhaps really like that, yes what were we talking to you about?

N.B. "What do you want here? You can't do that here!"
". . . I'm leaving for foreign countries, brother."
"Foreign countries?"

[N.B. I can't understand: I not I, one must live!

"Well, what of it? You're young."
Mikolka made up the answers in fine fashion: capable and talented. Often the thought came to me: the peasant works the soil, and he is perhaps a Newton or a Shakespeare. An apple falls and a thought is born and dies. If there were only education for all. One must not quarrel (about systems) but one must live. Machines are going to do the work. Even if they were in brick.]

Porfiry came to him.
"Do you know why you've come to me?"
In order *to assure myself even more about the sum of evidence.* You are a clever man, that's the way it is (?) You are a psychologist. Perhaps I myself did not realize clearly why I was attracted to you.
Nothing will happen.
"(N.B. So that you will not run away. Even if I didn't come, you would know all the same that I was tracking you. On the contrary I am now reassuring you, admitting my weakness to you.)"[22]
"(Give me your hand: I'll shake it.)"
"But if you are guilty before me?"
"Then, of course, I don't have anything to repent."
"I'll spend my life on my knees before you."[23]

Porfiry. "Perhaps I even think that I have acted illegally, but I believe in my conscience that I have acted well in coming to you and telling it to you directly. Perhaps you will think about it. Yes, surely, you will; I can tell by your look."[24]

---

[22] All I have to do is wait until you become ill. You'll tell everything when you become sick.

[23] Do you understand that: even after Mikolka came, I sat down, nevertheless, with the petit bourgeois. Have you understood why? If you haven't understood it, I'll tell you: I wanted to let you know that I was convinced all the same that you were the one.
"Well am I speaking to you now frankly?"

[24] Repent; one must not step over blood.

"Well, what can I say? I'll remain the same."

"But is it possible for a man like you to admit it in that way? What's the matter with you, for goodness sake?"

"I'll make one more remark: if you are thinking of laying hands on yourself, then leave a note, so that the innocent do not suffer."

"Lay hands on myself?"

"You're capable of it."

["No, that's not right; you won't lay hands on yourself; indeed you're really not capable. But there can come a minute, and in such a minute a man is not responsible for his actions; there have been cases like that."]

The End of the Novel

Raskolnikov goes to shoot himself.

Svidrigaylov: I'm happy to go to America now, but no one really wants to.

Svidrigaylov: To Raskolnikov on Hay Market Square:[25]

---

[25] I. a. *Svidrigaylov:* You'll shoot yourself; with your character you won't stay alive. You have two paths: either confess or shoot yourself. What playful signs . . . We are not busy . . . White Russians, *en grand.*

"And if we were sitting in the chamber of deputies, then you would bustle about with all our might [to topple the ministry] bustle about the finances—then what?"

"That would be lower than the present situation. More vile (as you wish, there's much that is noble in clean hands. But then I would not shoot myself)."

Only man would be more insignificant.

Listen you've drunk a lot of champagne. So it seems often, but what I just expressed is true and really hidden in me even though only a drop.

Lower:

To be sure we are becoming corrupted; we don't bother about obligations; we get slapped in the face and we hide; we have debased ourselves through and through, but it's freer that way. Nihilism of its own kind. There are two nihilisms and both points touch each other. Imagine it, here it is the eve of putting a bullet in my head, I'm talking things over frankly with you. Well, such a state is higher, freer, even though it is not as happy.

There you are; I wanted to and I shot myself.

Yes, I'm burning with love for my country, no, copy this and that, but don't reveal what's in you, burn but according to the rules.

Agree that one finishes by spitting at everything.

"You will shoot yourself, and I will also perhaps shoot myself."

"Have you noticed that recently more strange things have been happening? Two women drowned themselves; someone closed the cash box and threw himself out of the window. The times have become capricious. It's like the spiders, isn't it?"

Svidrigaylov is despair, the most cynical.

Sonia is hope, the most unrealizable.

[Raskolnikov himself should express this.]

He became passionately attached to both.

Name and Topic Index